3/99

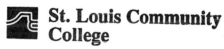

St. Louis Community College

Forest Park
Florissant Valley
Meramec

Instructional Resources
St. Louis, Missouri

THE FEMININE POLITICAL NOVEL
IN VICTORIAN ENGLAND

THE FEMININE
POLITICAL NOVEL
IN VICTORIAN
ENGLAND

Barbara Leah Harman

UNIVERSITY PRESS OF VIRGINIA
Charlottesville and London

The University Press of Virginia
© 1998 by the Rector and Visitors
of the University of Virginia
All rights reserved
Printed in the United States of America

First published 1998

♾ The paper used in this publication meets the
minimum requirements of the American National
Standard for Information Sciences—Permanence of
Paper for Printed Library Materials, ANSI
Z39.48-1984.

Library of Congress Cataloging-in-Publication Data
Harman, Barbara Leah.
The feminine political novel in Victorian England / Barbara Leah
Harman.
p. cm. — (Victorian literature and culture series)
Includes bibliographical references (p.) and index.
ISBN 0-8139-1772-7 (cloth : alk. paper)
1. English fiction—19th century—History and criticism.
2. Politics and literature—Great Britain—History—19th century.
3. Feminism and literature—Great Britain—History—19th century.
4. English fiction—Women authors—History and criticism.   5. Women
and literature—England—History—19th century.   6. Political
fiction, English—History and criticism.   7. Great Britain—Politics
and government—1837–1901.   I. Series.
PR878.P6H37   1998
823'.809358—dc21   97-25222
CIP

for my mother, Sylvia Harman
for my father, Sidney Harman

and for Bill, Julia, and Isabel

Contents

Preface

I BEGAN THINKING about this book when my older daughter was an
infant. Teaching *North and South*, I was struck by Elizabeth Gaskell's
remarkable description of Margaret Hale's emergence into the turmoil of a political strike: the sense of exposure, the prominence of
the female body in the crowd, the political power of the heroine's
inentions, and the complex interpretive problems that ensued, all
stood out with extraordinary clarity. But criticism of *North and South*,
I would discover, represented "Mrs. Gaskell" as a domestic novelist—a political novelist only by accident or on the side. From the
lookout of my own temporary domestic isolation, I could see that
this was not who Gaskell was at all. More importantly, I perceived
that the familiar notion of Victorian fiction as domestic fiction was
challenged by this novel, which would have more to tell me about
women's public lives in the nineteenth century than I could even
then imagine.

When I published my first essay on this subject in 1988, discussions of female publicity and of the relationship between public heroines and the "woman question" were scarce. A decade later the
critical map looks rather different. We know now more than we did
then about street women, independent women, new women, and
urban women. Still, we do not have a clear sense of what the literary
map looks like when we ask which texts might constitute a tradition
not of domestic novels by and about women but public novels by
and about women. Is there a tradition of feminine political novels in
the nineteenth century? If there is, what texts might constitute it?
This book suggests that there is indeed such a tradition and provides
one set of answers about how that tradition might be understood.

I have accumulated numerous debts in the long course of my
work on this project. I thank my students at Wellesley College, who
worked through many of the texts I present here (and some that I do

not), who listened eagerly to my discoveries and added insights of
their own. I am also grateful to my extraordinary student research as-
sistants, Laura Kotanchik and Alina Kantor. Laura gave several years
of her life to this project both here in the States and in England
where, among other things, she obtained photographs of the Ladies'
Gallery in the House of Commons so that I could see what it really
looked like. Our thanks to Lady Alexandra Wedgwood, architectural
archivist of the House of Lords, for helping us in this task. Laura's
imaginative resourcefulness, determined thoroughness, and unflag-
ging commitment over a period of several years have been an inspira-
tion. I am also grateful to Alina Kantor, who joined me in the final
stages of this work and found all the missing pieces—quickly, carefully, and without complaint about my schedule. Lindy Williamson
helped me with countless tasks and generally made my life easier.
Alina and Inna Kantor and their classmates Colleen Brownell and
Shana Whitehead provided the highest quality of child care imaginable, engaging and amusing my children so that they wouldn't notice
how much I was working.

It is one of the odd ironies of writing a book about female publicity that this book was written almost exclusively at home. Necessary materials were gathered through the superb services of the
Wellesley College librarians and the Interlibrary Loan Office. I am
indebted to friends and colleagues who read and commented on
parts of the manuscript over the decade it took me to complete it—
Rosemarie Bodenheimer, Mary Jacobus, Nancy K. Miller, Timothy
Peltason, Patricia Meyer Spacks, Margery Sabin, and Carolyn Williams among them. I also wish to thank an anonymous reader for
Texas Studies in Literature and Language whose thoughtful reading of
my article on George Gissing had a profound impact on the rest of
my work. I thank Karen Chase and several anonymous readers of my
book manuscript who saved me from errors and offered invaluable
advice and criticism, virtually all of which I took. One of these
anonymous readers suggested the current title of the book. Cathie
Brettschneider at the University Press of Virginia sustained her interest in this project for many years. Gerald Trett provided superb edi-
torial assistance and helped me through the maze of converting my
documentation system. ("Here there be dragons," he remarked; he
was right.) I have also been the beneficiary of generous support from
the National Endowment for the Humanities and, for more summers

than I can count, from Wellesley College grants for Scholarly Research.

A portion of the Introduction and chapter 2 first appeared in *Victorian Studies* 31 (1988): 351–74; reprinted by permission of the Trustees of Indiana University. A portion of chapter 1 was published in *Making Feminist History: The Literary Scholarship of Sandra M. Gilbert and Susan Gubar*, ed. William E. Cain (New York: Garland Publishing, 1994); reprinted by permission of the publishers. A portion of chapter 4 first appeared as "Going Public: Female Emancipation in George Gissing's *In the Year of Jubilee*" in *Texas Studies in Literature and Language* 34 (1992): 347–76; reprinted by permission of the University of Texas. I thank the publishers for permission to reprint these earlier versions of my work.

I also wish to thank my mother and my father for supporting me and valuing the rewarding public and private life I lead. The example each of them provides—of energy, intelligence, and grace—is always before my eyes. This book is dedicated, in part, to each of them.

In the long course of working on this project a second daughter joined the first. Together they added much joy, and not a little delay, to what has sometimes seemed a project without end. For their patience, and even interest, I am very grateful. I am certain that this book would not have been completed had I not enjoyed the almost unimaginable generosity of my husband, William Cain. Editor and critic, chief cook and household manager, intimate friend, I thank you. This book is also dedicated to you and to our daughters.

THE FEMININE POLITICAL NOVEL
IN VICTORIAN ENGLAND

Introduction:
In Promiscuous Company

IN THE SPRING OF 1840, when the World Antislavery Convention gathered at the Freemasons' Hall in London, the *Times* referred to "a very long and irregular discussion" about a motion to seat the women delegates from Pennsylvania and Massachusetts. Mingling women indiscriminately with men, seating them in mixed, or what Victorians would have called promiscuous, company, was considered by opponents to be "contrary to the custom and usage" of England, as was admitting them to "participation in public discussions." Predictably, the motion to seat the delegates failed.[1]

As Wendell Phillips, the Boston reformer and delegate to the convention, noted, the spurned women sat "behind the bar" instead of joining their male compatriots. When the founder of the American antislavery movement, William Lloyd Garrison, arrived at the convention after a delay at sea, he learned "that the women had been rejected as delegates" and promptly "declined to take his seat in the Convention." He and the women were "fenced off behind a bar and curtain, similar to those used in churches to screen the choir from the public gaze." Phillips remarked that through "all those interesting discussions on a subject so near his heart, lasting ten days, [Garrison] remained a silent spectator in the gallery." Dismayed by this turn of events, Garrison nonetheless wrote to his wife that he had not "visited this country in vain. The 'woman question' has been fairly started."[2]

Charlotte Brontë would have appreciated Garrison's response and understood the meaning of his important gesture. Her novels reveal that she was keenly attentive to the "custom and usage" of the country and to the difficulties attached to women's "participation in public discussions." Indeed, her representations of women's relationships to public life bear an uncanny resemblance to the happenings at the Antislavery Convention. In Brontë's novels women are often present at, but screened off from, significant public experiences. Like Garrison, who in this instance allied himself physically and symbolically with the women delegates, Brontë's women choose (however reluctantly) a spectator's vantage point on critical events.[3]

From the mid-nineteenth century onward, both in aftermath of the Antislavery Convention and as women increasingly sought access to the public sphere—to political discussion, to education, to the professions, and to the vote—the debate about female publicity took a more prominent place in the collective cultural discussion. In commentary on the reform of laws concerning women, in writing about women's higher education, in deliberation about the expansion of female employment opportunities, and in arguments about female suffrage, writers both defended and challenged the "sharply marked division" between private and public life, revealing the critical role it played in Victorian social and cultural experience and the extraordinary permutations through which it moved.[4] Debates about female publicity sometimes exposed an intense level of anxiety about women's engagement in the political sphere and thus the importance of strengthening the "bar" that divided them from it. But they also revealed the difficulty of maintaining the divisions upon which the opposition rested. As Elizabeth Gaskell would certainly have agreed, private and public life were indeed different realms in Victorian England; to deny this would be to disavow the movement from one to the other that is, so often, her theme. But distinctions between private and public have a tendency—in Gaskell's novels and elsewhere—to collapse in the very act of being constituted. The challenge is thus a double one: to identify the occasions when women enter the public realm and to acknowledge, at the same time, the enormous complexity of these moments and the interpretive complications that attend them.

My purpose in this book is to investigate, in the historical and literary record, the meaning of public life for nineteenth-century Englishwomen when it begins to emerge as a dangerously real possibility. I begin with the "woman's mission" arguments of the 1840s and 1850s because Charlotte Brontë and Elizabeth Gaskell read them and because domestic ideologists imagine a moral influence on public life for middle-class women while, at the same time, opposing their direct engagement in the political arena. In the works of such mid-century writers as Sarah Stickney Ellis and Sarah Lewis, it was frequently argued that woman's sphere must be separated from man's lest it be tainted by the connection. Participation in public life jeopardized the clarity of woman's position as disinterested analyst and observer, someone capable of *influencing* the public realm precisely because, in her separateness, she conserved the "abstract principles of right and wrong" by which public men would be guided.[5]

Ironically, the vision of woman as independent moral resource, a vision crucial for domestic apologists from Ellis to John Ruskin, was decisively undermined by the null status under the law of women in Victorian England. The operative definition in the period remained that of Sir William Blackstone, who, in his *Commentaries on the Laws of England*, described the legal situation of married women under the law of coverture: "By marriage, the husband and wife are one person in law: that is, the very being or legal existence of the woman is suspended during marriage, or at least is incorporated and consolidated into that of the husband: under whose wing, protection, and cover she performs everything; and is therefore called in our law-french a *feme-covert*." In stark contrast to Lewis's representation of woman as a figure of moral neutrality and thus integrity, Blackstone implies that her neutrality is really ontological emptiness or nullity. Blackstone's definition also ties what the writer and reformer Caroline Norton would call the "non-existen[ce]" of women, to their lack of self-definition. Women are unable to act in their own right because they cannot differentiate themselves from their spouses and make their actions, and their selves, distinct and visible. The incorporated woman is a protected woman, but, as Frances Power Cobbe, chair of the London National Society for Women's Suffrage, both humorously and grimly remarked when she wrote in support of legal reform in the 1860s, the proper emblem of woman's "absolute . . . Union" with man is the "Tarantula Spider, [for] when one of these delightful creatures is placed under a glass with a companion of his own species a little smaller than himself, he forthwith gobbles him up. . . . The operation being completed, the victorious spider visibly acquires double bulk, and thenceforth may be understood to 'represent the family' in the most perfect manner conceivable." A wife's union with her husband—which Blackstone first calls her "incorporation" and then her "consolidation"—is far from benign. To be incorporated is simply to be eaten alive, and to be represented in the flesh of the husband is to improve his self-representation at the cost of hers.[6]

The union of husband and wife and the disappearance of the wife into the husband had profound implications for female representation and, finally, for female participation in the public sphere. As the nineteenth-century jurist John Taylor Coleridge put it, clarifying the social consequences of coverture, the law "places the wife under the guardianship of the husband, and entitles him for the sake of both, to protect her from the danger of unrestrained intercourse with the world." The husband's "cover" translated into his guardianship and control over her public engagements, and until 1891, a husband could also confine his wife to the home against her will. One contemporary journalist saw his ability to do so as a necessary condition of married life. When the law was finally eliminated (in *Re. v. Jackson*) Eliza Lynn Linton wrote in *Nineteenth Century* magazine that "marriage, as hitherto understood in England, was suddenly abolished one fine morning last month!"[7]

When those who opposed reform considered the results of revising the laws governing married women, they saw that if women had property they would gain a troubling freedom of movement. In an 1868 parliamentary debate about the Married Women's Property Bill (an early petition on whose behalf Elizabeth Gaskell had added her signature; the bill was not passed until 1882), Gabriel Goldney argued that it would "so free a woman from restraint that in any quarrel she might have with her husband she would be enabled to say, 'I have my own property, and if you don't like me I can go and live with somebody who does.'" In a later debate Anthony Cooper, earl of Shaftesbury, asked, "Could she quarrel with her husband and eject him, or refuse him admission to her house; and, while keeping him out of it, might she admit everyone else?" The right to own property would give wives the power to control access to their own dwellings. A woman thus liberated, Shaftesbury contended, might convert a traditionally private place into a public space (a brothel) by admitting not "anyone" but rather "everyone" into her home. The consequence of the wife's ability to own property was sexual freedom, which in Shaftesbury's view was sexual permissiveness: "If she could act in that manner, he wanted to know how the conjugal rights of the husband were to be asserted."[8]

It is no surprise, in this context, that the movement to open higher education to women (first in secondary schools and later in universities) moved ahead cautiously, and always with an eye toward the possible impropriety that might attach to female students. In February 1865, when the syndicate investigating women's access to entrance examinations at Cambridge made its report to the university senate, it recommended (by a narrow margin) "that girls be admitted to the Local Examinations, on the same terms as boys. There were to be local committees of ladies, and care was to be taken to 'prevent undue publicity or intrusion.' No names of candidates or class lists were to be published." Young women who left home, and home duties, to be educated at Girton, Newnham, or at any of the other women's colleges that were established in the second half of the nineteenth century were understood to have left behind the protections of home as well. Anne Jemima Clough, the head of Newnham, was "very nervous lest her students should attract attention and criticism" and hence was guarded about their mode of living, outdoor activities, and style of dress. At the same time, Clough "did not like an individual to be sacrificed to a cause, however good," and memoirs of her life include intriguing accounts of her handling of this conflict. One Newnhamite remembered Clough's response when she received complaints of students "buttoning their gloves" in the streets: "I know, my dears, that you have a great deal to do, and have not much time; but I don't like people to say such things about you, and so, my dears, I hope you'll get some gloves that don't want buttoning."[9]

University students who left home to study did so with differing ends in mind: some prepared themselves to be well-educated wives; others prepared themselves for a life of work. But the concerns about impropriety appeared even more persistently in the writing of those who considered the consequences of women entering the professions. In "The Rights of Woman," published anonymously in *Blackwood's Magazine* in 1862, William E. Aytoun explored the implications of training women for careers and immediately warned of the impropriety of men and women working in close quarters together. In the case of the female lawyer, he maintained: "It is all very well to talk of professional honour; but we swear by the Knave of Clubs that if we found the wife of our bosom, whatever kind of gown she might be wearing, closeted with a rascally lawyer, we should force open the door with a poker, hit Mr. Sargeant Doublefee a pitiless pelt upon the numskull, and fetch madam home to expiate her offences by a week's solitary confinement." And in the case of the female doctor, he observed:

> *A married female M.D. must of course be prepared to sally forth at any hour of the night, if summoned by a patient. What husband would submit to such a gross infringement of the connubial contract? Nay, it may be questioned whether he would feel gratified by the information that his wife had been selected by some notorious debauchee as his confidential medical adviser. If a maiden, the case is even worse. No daughter of Esculapius would be safe for a moment if, under professional pretexts, she might be decoyed into any den of infamy. Nor would the public sympathy be largely lavished upon the victim of such an outrage.*[10]

In Aytoun's view the real danger of women entering the professions is the grave risk—indeed the inevitability—of seduction and betrayal. In his first example the wife's law robes can't quite be distinguished from more intimate garments, and the husband's only recourse in the presence of his wife's infidelity is violently to substitute his poker for someone else's and to punish his wife for venturing into the world by confining her to home. In Aytoun's second example the husband's loss of connubial rights is only part of the problem. When his wife "sall[ies] forth" it is only to be seduced by her patients. The powerlessness of the wife—or the maiden—is here imagined as an antidote to her adventurousness, as her rape is a kind of punishment. In the midst of its own burlesque, the cruelty of the final assertion that a violated woman would win no sympathy for her plight reveals the author's hostile, punitive intentions.

The association between access to public life, freedom of movement, and sexual impropriety appears insistently in the documentary material on the suffrage movement as well. In response to John Stuart Mill's proposal to amend the 1867 Reform Bill so that it would extend the vote to unmarried women (including widows), John Burgess Karslake said in parliamentary debate that Mill's arguments "all pointed to the admission of married women":

> *The law of the land of the present day had deliberately settled that the wife should be absolutely and entirely under the control of the husband, not only in respect of her property, but of her personal movements. For example, a married woman might not "gad about," and if she did her husband was entitled to lock her up . . . [for] undoubtedly the husband had entire dominion over the person and property of his wife. He thought, then, it was clear that votes could not be given to married women consistently with the rules of law as regarded property and the husband's dominion over the wife's movements.*

Karslake identifies voting with having the right to move freely, to "gad about" in the world. And he identifies the husband's "entire dominion" over the wife's movements with the impossibility of extending her the vote. Even George Bowyer, who did not oppose Mill's amendment, presumed that Mill would recommend that women "use voting papers [absentee ballots], for it would be manifestly indecorous for them to attend the hustings or the polling-booth." Female participation in public life, and female public appearance itself, would so compromise a woman's virtue that the only way even a proponent of the vote like Bowyer could imagine its success would be to convert a public into a private act—to make women vote in absentia, in the privacy of their own homes.[11]

But the suffrage was understood by its opponents to be more than an "unseemly spectacle." William Gladstone referred to its "unsettling, not to say uprooting, of the old landmarks of society," and John Pleydell Bouverie declared that the suffrage "was in reality disturbing the whole foundations of society and obliterating the distinction of sex, and ignoring the functions of the sexes in society which have existed in all times and in all civilized communities."[12] The notion that every existing aspect of culture would be altered by women's participation in political life was disputed by proponents of the measure, who made their arguments on the grounds of citizenship, agency, civil rights, and representation. Nevertheless, the arguments persisted throughout the nineteenth and into the twentieth century, exploding into prominence when the constitutional tactics of the suffragists became the militant tactics of the suffragettes.

From the 1840s to the turn of the century, reformers sought to redefine female identity and gain for women access to the public sphere, while opponents defined public life as a prohibited realm for women, associated with indecorous self-display, illicit sexuality and infidelity, and the destruction of the family. As late as 1892, when the liberal reformer William Gladstone considered in a letter to Samuel Smith the consequences of extending the vote to women, he claimed to fear "lest we should invite [the female voter] unwittingly to trespass upon the delicacy, the purity, the refinement, the elevation of her own nature, which are the present sources of its power." Gladstone's description of the problem would have sounded familiar half a century earlier, so little does his language vary from that of domestic ideologists in the 1840s. But Gladstone also admits that "in the Universities, in the professions," in what he calls "the secondary circles of public action" women have indeed studied and labored and acted, though he argues that "we have [still] done nothing that plunges the woman as such into the turmoil of masculine life."[13]

Gladstone's letter is important, however, not so much for its reiteration of the familiar position (public life is chaotic and tumultuous; women who enter it will violate their purity and damage their delicacy) but rather for its revelation about the relationship of private to public experience: "I am not without the fear lest beginning with the State, we should eventually be found to have intruded into what is yet more fundamental and more sacred, the precinct of the family, and should dislocate, or injuriously modify, the relations of domestic life."[14] In the midst of an insistence that private life must assiduously be distinguished from public life, Gladstone's letter makes perfectly apparent that they are intimately connected and that their separation is impossible to maintain. As Gladstone himself understands, to legislate one is automatically to legislate the other; to decide on a public matter is to influence —to intrude upon, to dislocate, to modify—a private one, because the two spheres are entirely dependent on each other for their mutual distinction and definition. Indeed if the material we have looked at thus far suggests how Victorians sexualize the public realm and thereby make it the scene and setting of private matters, what Gladstone's letter points to is the inevitably political character—in certain ways the manifestly *public* character—of private life. For while it looks as though legislating the vote is legislating a public issue, Gladstone understands that to decide public issues is to determine the "relations of domestic life." His statement is really an admission of the deeply political underpinnings of domesticity and privacy and an acknowledgment that female private life cannot escape entirely the "turmoil of masculine life" because in one sense it is already governed and defined by it. Gladstone appears to invoke the familiar liberal principle that the "right to privacy," the "right to be left alone" in one's intimate relations, should always be protected by law. But this right is here invoked to protect—to legislate by not legislating—that particular version of domestic relations otherwise known as the status quo.

Gladstone makes an interesting distinction between what he calls the "secondary circles of public action" and what he must have considered the primary circle of action—the vote. Access to this last circle, he claims, would plunge "the woman as such into the turmoil of masculine life" because direct political action is the most "masculine" activity and the most dangerous form of publicity. In Gladstone's view the vote is the last and also the deepest masculine preserve. But as I have already suggested, his language elsewhere makes the point that such distinctions—between one circle and another, between private and public—are *not* easy to draw even when they seem on the surface to be clear. Gladstone's letter reveals that the private domain is less a realm of freedom than a realm of constraint, a legislated condition proscribed by those who control the public sphere. As we have already seen elsewhere, the public realm for women is linked not merely to political action but to self-manifestation and self-display—and, at the same time, to the intimacy and illicit sexuality that might otherwise be thought properties of the private realm. Gladstone identifies clearly the public activity he seeks to prohibit; at the same time his language complicates any simple sense of the private/public distinction.

As the documentary materials of the British women's movement make clear and as the novels that I explore demonstrate, female public appearance was actively contested from the 1840s onward, but the resistance emerged in order to meet a wide range of efforts to cross the boundary from private into public life. Some of these efforts occurred in political arenas and some occurred in literary ones. Indeed, it is often possible to detect in nineteenth-century fiction direct evidence of the impact of the "woman question" debate on fictional representations—though it is equally the case that some novelists press the debate further than contemporary participants, just as some react against it as if to protect themselves from its impending consequences. Novelists, after all, are both participants in, and fabricators of, their worlds.

My intention in the pages that follow is to identify the occasions, describe the conditions, and chart the complications of women's emergence onto the public stage through a literary subgenre that I have called "the feminine political novel." This subgenre includes texts in which female characters participate in the public universe conventionally understood to be owned and occupied by men—the world of mills and city streets, of labor and strikes, of Parliament and parliamentary debates, of national celebrations and urban investigations, of outdoor public speaking and political activism. A number of these novels have been discussed elsewhere, but some have not been examined at length, and they have not been examined as a group, either in relation to each other or to developments in the emerging British women's movement. In my view they need to be studied in this manner because together they tell a story about a different tradition in the Victorian novel—not the tradition of domestic fiction and, perhaps more pertinently, not the tradition of the public woman as fallen woman.[15] Instead, these novels reveal the way in which nineteenth-century English writers began to think about female transgression into, and occupation of, the public sphere and then about the often vexed consequences of women's public appearances. In the texts that I identify, female characters have a defining public moment; that experience and responses to it also dismantle the private/ public distinction in the very act of illuminating it. This is not, however, to suggest that the erosion of distinctions signifies the meaninglessness of the categories and thus the impossibility of truly imagining female public action. It is rather to assert that the dismantling or redefining of categories is yet another way in which the private/public boundary is traversed.

Feminist historians like Lee Holcombe, Judith Walkowitz, Martha Vicinus, Jane Lewis, and others have been examining for some time what Vicinus has called the "widening sphere" of women's lives.[16] But feminist work in literary criticism has not predominantly focused on female publicity. Even Catherine Gallagher's influential book *The Reformation of Industrial Fiction* (1985), which took seriously the role of female heroines in "condition of England" novels and interpreted women's presence on the industrial stage as a sign of the breakdown of traditional boundaries, still understood the engagement of women in public activities as inevitably doomed. In Gallagher's reading of industrial fiction, the woman (and the family) function "as either a model or a school of social reform" and must therefore, "paradoxically, be separated from and purged of the ills infecting the public realm. While trying to obliterate the separation of public and private life," Gallagher repeatedly suggests, "these novels reinforce that separation." Like many writers on women's public lives, Gallagher would make claims for female progress that she both proffered and withdrew.[17]

Mary Poovey's *Uneven Developments* (1988) considered a series of what she called "contested images" of gender (in the lives and works of Caroline Norton, Charlotte Brontë, Florence Nightingale, and others) in order to identify the "ideological work" that they performed. The "jeopardizing" representations of womanhood that she explored again threatened "to erode the supposedly fixed boundary between the private and the public spheres." But although Poovey insisted on the way that they "collapsed the separation," she too returned repeatedly to the notion that the culture used the subversive power of these representations to "shore up the distinctions" that their presence might seem to have challenged.[18]

Nancy Armstrong's influential *Desire and Domestic Fiction* (1987) took the rather different tack of seeking to reinvigorate our notion of the private sphere. Unlike her predecessors, Armstrong celebrated female domesticity, arguing that "those central functions which we automatically attribute to and embody as women . . . have been just as instrumental in bringing the new middle class into power and maintaining their dominance" as the economic and political work normally attributed to public men. Armstrong addressed the split between private and public by writing what she called the "political history" of domestic life—political because it served the social function of "contain[ing] disorder within the household and giving it a female form."[19]

Armstrong validates the universe of private values instead of seeing it as secondary to the realm of power in which men operate effectively. Of course it is not her purpose to discern evidence of the emergence into public life of Victorian heroines or to detect the pervasive challenges to the division of spheres, a division that Armstrong not only accepts but acclaims. Mary Ryan's *Women in Public* (1990) sought, in the American examples that she investigates, to identify in the lives of women the very "points of entry" that Armstrong had conceded to others. The task before us, as Ryan put it, is to "go defiantly in search of women in public." Ryan lauds the opening of new space to women as she describes "the exhilaration of the ceremonial, the freedom of the street, the empowerment of political engagement, and the human possibilities of the public sphere."[20]

Like Ryan's ordinary American women in real public places, Judith Walkowitz's Englishwomen in *City of Dreadful Delight* (1992) can be identified by their "forceful entry into the world of publicity and politics." Walkowitz distinguishes a mid-century vision of the dangerous and endangered female public figure from a late-Victorian vision in which a wide range of public figures "made their public appearances . . . in relation to the urban panorama." Her principal example of the mid-century public woman is still the prostitute, the woman who brings into view "the permeable and transgressed border between classes and sexes." I shall suggest that mid-Victorian England provided other instances of women in public places—Brontë's Shirley and Gaskell's Margaret Hale among them—illustrations at once different from and continuous with later examples of girls in business, women speakers, and female explorers of urban space. Still, Walkowitz's description of the emergence of the latter provides a powerful historical context for the literary representations I shall study in the novels of Meredith, Gissing, and Robins.[21]

Ryan and Walkowitz, both historians, prepared the ground for Deborah Nord's *Walking the Victorian Streets* (1995). Nord is interested in the female "urban spectator" whose transgressions bring with her the "vexed sexuality her position implies." In the new paradigm of the urban female wanderer, the central wanderer is still a fallen woman—"a partner in urban sprees" who sometimes functions as a symbolic means of "quarantining urban ills," and sometimes as "an agent of contamination and connections." Like Ryan, Nord assumes that women are present on the urban scene. Both women writers and female characters, she notes, have public lives that are marked by conflict and tension—"by the struggle to assume authority in a sphere of masculine concerns and by anxiety about the public exposure that attends such authority." But like Gallagher and Poovey, Nord contends that it is impossible for female urban spectatorship to move beyond the taint of exposure. Public gestures provide their own significant satisfaction, "and yet they also expose women to trauma and nearly irreversible disgrace." Though Nord builds on recent studies of women in urban spaces, providing the literary counterpart to Ryan's and Walkowitz's historical accounts, she still sees the public woman as a tainted woman whose contamination is both unavoidable and limiting.[22]

The novels I have selected center on scenes of female public experience— what Ryan describes as "points of entry" and Walkowitz calls occasions of "forceful entry"—but my examples are not primarily associated with fallen women. Instead, they explore the complex connections between private and public life in varying forms of engagement. Although I agree with Walkowitz and Nord that the public woman's affiliations with the prostitute must be acknowledged and understood, I have focused on public women who, though threatened by the taint of exposure, interestingly move either around, beyond, or through it. In Charlotte Brontë's *Shirley* (1849)— a transitional novel for my purposes—the known risks of exposure cause the heroine to refrain from direct engagement in public affairs and to seek instead indirect access to what Brontë calls the "struggle for money, and food, and life." With a keen perception of the risks of female publicity in the late 1840s, Brontë describes a heroine who finds indirect means to effect her charitable designs and who witnesses, even though she cannot directly participate in, the novel's central riot scene. This heroine conserves her unsullied character for intimate, rather than public, expression, but Brontë interestingly configures intimacy *as display*. In Elizabeth Gaskell's *North and South* (1854–55) Margaret Hale throws herself "into the mêlée" of an industrial strike in one of the most extraordinary scenes of public exposure in the Victorian novel. Margaret suffers the misconstruction of character that Shirley had feared, but Gaskell transforms Margaret's sense of sexual taint into mature sexual self-acknowledgment; she celebrates, rather than resists, the connection between private and public life, suggesting that the link is powerful and transformative.

For George Meredith, writing several decades later and in the midst of heated debates about women's rights, the heroine in *Diana of the Crossways* (1885) finds courtship and parliamentary politics indistinguishable (as courtship and industrial knowledge are in *North and South*). Meredith's Diana, loosely modeled on the activist Caroline Norton, explores the heroine as parliamentary advisor, writer, and even political blackmailer, though Meredith both invokes and severs the connection between publicity and private sexuality that is so prominent in Gaskell's novel. He insists instead on his heroine's chastity even as he describes both her increasing political engagements and the development of her passionate nature. Perhaps more than any other novelist, Meredith was eager both to see the relationship between public women and scandal and to separate the scandal from the woman. In *Diana*, as in earlier novels like *Beauchamp's Career* (1875) and *The Egoist* (1879), Meredith thinks about female publicity in relation to more problematic forms of male publicity and creates heroines who challenge prior conceptions of women's lives.

Nancy Lord, in George Gissing's *In the Year of Jubilee* (1894), participates in a national celebration and involves herself in public adventures during and after Queen Victoria's Jubilee Day celebrations. Nancy's public "sprees" are explicitly tied to her eventual fall and ensuing pregnancy. But Gissing is suspicious both of illicit, and of legitimate, public engagements in the late-Victorian city: he reconfigures both privacy and publicity in the unconventional marriage with which his text concludes as a way of resolving not merely the specific dilemma of female publicity but the larger dilemma of a world grown increasingly public and commercial. Finally, in Elizabeth Robins's suffrage novel, *The Convert* (1907), the heroine's main interest is the occupation and redefinition of public space. Vida is the central "convert" of the novel, but she seeks as well to convert the terms I have identified above—to reconceive the meaning of female privacy, to manipulate the connection between publicity and sexual impropriety, and, most importantly, to reimagine the public realm as the site for noble and meaningful action for women. Vida's speeches in Trafalgar Square offer perhaps the most direct examples of female political engagement, but as we shall see, they gain power from the history of female public appearance that precedes them.

What has absorbed me about the novels and scenes I describe are their extraordinary permutations on a set of repeating themes. As we move from the 1840s to the first decade of the twentieth century, the narratives become increasingly public—from Brontë's restraint, to Gaskell's transgressions; from Meredith's mergers, to Gissing's complex reconfiguration; and from these, to Robins's reappropriation of public space, a reclamation at once celebratory and, it should be noted, mournful. But the questions with which they deal, while taking decidedly different forms, remain in essence the same: How can one maintain one's "character" in the presence of efforts to misconstrue it? What is the relationship between meaningful public action and the desire for intimate recognition? Is it possible successfully to assert a rebellious impropriety, or must female publicity be assiduously distinguished from its dangerous cousin? Can the public realm be reclaimed for women, and if so, at what cost?

The novelists on whom I have focused in this book address these questions in terms that, as a literary critic, I find compelling and complex. Because they consider women in relation to politics—to Luddite riots, industrial strikes, parliamentary politics, national celebrations, and open-air political meetings—the questions they explore offer rich, if often disquieting, insights into cultural history. To be sure, other novelists in the period also examine female publicity— exploring women who "fall" (George Moore's *Esther Waters* and Thomas Hardy's *Tess of the D'Urbervilles*), navigate urban settings (Charles Dickens's *Bleak House*), go on stage (Geraldine Jewsbury's *The Half Sisters* and Wilkie Collins's *No Name*), stray from home (George Eliot's *Mill on the Floss*), or have illicit public lives that exist only in the imaginations of others (Anthony Trollope's *He Knew He Was Right*). All of these novels would benefit from examination in light of the questions that this book raises. But by concentrating on the "feminine political novel" I have sought to sharpen my investigation and to bring to bear on the most openly political examples of female publicity the questions that I have identified. These novels are uniquely suited to interpretations that are illuminated by their connection to the politics of the British women's movement, as I hope the pages that follow will demonstrate.

I

Public Restraint and Private Spectacle in *Shirley*

I.

IN A REVEALING letter written to her publisher and friend George Smith about the completion of *Villette*, Charlotte Brontë declared, "You will see that [it] touches on no matter of public interest. I cannot write books handling the topics of the day; it is of no use trying. Nor can I write a book for its moral. Nor can I take up a philanthropic scheme, though I honour philanthropy; and voluntarily and sincerely veil my face before such a mighty subject as that handled in Mrs. Beecher Stowe's work, 'Uncle Tom's Cabin.' "[1] Brontë proved that she meant what she said about "honour[ing] philanthropy" when she held back the publication of *Villette* (1853) to permit Elizabeth Gaskell to publish her own, more "philanthropic," novel earlier in the year, noting that " 'Villette' had no right to push itself before 'Ruth.' There is a goodness, a philanthropic purpose—a social use in the latter, to which the former cannot for an instant pretend."[2]

Villette would be one of Brontë's most autobiographical novels, reconceiving her earlier attempt in *The Professor* (1846; published posthumously and written from the perspective of a young male teacher) to write about her experiences as a pupil and pupil-teacher in Brussels in 1842 and then again in 1843–44, as well as to represent and reinvent her intense attachments to George Smith and Constantin Héger. But the novel would also explore, despite her assertions to the contrary, Brontë's strong feelings about female independence, education, and work—topics that had currency in the 1840s and that would prove frequent subjects of discussion in her correspondence. Brontë kept in touch with her school friend Mary Taylor, who emigrated to New Zealand with the intention of finding there the sort of employment that was unavailable to unmarried Englishwomen, and Taylor's activities were a subject of conversation in the Brontë household and in Charlotte's letters to common friends. Brontë's letters to her editor, William Smith Williams, about his children also reveal her belief that education and independent labor were as important to young women as to young men.[3]

Still, what seems most interesting about the *Villette* letter (and then about her agreement to delay publication) is the language Brontë uses to describe her relationship to "matter[s] of public interest." Brontë "honour[s]" what she considers Stowe's "philanthropic" gesture, and her response is to "voluntarily and sincerely veil my face before such a mighty subject" (the slavery and race question)—suggesting in her choice of words a sense of humility in relation to great public causes and, one suspects, in relation to authors who might be seen as relinquishing self-expression in order to write on behalf of others' needs. Perhaps most importantly—and I will have more to say about this later—her words suggest her own mediated relationship to matters of public import, a mediation that manifests itself here in sincere, voluntary self-screening (I "veil my face"), and in the quite literal act of authorial self-postponement that her willingness to delay the publication of *Villette* represents.

Of course Brontë means to make a point about the difference in her current attitude toward "public" writing (at the time of *Villette's* completion) and her former one (at the time of *Jane Eyre* and *Shirley's* completion), and in any case she would likely have made a distinction between women's causes like equality and employment and larger public causes like slavery. Still, her comments illuminate *Jane Eyre* (1848) and *Shirley* (1849) as well as *Villette*. If the author of *Villette* steps to the side and veils her face before "mighty subject[s]," the heroines of her other novels, whose relationships to persons with social status and access to the world (*Jane Eyre*) or to events of social and political significance (*Shirley*) do the same—mediating their relation to public life, sometimes in extraordinary ways.

Jane Eyre presents us with a heroine whose marginal social status as the unwanted, orphaned member of her aunt's household is embodied by her self-seclusion in the window seat of the breakfast room at Gateshead Hall—from which perspective of "double retirement" (she is protected both by the window seat's draperies and by her own mental disengagement) she is able, at least at times, safely to observe and criticize the small social world of her aunt's family.[4] Jane's retirement is always at risk as is her position of veiled observer, because her cousin John Reed won't leave her in peace, instigating, in part, the scenes of rebellion that eventually lead to Jane's departure. Even at Thornfield Hall, where Jane likes to "gaze without being observed" when Rochester has company (203), she finds herself in the presence of another veiled observer, who uses his gypsy disguise to penetrate her disguises and flush out her secrets (chapter 29). Rochester's notion that the way to get to Jane is to approach her in disguise himself suggests (accurately I think) his understanding of her mediated relation to social experience: he needs to catch her off guard or he won't penetrate her veil.

Charlotte Brontë liked her own disguises and gave up with reluctance the use of her pseudonym. She continued to sign herself "Currer Bell" in letters after 1848 (when her identity became known to her publishers), even suggesting in 1853 that a new pseudonym be invented for the author of *Villette*. (Naturally, George Smith rejected the idea.) In letters to Smith, Brontë enjoyed talking about herself in the third person, and she liked as well the disguise that she assigned to him—sensing that these covers protected her from the risks associated with exposing her feelings in her own person and provided her with the freedom to say things that she might otherwise have kept to herself. In one letter, thanking George Smith for replacing a book lost in the mail, she leaves to "the 'close-fisted' Head of the Establishment" (one version of Smith) "the duty of reprimanding Mr G——e S——th; they may settle accounts between themselves—while Currer Bell looks on and wonders but keeps out of the mêlée." This complex way of expressing her thanks acknowledges an aspect of himself that Smith has presented to her (the "hard-headed man of business" side) while also acknowledging the generosity of her publisher's frequent packages. She lets Smith know that she sees what he is doing and appreciates it, and at the same time doubly distances herself from the imaginary battle between the two Smiths by thanking "them" in the person of Currer Bell and by refusing to engage in the "mêlée" ("a mixed or irregular fight between two parties of combatants")—even though her own fiction has created it.[5]

Even during the period in which Brontë described herself as someone who "no longer walk[ed] invisible," she was content, as many women in the late 1840s would also have been, to serve as a witness to events in which she might easily have imagined herself participating. She regretted missing, because of the poor health of family members in May 1850, the Royal Literary Fund Society Dinner—not because she wanted, or imagined that she could have, a place at the table, but because she could have listened, from her seat in the Ladies' Gallery, to the afterdinner speeches of important literary figures like Charles Dickens and William Thackeray (women were "ineligible to attend the actual dinner"). She was able to satisfy, on a trip to London later that month, her desire to visit the Houses of Parliament—a trip that also included excursions to the opera, the offices of the *Times*, the General Post Office, and the Royal Academy. As a visitor to Parliament, Brontë would also have to sit in the Ladies' Gallery: women were not permitted to sit in the more open and accessible Visitors' Gallery where Charlotte's companion, George Smith, would sit, and he described his difficulty in reading her face to determine when she was ready to leave. Charlotte is reputed to have replied, in response to his remark that all eyes "seemed to be flashing signals to me" that she "did not wish to go away" and that "perhaps there were other signals from the Gallery"—an assertion on Brontë's part that, perhaps unlike others, she was attending to the speeches on the floor and not to her handsome host (at least so she said).[6]

Brontë accepted, in herself and in her culture, the mediated stance of the female public figure at once engaged and disengaged. She would not have said that women were inevitably barred from interest in public causes—as her comments and actions in relation to Stowe and Gaskell indicate. But her own interests, and her conception of what was both possible and customary, coincided—producing a transitional stance in relation to public matters, a mediated or veiled relation to public causes, that Brontë would find, as she did in her letters to George Smith, both protective and liberating.

In an 1848 letter discussing the novel that would eventually become *Shirley*, Brontë told her editor, William Smith Williams, that she "often wish[ed] to say something about the 'condition of women' question—but it is one respecting which so much 'cant' has been talked that one feels a sort of repugnance to approach it." Brontë's letters to Elizabeth Gaskell also indicate that she was familiar with the debate about women's roles that emerged in the 1840s, as a response to Gaskell written in 1850 (the year following the publication of *Shirley*) confirms. Gaskell, whose own letter to Brontë is lost, must have asked her whether she read the *Westminster Review*, for Brontë replied that, though it was "not a periodical I see regularly," she had "got hold of a number—for last January, I think—in which there was an article entitled 'Woman's Mission' (the phrase is hackneyed), containing a great deal that seemed to me just and sensible. Men begin to regard the position of woman in another light than they used to do; and a few men, whose sympathies are fine and whose sense of justice is strong, think and speak of it with a candour that commands my admiration." The article to which Brontë refers appeared, just as she recalled, in the January 1850 issue. The piece is a review of a book entitled *Woman's Mission*, usually attributed to Sarah Lewis, in its thirteenth edition in 1850 (it was first published in 1839 and there would be more editions in future years). The work is said to be based on Aimé Martin's "The Education of Mothers" (L'éducations des mères), and it belongs to a larger group of mid-century texts on domestic ideology, including those by Sarah Stickney Ellis, whose *Women of England, Their Social Duties and Domestic Habits* (1839) extended itself into *Daughters* (1842), *Wives* (1843), and *Mothers of England* (1843). It is no wonder that by 1850 Brontë found the phrase "woman's mission" to be "hackneyed"—much as she thought there was too much "cant" in talk about the "woman question." But the fact that she believed these things suggests that she was well acquainted with the substance of the "woman's mission" and "woman question" arguments.[7]

A review essay published anonymously by T. H. Lister entitled "The Rights and Conditions of Women" is typical of articles on this subject. Lister considers works on what he calls "the education, rights, and condition of women," the existence of which, in the early 1840s, "sufficiently proves that increased attention has been directed to that subject." Like a later reviewer of *Woman's Mission*, whose essay Brontë comments on in her letter to Gaskell, Lister admires Lewis's chapter on woman's "influence" and finds appealing its "application to woman's duties." He quotes from *Woman's Mission* the assertion that women should participate in political power

> *as* moral *agents, as champions of right, in preference to the expedient. The immense influence which they possess, will be most beneficial if allowed to flow in its natural channels; namely, domestic ones. The political feelings of women are more likely to be guided by the abstract principles of right and wrong, if they themselves are restrained from the public expression of them. . . . It is of the utmost importance for men to feel, that in consulting a wife, a mother, or a sister, they are appealing from their passions and prejudices, and not to them, as embodied in a second self.*

Lister is frighteningly clear about the consequences that will ensue if women relinquish the role of moral agent and seek a more active form of public or political participation. He asserts—and I would claim that Brontë understood the force of this cultural argument only too well—that

> *women, as a class, cannot enjoy, at the same time, the immunities of weakness and the advantages of power. They may take their stand upon the latter ground, but in order to do so with safety they must* possess *the power which they assert. If they assume only the* appearance *of sharing it with man, and are invested with a privilege which their inferiority in numbers prevents them from using for their own benefit as a class, they will, while mocked with the shadow of authority, have excited a spirit of jealous opposition, which would deprive them of the advantages which man now yields without reluctance.*

Lister's point conceals a threat—or rather a number of threats. Men offer their chivalrous protection of the weak *to* the weak. Those who "take their stand upon the latter ground"—the ground of power—surrender the "immunities" that are granted by those charged with the protection of the weak. Should women assume power, Lister suggests, they would lose the protection upon which they depend and would become subject to attack. They had better, then, fully "possess the power which they assert," for if they merely assert it and do not possess it, they will excite "a spirit of jealous opposition" which they will not be in a position to oppose.[8]

Lister's language of sex warfare as a kind of class warfare in which women as a group will be outnumbered is striking. So are the open assertions that male "deference, tenderness, and courtesy" are paid to women because of their weakness, and the related threat that "ostensible power" and "competition" will put men on the defensive and bring about the speedy end of the "spirit of chivalry."[9] As we shall see when we turn to Brontë's *Shirley*, the heroine of that novel seems keenly aware of the risks associated with ostensible, or revealed, power and of the threat that underlies the recommendation that women retain moral authority but refrain from engaging openly in public affairs.It is not difficult to imagine in this context why Brontë figured herself "veil[ed]" before issues of great public import. Indeed, one thing that the reviews of *Woman's Mission* consistently reveal is how easy it is to see the text both as a source of female power and as a source of female powerlessness. Brontë's response to the later 1850 review indicates as much, and Lister's article makes clearer why this is so.

Brontë's letter to Gaskell intimates that she approved of the later article's favorable reading of *Woman's Mission*—though she also voiced reservations about it. The article invokes those who "regard the spiritual organization of man and woman to be one and the same, modified [only] by circumstance," and it implies through exaggeration that this view cannot be accurate: "This view of the case may be the right one—may be the one that time shall prove true on earth, and in some other sphere; physical strength equalized, its necessity perchance gone, sex destroyed, the streams of light descending from the Infinite on each, [they] shall be known to be the same, differing only in degree." The writer, of course, assumes that no such thing will occur and is determined to demonstrate, as Lewis had herself, that the "the native, elementary spiritual difference between man and woman" is the "great difference . . . that throws all others into the shade."[10]

Brontë would have admired several things in the 1850 article. First, she would have found appealing here—and this is true of all domestic ideology tracts in the period—the transformation of woman from ineffective and helpless creature into moral and spiritual guide: "She sends [man] from her with all the subtle threads of his being in firmer tension, and remembering only that he too 'is a little lower than the angels.' She can make him work, and dare even death for his work, and his heart ever beating with the love of the highest love. She can do this without knowing it, and because her *genius* is *influence*." Citing Aimé Martin, the reviewer agrees that "women do 'give the tone to morals,' that nothing which they really dislike,—from their souls disapprove,—can live. Man . . . has no standard of his own by which to regulate his conduct to woman, but uses hers."[11]

This is the view most clearly expressed in the text of *Woman's Mission.* Women operate as "moral agents; as representatives of the moral principle." Although women's political influence must "flow in its natural channels, viz.: domestic ones,—because it is of the utmost importance to the existence of influence that purity of motive be unquestioned," still this role is a form of "public participation," of "interfere[nce] in politics," that has largely gone unnoticed. What is interesting about *Woman's Mission,* however, is that it recognizes, indeed brings to the fore, the contradiction that is embedded in its proposal: "It seems somewhat irrational to condemn women to obscurity and detail for their field of exertion, while men usurp the extended one of public usefulness," or, as Lewis puts it elsewhere, "to induce women to acquiesce in a plan, which, assigning to them the responsibility has denied them the *éclat* of being reformers of society." Yet this is exactly what Lewis has in mind. Affirming the moral and intellectual power of women, she still wishes to see them "removed from the actual collision of political contests," and "*screened,*" as she puts it, "from the passions which such engender" (italics mine). Thus screened, woman maintains her purity and disinterestedness: "she brings party questions to the test of unalterable principles of reason and religion; she is, so to speak, the guardian angel of man's political integrity." Caroline Helstone's moral renovation of Robert Moore in *Shirley* will resemble, in many ways, just this view.[12]

Lewis argues that, even though women are thus removed from the political arena, they are not in fact removed from politics: "Governments will never be perfect till all distinction between private and public virtue, private and public honor, be done away . . . And shall it be said that women have no political existence, no political influence, when the very germs of political regeneration may spring from them alone?" Lewis first splits private from public events and then contends that ultimately "all distinction" must "be done away." Once woman's role as moral arbiter, as repository of unalterable moral principle, is established, then private life will be inextricably connected to public life—however impassable the gulf may in other ways be. The inherent contradiction in Lewis's position, as in the position of all domestic ideologists of the period, lies exactly in the insistence that women preserve their purity and disinterestedness, their separateness, and at the same time experience in some abstract or theoretical sense, the loss of distinction between public and private life that their influence will create.[13]

The *Westminster Review* author goes further, however, in suggesting that characteristic female traits often disparaged by others, traits like "tact . . . [which is] perhaps nothing more than refined dissimulation," are really evidence of something greater in women, of "a power stirring within them necessitating some expression of itself, undirected as yet by Christian law! And what work, what aims must we propose to her, that she shall so direct her power?" This question becomes a central one in the essay: what aims must we propose to her?[14]

The reviewer suggests that "weary, busy inactivity of mind" must end and that women must "act": they are "emerging . . . feeling around for safe channels through which the life-blood of [their] soul[s] may flow. . . . And all we can hope for them is that they may be allowed, incurring less and less odium thereby,—to choose their work and do it." The reviewer imagines a wide variety of work—work that it is hard to imagine Sarah Lewis recommending: "lecturing, public reading, the profession of the dissenting clergyman" as well as "employments fitter for the woman's nature"; even women who need not work for money should work because "loving service may win treasures our gold alone could not have procured us."[15]

As the situation of *Shirley*'s Caroline Helstone, and of Jane Eyre too, testifies, Brontë believed that women needed "exercise for their faculties, and a field for their efforts"; she would thus no doubt have admired and approved of the view that, at no cost to their womanliness, women might "direct [their] power" and "emerge." But Brontë also emphasizes, in her comments at the end of the letter to Gaskell, what is problematic to her in the *Westminster Review* article: "They say, however—and, to an extent, truly—that the amelioration of our condition depends on ourselves. Certainly there are evils which our own efforts will best reach; but as certainly there are other evils—deep-rooted in the foundations of the social system—which no efforts of ours can touch; of which we cannot complain; of which it is advisable not too often to think." It is difficult to know in detail what Brontë refers to here—exactly which evils are "deep-rooted in the foundations of the social system." Perhaps she senses in the midst of this extraordinary call to action, a countercall to inaction or, to put it another way, a failure to explain how the activity prescribed above might ever come to pass. Quoting Emerson's "Essay on Manners" and then repeating the phrase often, the reviewer insists with Emerson that "I believe only herself can show how she shall be served." The implication of this remark, especially as it emerges and reemerges in the essay, is that "woman must take a full share in the accomplishment of such a state of things, and that without her it must remain undone." Or, later, "whatever she can be she may; and that social or other laws have clauses inimical to her welfare is her own affair. She has not really cared to erase them, as yet."[16]

Brontë's comment to Gaskell suggests that while she is moved by the vision of "a power stirring within [women] necessitating some expression of itself," she has also concluded that "safe channels" are hard to find, that the social system is inhospitable to the expression of direct female power, and that individual efforts are hopeless against such a system. Brontë's reluctance even to name the evils—the reluctance to complain, even to think—discloses that the evils are indeed unspeakable and that the clear path toward expression the reviewer identifies is in Brontë's view a path that is hindered or blocked.

Brontë also commented in an 1851 letter to Gaskell on another essay in the *Westminster Review* now regularly attributed to John Stuart Mill's wife, Harriet Taylor. The article begins by describing the American women's movement (and its association with the abolitionist movement), citing the demands adopted by the Women's Rights Convention of October 1850 held in Worcester, Massachusetts, whose resolutions bear on education, equal access to "productive industry," and "coequal share in the formation and administration" of laws. Brontë appreciated the complaint—one of a larger set of complaints about things that are "permitted to one person and interdicted to another"—that "even in the exercise of industry, almost all employments which task the higher faculties in an important field, which lead to distinction, riches, or even pecuniary independence, are fenced round as the exclusive domain of the predominant section." She would also have agreed with the essay's assertions that

> many persons think they have sufficiently justified the restrictions on women's field of action, when they have said that the pursuits from which women are excluded are unfeminine, and that the proper sphere of women is not politics or publicity, but private and domestic life. . . . We deny the right of any portion of the species to decide for another portion, or any individual for another individual, what is or is not their "proper sphere." The proper sphere for all human beings is the largest and highest which they are able to retain.

Brontë remarked to Gaskell that "if there be a natural unfitness in women for men's employment there is no need to make laws on the subject; leave all careers open; let them try; those who ought to succeed will succeed, or, at least, will have a fair chance; the incapable will fall back into their right place."[17]

What Brontë objected to in the article emerges, I believe, as Harriet Taylor explores what she considers "the foundations of the subject . . . the real question":

> When, however, we ask why the existence of one-half the species should be merely ancillary to that of the other—why each woman should be a mere appendage to a man, allowed to have no interests of her own, that there may

*be nothing to compete in her mind with his interests and his pleasure; the
only reason which can be given is that men like it. It is agreeable to them
that men should live for their own sake, women for the sake of men. . . .
The meaning being merely, that power makes itself the centre of moral obligation, and that a man likes to have his own will, but does not like that his
domestic companion should have a will different from his.*

Surely this is what Brontë had in mind when she wrote to Gaskell that John
Stuart Mill (whom Brontë mistakenly thought to be the essay's author) was
unable to imagine between men and women "self-sacrificing love and disinterested devotion." The essay's analysis of the relations between the sexes would
have seemed to Brontë hardly less oppositional than Lister's proposition that
expressions of female power would trigger gender warfare.[18]

As representations of her heroines reveal, Brontë yearned for a wider field
of action for women, and in the essays that she read she consistently valued and
praised those who argued on behalf of wider opportunities for them—in moral
life, politics, education, and employment. She both honoured, and distanced
herself from, writing on great public causes, her ambivalence revealing itself in
the assertion that she "veiled herself" before "matters of public import." But
she resisted the idea that women were responsible for accomplishing changes on
their own in a society whose fundamental presuppositions about their roles were
unspeakable—even though she found spoken descriptions of these presuppositions, such as those in Harriet Taylor's essay, disturbing. These complex and
sometimes contradictory views found their literary expression in Brontë's novels,
perhaps most fully in *Shirley*. In the character of Miss Keeldar, Brontë imagines
(as she sometimes does in her letters) what a woman might do if she were a man
of public stature; but she also perceives that Shirley stands in the position of a
man without actually being one, and that her role is both extraordinary in its
play of opportunities and limited in its actual powers.

In that curious space between being a woman and playing at being a man,
Shirley gains access to public experience even while she refuses direct participation in it. She identifies herself symbolically with the opposite sex and also
"veils" or screens herself from direct public participation in a pivotal scene that
I shall explore in detail. Furthermore, her insistence on preserving the conventional distinction between publicity and privacy—even as her male role-playing
undermines it—serves to protect a private realm whose combative and ener-
gized sexuality sustains the belief that men and women can transcend the social
order, simultaneously mirroring and substituting itself for the recognition that
public life might provide. While *Shirley* does not offer the spectacle of unme-

diated female publicity—as such later novels as Gaskell's *North and South*, George Meredith's *Diana of the Crossways*, and Elizabeth Robins's *The Convert* will do— it does explore a mediated or veiled version of public experience that functions powerfully in the text. It also describes a counterrealm of intensely eroticized privacy (this is what Brontë feels Mill is unable to imagine)—what I will here call the "spectacle of intimacy"—that finally substitutes for the public spectacle that Shirley desires yet resists. The novel challenges our sense of the conventional distribution of public and private endeavor, at once affirming, undermining, and recreating the public/private distinction.

These challenges occur on a number of different levels: in the life and conduct of the mill operator Robert Gérard Moore, who complicates the conventional distribution of public and private endeavor by dangerously conflating them and performing the functions of both; in the character of Shirley's friend Caroline Helstone, who (not coincidentally) finds herself without any sphere of activity or operation at all; and in the heterogeneous, paradoxical activity of Shirley who at once subtly explores, openly embraces, and aggressively refuses the public realm that the novel represents and the gender conventions that it investigates.

II.

Our first introduction to Robert Moore is through the speech of Caroline's uncle and guardian, Mr. Helstone, who finds Moore's sense of self-containment surprising. Moore wants no helpers on a night when there is a fair "chance of a row" or, worse, a "riot," as new machinery is brought to his mill in defiance of the frame breakers' threats.[19] But Helstone considers Moore's proud isolation and comfortable sense of self-containment inappropriate and "careless"; he "sits in the counting-house with the shutters unclosed; he goes out here and there after dark, wanders right up the hollow . . . just as if he were the darling of the neighborhood"—which, clearly, he is not (48).

This early description of Robert Moore speaks to his self-sufficiency but also to his easy appropriation both of what is outside and what is in. Isolated in "his individual person from any community amidst which his lot might temporarily happen to be thrown" (60; among other problems, he is Anglo-Belgian), he nevertheless extends his personal boundaries to make a world around himself within which he feels comfortable and complete. The world of the countinghouse reaches to the neighborhood and thus there is no need to close the shutters.

Moreover, within the world thus defined, it is Moore's "fancy . . . to have every convenience within myself, and not to be dependent on the femininity of the cottage yonder for every mouthful I eat or every drop I drink. I often spend the evening and sup here alone, and sleep with Joe Scott in the mill. Sometimes I am my own watchman" (58). Though Moore makes a point of his independence and solitariness, he also stresses here the self-sufficiency that this brings. He likes the idea that, in serving as his own watchman, he can operate entirely by himself, but he also appreciates the fullness of his role: he can be the watcher and the watched, just as he can also be the cook and the consumer of mutton chops. When he asks his visitor and erstwhile dinner guest, Malone, whether the latter is party to "the secret of keeping the juices [of mutton chops] in," one feels that this is Moore's own great talent. He is self-contained but also self-complete; his recesses are "well-stored" (58).

As Malone correctly remarks, Moore is "not under petticoat-government . . . destined to be ruled by women" (59), but this is because he performs women's roles for himself: although the cottage is his real home (staffed by his sister), he keeps himself company, makes his other home—the countinghouse— comfortable, superintends his own stores, cooks and eats his own food.

There are two interesting problems associated with this mode of being. First, as Caroline Helstone notes, Moore's sense of independent agency is as-sociated with a problematic "manner" towards his workers (99). Caroline com-pares Moore to Shakespeare's Coriolanus, telling him: "You must not be proud to your workpeople; you must not neglect chances of soothing them, and you must not be of an inflexible nature, uttering a request as austerely as if it were a command" (117). Caroline worries about Moore's habit of alienating those who work for him and sees in his proud solitariness and independence the danger that, like Coriolanus, he too will be hated, and banished, by his people. Al-though she doesn't say so, his solitary self-sufficiency is also a risk to her because it speaks to her superfluity. Moore literally appropriates, and renders unnecessary, her female talents.

Moore's treatment of his workers and his treatment of Caroline are hence associated from the beginning of the novel. In his relationship to both he is a failed paternalist—because he insults the poor and treats them haughtily (118), focusing entirely on his own will to succeed; and because he similarly refuses, at least at the start, to figure importantly in Caroline's life, thus denying her the only role (loving him) available to her. Moore claims that he has no more time for romance than for friendly relations with his workers; his aim in life, he tells Caroline, is that of "patching up his broken fortune, and wiping clean from his bourgeois scutcheon the foul stain of bankruptcy" (144). Moore sees his own economic condition in moral terms—bankruptcy is a stain on his (bourgeois) breast—and though Caroline lets him off the hook in this difficult conversation (he is telling her directly that he has no time for romance)—she clearly judges this view of matters to be a mistaken one.

The moral tone Caroline exhorts Moore to take up in their Coriolanus discussion honors the humanity of others and sympathizes with their condition quite apart from the economic impact on him. Like a good proponent of the "woman's mission" argument, Caroline urges Moore to have a moral life independent of public exigencies, and she is careful to point out that she thinks he is capable of such feeling. It is his *manner,* she remarks, that is faulty, not his character. Moore's conflation of moral and economic matters (the phrase "foul stain of bankruptcy" captures this) collapses separate universes—collapses private and public concerns—in a way that is different from, but related to, his male appropriation of feminine practices in the mutton-chop scene and his conversion of the countinghouse into a snug home. The difficulty that Moore's behavior causes Caroline is precisely that, in a world in which she is expected to occupy a very traditional version of the private sphere, Moore has in fact appropriated that sphere and emptied her very constricted world of its already limited interests.

Caroline thereby becomes a perfect example of what mid-century writers would call the "redundant" or "superfluous" woman.[20] In the simplest sense, she has no one to marry, but her problem with Moore is more troubling than that. His well-stocked house empties her house of its meanings; his self-sufficiency at home renders her ministrations unnecessary; and his ability to turn countinghouse into living quarters, like his rendering of economic matters in moral terms, exemplifies the way he has merged private with public in his own person, rendering Caroline's very being unnecessary.

No wonder Caroline eventually sickens and fades. Her various efforts to find "an occupation" are all doomed to failure. The only interesting and pleasant way she might "mak[e her] way in life" would be available to her "if [she] were a boy"—she could apprentice herself to Robert's trade and learn to do the countinghouse work—but, needless to say, she is not a boy (99, 98); she considers being a governess, but her uncle forbids it and she hears enough disastrous news about this profession to relinquish the idea. The only labors available to her are those recommended by her uncle—"stick to the needle—learn shirt-making and gown-making, and pie-crust-making, and you'll be a clever woman some day" (122)—and those associated with the dreaded "Jew-basket" or "Missionary-basket" (so called because the proceeds from sales were used to convert Jews and regenerate blacks) that Caroline considers an "awful incubus" (134). Filled by "the willing or reluctant hands of the Christian ladies of a parish" with "pin-cushions, needle-books, card-racks, work-bags, articles of infant wear, &c.," its contents are then "sold per force to the heathenish gentlemen thereof, at prices unblushingly exorbitant." Brontë continues, "Each lady-contributor takes it in her turn to keep the basket a month, to sew for it, and to foist off its contents on a shrinking male public. An exciting time it is when that turn comes round: some active-minded women, with a good trading spirit, like it, and enjoy exceedingly the fun of making hard-handed worsted-spinners cash up, to the tune of four or five hundred per cent. above cost price, for articles quite useless to them" (134).

The Jew basket stands out in the novel as an example of fraudulent female labor and trade. To begin with, the women themselves are made slaves by their own labor, having no choice in the matter of contributing to the basket. And they sell to men who are heathens too—"hard-handed" creatures who must be cultivated by purchasing female goods. Furthermore, the women's labor has no authentic value attached to it, since they make what the men do not want to buy—small, invented commodities (the hyphens indicate the ways in which articles have been cobbled together in order to create new, if unnecessary, objects), or else items of exclusive interest to women (infant clothes), or both. And finally, those who buy them have no choice about their purchases and must nonetheless pay usurious prices for them. The devaluation both of the female labor involved in the making of these delicate pseudo-objects, and of the trading practices in which their value is (dis)established, is particularly notable in a novel in which female work, or rather the lack of it, is an authentic subject.

Caroline's "brain lethargy," her sense of dislocation ("Where is my place in the world?" 190), and her eventual physical decline are all functions of the double absence I have been describing: there *is* no authentic "woman's place" in this novel (it has been occupied by men), and there is no place outside woman's place either.

III.

When we are first introduced to Brontë's title character, it is immediately clear that Shirley stands in the place of an absent male heir and comes into view in the novel precisely at the moment when she achieves her majority and takes independent possession of her property.[21] Her parents, wanting a son, have given her "the same masculine family cognomen they would have bestowed on a boy, if with a boy they had been blessed" (211), and her "property of a thousand a-year" has "descended, for lack of male heirs, on a female" (208). Shirley is at once well-placed and oddly misplaced. Her presence calls up the absent male figure whom she both plays and replaces: that "brave but gallant little cavalier," "an esquire," "Mr. Keeldar," "the first gentleman of Briarfield" (212, 213, 215, 326).

Critics of the novel have been almost unanimous, however, in expressing the view that Shirley's role-playing is an empty gesture. Helene Moglen suggests that Shirley's "redefinition [of her role] is only a game. 'Captain Keeldar' is a collection of postures, gestures, and words: a child who, at the sufferance of adults, plays at being one of them." Sandra M. Gilbert and Susan Gubar refer to the "recurrent and hopeless concern with transvestite behavior" in Brontë's work, noting that "there is something not a little foreboding about the fact that independence is so closely associated with men that it confines Shirley to a kind of male mimicry." And Rosemarie Bodenheimer speaks of "the self-consciousness of [Shirley's] play-acting at masculinity" as "itself a recognition that women do not command power in the public realm."[22]

But, in my view, Shirley's role-playing also functions importantly and positively within the text—as it does in Brontë's letters to George Smith. To begin with, her "male mimicry" violates boundaries and manipulates categories in ways that challenge any simple placement of her gender and thus her social and sexual role. She uses her male disguise to play with, baffle, cover, and confuse her male interlocutors, not to affiliate herself with them. Rather than signaling a fatal identification with the male, as Gilbert and Gubar propose, her complex performances embody a refusal wholly to confine herself to the experiences of one sex or the other. They also suggest her desire to "cover" herself (in undecideability) and prevent others from penetrating and fixing her character even as she gains access to a wider range of experiences than she would otherwise have. Disguise is here composed of verbal and behavioral gestures instead of, as in *Jane Eyre* (Rochester's gypsy) and *Villette* (Lucy's stage performance), sartorial ones. Still, Marjorie Garber's insight that transvestism is really about "category crisis," and hence represents an important "failure of definitional distinction," is revealing about Shirley's situation as well.[23]

The confusions associated with Shirley's character have as a basis the fact that she doesn't *play* at being a millowner; she *is* a millowner. Yet she is acutely conscious of the sense in which she plays at being a man:

> *There was business to transact. Business! Really the word makes me conscious I am indeed no longer a girl, but quite a woman and something more. I am an esquire: Shirley Keeldar, Esquire, ought to be my style and title. They gave me a man's name; I hold a man's position: it is enough to inspire me with a touch of manhood; and when I see such people as that stately Anglo-Belgian—that Gérard Moore before me, gravely talking to me of busi-*

ness, really I feel quite gentlemanlike. You must choose me for your church-
warden, Mr. Helstone, the next time you elect new ones: they ought to make   (213)
me a magistrate and a captain of yeomanry.

In this scene, as in others, Shirley enjoys the fantasy that she is a man, but plays
with it openly before Mr. Helstone, who eagerly participates in what is clearly
marked as a fiction. He tells her companion, Mrs. Pryor, to "take care of this
future magistrate, this churchwarden in perspective, this captain of yeomanry,
this young squire of Briarfield, in a word: don't let him exert himself too much:
don't let him break his neck in hunting: especially, let him mind how he rides
down that dangerous hill near the Hollow" (215). Helstone goes along with
Shirley's presentation of herself as a man, all the while recommending to her
guardian that she be protected like a woman.

Brontë's portrayal remains mixed. Shirley may not be a man, but in certain
ways she behaves like one. "I like a descent," she replies, "I like to clear it rapidly."
And when asked if she likes the countinghouse and "the trade? The cloth—the
greasy wool—the polluting dyeing-vats?" she replies, "The trade is to be thoroughly respected" (215). She needs to be warned by Mrs. Pryor not to "allow
the habit of alluding to yourself as a gentleman to be confirmed: it is a strange
one. Those who do not know you, hearing you speak thus, would think you
affected masculine manners" (217).

In short, Brontë makes it difficult for us absolutely to place and identify Shirley. The sphere she occupies and the role she performs are decidedly
Robert Moore's—she is his landlord; she is physically fearless (267; as he is,
63); she shares in his attitude toward the poor ("if they bully me, I must
defy; if they attack, I must resist," 268); she even whistles like him. But unlike
the uncompromising Moore, she is a savvy, compromising politician who
knows that she is not a man and who has a keen understanding of her curious
status.

When Shirley develops her plan of aiding the poor (hoping, in large part,
to quell their anger and control the potentially explosive social situation that
Moore always aggravates), she is careful to present it to the rectors so as not to
alienate them. First the plan is drawn up not in Shirley's but in the subdued
Miss Ainley's hand—which wins one rector's immediate approval. But Mr. Helstone "glanced sharply round with an alert, suspicious expression, as if he ap-
prehended that female craft was at work, and that something in petticoats was
somehow trying underhand to acquire too much influence, and make itself of
too much importance" (272). Shirley is quick, however, verbally to undermine
her agency in the matter: " 'This scheme is nothing,' said she, carelessly; 'it is

only an outline—a mere suggestion; you, gentlemen, are requested to draw up rules of your own' " (272).

Brontë remarks that Shirley "smil[ed] queerly to herself as she bent over the table where her [writing case] stood"—in other words, while she faces away from the company of men and from Helstone in particular. As she presents Helstone with pen and paper for his signature, she holds her hand out and "beg[s] permission" to seat him at the table. The moment is odd and awkward for Helstone, who suspects that he is being manipulated but can't figure out how or where to penetrate and expose the scene. Shirley's manner is both that of a gracious wife and a gentlemanly host (the first provides him with his writing materials, the second pulls out his chair and offers to seat him) and Helstone doesn't know how, or to whom, he should respond. When he finally mutters, "Well—you are neither my wife nor my daughter, so I'll be led for once; but mind—I know I *am* led; your little female manoeuvres don't blind me," he appears to have fixed her gender and penetrated her guise (273). It is your intention, he seems to say, to be so gracious to me that I can't refuse—as a wife or daughter *plays* a subservient role while exercising her power under cover.

But Shirley upends him in an equally playful, but unnerving and disorienting, reply: " 'Oh!' said Shirley, dipping the pen in the ink, and putting it into his hand, 'you must regard me as Captain Keeldar to-day. This is quite a gentleman's affair—yours and mine entirely, Doctor (so she had dubbed the Rector). The ladies there are only to be our aides-de-camp, and at their peril they speak, till we have settled the whole business' " (273). Shirley's response is brilliant. If Helstone feels he is being led by the nose, then Shirley will immediately admit to her participation—thus undercutting and disavowing the accusation that she is manipulating him. But if he also resents being led by a woman (he dreads what the men call "petticoat government," though his wife is dead and he has no daughter), then Shirley will insist that she is not a woman, that she is "Captain Keeldar to-day" and so he needn't worry. She establishes this masculine vision of herself by articulating, almost to the point of embarrassment, Helstone's own views about the way the world should work, delivering the world to him just as he likes it to be: things like this are always a gentleman's affair; the ladies are auxiliary to the entire matter; their silence permits the men to take care of business as men obviously should. Let us grant all this, she seems to say: I'm willing enough to describe the world as you would like it to be!

Perhaps Helstone takes her response as a concession, because he sees in it an indication that Shirley intends in her actions no fundamental revision of the cultural conditions of his world. Her willingness to articulate, and by articulating somehow grant, his sense of the proper distribution of male and female power reassures him enough to proceed. But perhaps, too, Helstone doesn't want what Brontë later calls his "inward nature" read out any further. By articulating in public Helstone's private views, Shirley opens him up to scrutiny in a way that he can't wish her to resume. Brontë notes that he "smiled a little grimly" as he began to write, indicating simultaneously that he is satisfied and that he is not— or, rather, that his grounds for argument have been removed, even if he hasn't actually been the victor.

As Helstone moves forward into the general debate, letting his struggle with Shirley lapse, she stands "behind the rectors, leaning over their shoulders now and then to glance at the rules drawn up, and the list of cases making out, listening to all they said, and still at intervals smiling her queer smile—a smile not ill-natured, but significant: too significant to be generally thought amiable. Men rarely like such of their fellows as read their inward nature too clearly and truly" (273). Shirley's queer smile would indeed not be thought amiable if it could be seen; but Shirley stands behind the rectors and is careful not to reveal herself. (The last time she smiled like this, she faced away from the company and toward her writing table.)

Brontë's subsequent remarks about what is "good for women" function as a valuable commentary on Shirley. "It is good for women," she observes,

> *to be endowed with a soft blindness: to have mild, dim eyes, that never pene-*
> *trate below the surface of things—that take all for what it seems: thousands,*
> *knowing this, keep their eyelids drooped, on system; but the most downcast*
> *glance has its loophole, through which it can, on occasion, take its sentinel-*
> *survey of life. I remember once seeing a pair of blue eyes, that were usually* (273–
> *thought sleepy, secretly on the alert, and I knew by their expression—an ex-* 74)
> *pression which chilled my blood, it was in that quarter so wondrously unex-*
> *pected—that for years they had been accustomed to silent soul-reading. . . .*
> *she was the finest, deepest, subtlest schemer in Europe.*

This authorial intrusion is both spectacular and odd—a reference to the future Madame Beck of *Villette*—and establishes a hierarchy of watchfulness: from women as a group for whom it is thought good that they should have "dim eyes" that don't penetrate; to that subgroup of thousands who, "knowing this" (i.e., knowing this is thought good), pretend to blindness and keep their eyelids "drooped, on system" (partially down, intentionally and regularly) so that they can, now and again, see what's going on; to a further subgroup—"the most downcast"—who still, on occasion, take their "sentinel-survey"; and finally to that ultimate sleeper with the blue eyes who appeared entirely downcast but kept her sentinel-survey year in and year out. She was the "subtlest schemer" of all because her keeping of the watch was so invisible, so unexpected. If the schemer Brontë has in mind is indeed Madame Beck, then she is also a violator of the privacy of others, a woman motivated not by politics (as Brontë's language here suggests) but by self-interest.

Shirley herself resides in the middle of this range. Neither dim-eyed nor the subtlest schemer, she pretends to blindness in order to cover her ability to see and to penetrate, but she likes hinting at her knowledge, giving intimations of the power it implies. Brontë raises the specter of the ultimate schemer whose physiognomy is entirely unreadable and whose aim is not knowledge but rather duplicitous action; and yet Shirley is distinguished from her in the final lines of the chapter. When the work of the day is done and a glass of wine is raised in toast, "Captain Keeldar was complimented on his taste; the compliment charmed him: it had been his aim to gratify and satisfy his priestly guests: he had succeeded, and was radiant with glee" (274). The male pronouns return us to Shirley's performance as "Captain," while the phrase "radiant with glee" is decidedly female. The combination of the two suggests that Shirley's role-playing provides her with a useful, because baffling, disguise. As the pretense of blindness offers the opportunity to observe unnoticed, the pretense of masculinity defuses Shirley's feminine maneuvers—while her willingness to point to the disguise unnerves and confuses, even while it relieves, her guests.

IV.

In the critical and central riot scenes that soon follow, Helstone once again addresses Shirley in her Captain's guise and asks her to stay with Caroline in his absence. " 'Now,' interrupted Shirley, 'you want me as a gentleman—the first gentleman in Briarfield in short, to supply your place, be master of the Rectory, and guardian of your niece and maids while you are away?' " Helstone replies, "Exactly, captain: I thought the post would suit you. . . . *you*, who bear a well-tempered, mettlesome heart under your girl's ribbon-sash." Here, as elsewhere, Shirley will supply the place of a man—refusing a carving-knife for a weapon (that "lady's knife" will go to Caroline), and demanding instead a "brace of pistols" as Helstone prepares them for the possibility of a "disturbance in the night" which he does not identify (326).

Shirley makes it clear, however, that, despite Helstone's expectations that "we have no idea which way he is gone . . . nor on what errand, nor with what expectations, nor how prepared," she nevertheless "guess[es] much." And Caroline herself suspects "something." Shirley is properly struck by the discrepancy between the gentlemen's expectations of their ignorance—they "think that you and I are now asleep in our beds, unconscious" and the reality of the matter, which is that the two are very much on the alert (328).

The scene that follows begins with the remarkable visual image of Shirley, armed with her brace of pistols, "passing through the middle window of the dining-room" (a glass door) in order to be close enough to hear the conversation of the rioters as they pass the rectory on their way to the mill. Karen Chase has highlighted the importance of Brontë's spatial language, arguing that in Brontë's most "spatially *articulate*" novel, *Jane Eyre*, characters are "ceaselessly engaged in the opening and closing of windows and doors, the ascending and descending of staircases, the crossing of thresholds."[24] Though this is indeed a better description of *Jane Eyre* than of *Shirley*, the consciousness of outside and inside is intense in both novels. That is why the ease of Shirley's movements, the absence of impediments both internal and external, is so stunning, and this is even more significant because of the clear danger inherent in the women's situation.

What they overhear is talk of a possible intrusion into their home, the murder of Caroline's uncle, and the silencing of any woman who might hear them and raise the alarm—terrifying material to listen to when you are standing a foot away, shielded only by a "leafy screen" of shrubs (329). As Asa Briggs has noted, "attacks on mills, personal attacks, [and] home invasions (to steal weapons)" were common during the Luddite period in which *Shirley* is set, so that the women have reason to believe that they are very much at risk.[25]

When the barking of the rectory dog causes the rioters to fear that Helstone will awaken, their band moves on, leaving Caroline and Shirley behind. Shirley's response is a realistic one. She was prepared to fire her gun, and would have given the intruder "a greeting as he little calculated on," but says to Caroline that she could "not have effectually protected either you, myself, or the two poor women asleep under that roof" (331). This may seem to undercut Shirley's power, but Helstone could hardly have done better on his own. The two young women must next cross the fields to warn Robert Moore of the impending attack. Shirley is "surefooted and agile" while Caroline is "more timid, and less dexterous," but both are bold, resolute. It isn't until the end of their journey that shots ring out ("I thought we were dead at the first explosion," 333) and the sense of danger becomes evident.

From this point forward, Caroline and Shirley are thwarted in their desires and, in one sense, become "superfluous" to the main action (334). Both, it turns out, are frustrated in their effort to warn Moore of the impending danger—first, because they have arrived too late, and second because, as Shirley soon realizes when she detects the sentinel at the door, Moore is prepared already. But Shirley also thwarts Caroline's desire to rush forward and help her lover.

This time—in contrast to the earlier scene in which she passed so effortlessly from inside to outside with Caroline following behind—Shirley "clasped [Caroline] round the waist with both arms and held her back. 'Not one step shall you stir,' she went on authoritatively. 'At this moment, Moore would be both shocked and embarrassed, if he saw either you or me. Men never want women near them in time of real danger' " (333). Shirley's response reveals her familiar identification with male interests: she knows what men do and do not want. More significantly, however, it reveals her utter distance from them. Shirley insists on the separation between men and women; she insists that Caroline not mix romance with work, not mix private motives with public ones, not mix women with men. Moreover, Shirley repeats in her argument Moore's own view of his self-sufficiency. While Caroline must keep her love to herself and not bring it into the mill, Moore can have both his mill and his love—since his mill *is* his "lady-love" (333). Everything, in other words, resides on his side of the equation, nothing on hers.

Shirley's reading of their collective situation is, in one sense, an obvious disappointment in the novel—as critics have generally agreed. These women emerge from their dining room, pass effortlessly through the glass door, cross the dangerous fields, and arrive at the mill, but they may not mix with the men to whom the scene belongs: they may not emerge. Shirley's ownership of the mill is never mentioned and indeed has no bearing on the upcoming events. Nor, it seems, is her male persona welcome here. The women's only effectual act, Shirley will soon suggest, is their late arrival at the mill (mostly Caroline's fault as an inexperienced, if willing, climber of hedges)—since it saves them the "trouble of a scene" (334).[26]

Shirley has intriguing reasons for wishing to avoid such a scene: she imagines herself and Caroline bursting in on a room full of men all engaged in different versions of decidedly male behavior (they are either smoking, swaggering, sneering, or drinking, and Moore is in his "cold man-of-business vein," 334). The men are at their ease in this male preserve of the countinghouse, and they are also masters of the situation (this is why they *are* at ease); but in Shirley's projected fantasy of the scene, the women enter "toute éperdue"—completely frantic—because, having misread the situation, they think the men are in immediate danger. Moreover, their distraction and confusion are clearly set against the confidence and mastery of the men. And so the women at once expose their ignorance and undermine their own vision of themselves as acting out of "duty" and with "wisdom" (331).

Shirley does not wish to be at a disadvantage when it comes to knowledge. Her power, in this scene and in others, comes from knowing, and knowledge comes from managing her own mode of appearance, from controlling, often by confusing, the perception of her identity. This is why Shirley says, as she becomes for Caroline (and for us) the main narrator of the battle's action, "I am glad I came: we shall see what transpires with our own eyes: we are here on the spot, and none know it. Instead of amazing the curate, the clothier, and the corn-dealer with a romantic rush on the stage, we stand alone with the friendly night, its mute stars, and these whispering trees, whose report our friends will not come to gather" (334–35). From Shirley's point of view, the women's courage, combined with their self-restraint, has placed them in a highly unusual position. They are right on the scene, "here on the spot," of this crucial political struggle, and they can watch the battle unfold even if they cannot engage directly in its actions. Seeing with their "own eyes," and being "here on the spot," are not identical with dealing and receiving blows (336), but seeing and being there are not insignificant, either. Shirley and Caroline glean their own information about, and have their own experience of, this struggle for "money, and food, and life" (333), and their experience is uncensored and unmediated by the men who would otherwise report (or not report) it to them.

What they do not do is participate directly in the action and, equally importantly, insist on their own public appearances upon this stage. Still, Shirley's language *is* theatrical (it is the language of public appearance) just as her imagination of the setting is theatrical (it suggests performance before an audience). But in refraining from entering the mill, the women change their audience in a very significant way. In place of the "the curate, the clothier, and the corn-dealer"—all identified here in their public roles—the observers of their action are the friendly (because obscuring) night, the mute stars (who are not in a position to report on them if they could), and the whispering wind (which might report, but whose report isn't sought). The women's presence on the scene—which, if not the central action of the night, is still an action of some standing—has only inhuman observers. The women are witnesses, but they are themselves unwitnessed.

Their role as spectators is reaffirmed when Brontë states that the women wonder whether "a juncture [would] arise in which they could be useful" and that Shirley in particular would have given "a farm of her best land for a chance of rendering good service"—only to declare, moments later, that "the chance was not vouchsafed her; the looked-for juncture never came" (337). As the day dawns, however, the power of the event and the importance of seeing it, emerge as well. The women perceive that "just here in the centre of the sweet glen, Discord, broken loose in the night from control, had beaten the ground with his stamping hoofs, and left it waste and pulverized" (338). The ruin of the mill, the bloodied weapons, the dead body, the wounded and writhing men who "moaned in the bloody dust" are all visible to them. Brontë will later observe that in Shirley's experience the scene "was one unparalleled for excitement and terror by any it had hitherto been her lot to witness" (341).

Brontë also tells us that the only reason the women are able to witness the scene is that "they could see without being seen" (337). Their situation as un-witnessed witnesses is crucial, and Shirley will maintain it by holding Caroline back yet one more time before the scene draws to a close. She will warn her not to "make a spectacle" of herself (338); she will maintain that if Caroline "showed [herself] now" she would "repent it an hour hence" (339); and she will insist that Robert must be "unmolested" in his work (339). In all of these instances, but especially in the last one, Shirley makes a connection between female public appearance and imputations about its sexual meaning. Shirley's repeated restraint of Caroline—against which Caroline struggles in vain—is an effort to disengage or uncouple a familiar, and to Shirley unwanted, association between female public appearance and unconstrained sexuality. "Restrained from the public expression" of "political feelings," Caroline is also protected from displaying her "passions" (the words, as noted above, are Sarah Lewis's).

In exposing their bodies where ordinarily no female bodies are seen, in making spectacles of themselves by virtue of the extraordinariness of their appearance, women who enter a public domain managed and controlled by men (as this one assuredly is), introduce the issue of sex where it hasn't been introduced before. This is why Shirley earlier refers to their (aborted) emergence into the countinghouse as a "romantic rush on the stage" (335) and why she vigorously counsels Caroline against "showing" herself. When she says that Robert must be "unmolested," she means that he must not be bothered. But she means too that he must not be wept over, petted, embraced. There is no doubt in Shirley's mind that Caroline's action—and indeed *both* of their actions had they entered the scene together—would have been construed in romantic and sexual terms. To introduce the female body into the world of "serious work" (339) is inevitably to raise the issue of sex in an unexpected place, to name (and limit) the motives of the actors, to fix them sexually, indeed to reduce them to sex.

Finally, such an action is, in Shirley's view, a *dis*empowering one, and for two reasons. First, Shirley knows that the women's actions *will* be misunderstood—their intention had been to warn Moore, to "render good service" if that had been possible—but their actions will be interpreted sexually if their presence is discovered. Discovery will take from the women the one source of power they have—the power that resides in their knowledge and in the men's ignorance of their knowledge. To "see without being seen" is, then, to get as close as one can to the serious work of the world without relinquishing one's cover and, further, one's access to knowledge. To see without being seen—to veil oneself—is also to avoid having one's actions misconstrued and thereby to avoid being "taunt[ed]" with the "misconstruction." On the other hand, to maintain one's cover is to give oneself an edge in the unequal balance of power between men and women. "We will steal in as we stole out," Shirley concludes: "None shall know where we have been, or what we have seen to-night: neither taunt nor misconstruction can consequently molest us" (340). To Shirley, their invisibility on the scene both protects them from (sexual) misinterpretation and molestation and provides them with a source of power that derives from the imbalance in knowledge to which they may now lay claim.[27]

Bodenheimer is right to assert that "the women's midnight escapade to witness the attack, an important and radical secret to Shirley, is entirely periph-eral to the course of public events," part of "a strictly limiting perspective on the romance of female rescue." But this assertion does not capture the magnitude of importance to the women of the unmediated knowledge they gain, does not recognize the difference between "being here on the spot" and not being present at all. Terry Eagleton calls the raid on the mill "the central dramatic incident of the novel" yet oddly insists that it is "empty because the major protagonist, the working class, is distinguished primarily by its absence." Why Eagleton says this is perplexing. The working class *is* present at the mill—they can be seen at-tacking, and their bloodied bodies are described in the aftermath of the battle. The obvious thing to notice is that it is the *women* who are distinguished by their marginality—but Eagleton overlooks this point because he has a different case to press. When he does speak of Shirley and Caroline's role, he argues that the women "don't really see [the battle] either"; their "response is auditory." This is not true, either. Eagleton confuses the scene at Helstone's house (where the women listen from behind the hedge) with the scene at the mill (where they "see without being seen") and fails to take seriously the importance Shirley attaches to her presence at this critical event.[28]

Gilbert and Gubar are also mistaken about the mill scene, contending that "when the workers . . . break down gates and doors, hurling volleys of stones at the windows of the mill, Caroline and Shirley are divided in sympathy be-tween owners and workers and effectively prevented from any form of partici-pation." But Caroline's and Shirley's difference of opinion has nothing to do with owners and workers and everything to do with a difference of perspective on the risks of female publicity. Gilbert and Gubar go on to claim that Brontë's heroines "are so circumscribed by their gender that they cannot act at all," yet as Shirley's interpretation of events suggests, she believes that they *have* acted. This is not to disagree entirely with those like Robert Keefe who profess that the women are "excluded from the world of deeds" or that their action is not the sort of "heroic activity" one might wish. But it is to maintain that their presence on the scene is an action of very real importance and significant standing.[29]

When Miss Keeldar and Mr. Moore meet the next day, Shirley wonders, "Acute and astute, why are you not also omniscient? How is it that events transpire, under your very noses, of which you have no suspicion? It should be so, otherwise the exquisite gratification of out-manoeuvring you would be unknown. Ah! friend, you may search my countenance, but you cannot read it" (351–52). Moore replies, "What have you and she been doing? . . . What is your mutual mystery?" (352); but Shirley isn't telling. Not being seen comes here to mean more than not being misconstrued; it comes to mean not being read at all. Shirley's impenetrability, her mysteriousness, her secrecy, puts her out of reach of Moore's mastery—and this is precisely where she wishes to be.

In a related scene, when Shirley defends Moore's actions at the mill in vigorous terms—only to have Hiram Yorke mistake her political views for romantic ones, to merge the very divergent realms that Shirley kept so decidedly separate at the mill—the result is similar. Yorke is convinced, by the spirited nature of her speech, that Shirley is not defending a compatriot but a lover, and Shirley seems on the verge of losing control both over the interpretation of her character and over her corresponding insistence that personal and political matters be kept apart. When Yorke asks, "When [the wedding] is . . . to be?" (358), Shirley "gazed at the questioner with rising colour; but the light in her eye was not faltering: it shone steadily—yes—it burned deeply. 'That is your revenge,' she said, slowly: then added; 'Would it be a bad match, unworthy of the late Charles Cave Keeldar's representative?' " (359). Shirley's suggestion that Mr. Yorke seeks to "revenge" himself upon her for asserting so animatedly a set of political views different from his own reveals the combative struggle for power that underlies even this spirited friendship.

But in the discussion that ensues (about whether or not Moore is a gentleman), Shirley and Mr. Yorke are really having two different conversations—one about Robert Moore, and another, invisible, one about Louis Moore. Here, as elsewhere, Shirley takes a secret pleasure in speaking on behalf of her real lover (Robert Moore's brother), in uttering his name and defending his character, without letting her interlocutor know that she is doing so. Shirley acts—or here, speaks—under cover. She discerns what Yorke is doing, but he is unable to penetrate her; and the result is that she regains the position that, when her color rose, she seemed momentarily to have lost:

> *"Moore is a gentleman," echoed Shirley, lifting her head with glad grace. She checked herself—words seemed crowding to her tongue, she would not give them utterance; but her look spoke much at the moment; what—Yorke tried to read, but could not—the language was there—visible, but untranslatable—a poem—a fervid lyric in an unknown tongue. It was not a plain story, however—no simple gush of feeling—no ordinary love-confession—that was obvious; it was something other, deeper, more intricate than he guessed at: he felt his revenge had not struck home; he felt that Shirley triumphed—she held him at fault, baffled, puzzled; she enjoyed the moment—not he.* (359)

Yorke fails on several fronts: he fails to implicate Shirley in the confusion of public statement and private feeling (thus failing as well to taint her impartial stand); he fails to understand her and to reduce her to a romantic creature whose emotions are written on her face; and he fails both to revenge himself and to enjoy the experience. More importantly, perhaps, the scene is compelling for the way Shirley represents herself in it—as Brontë puts it, she is "visible, but untranslatable." This reading of her puts a striking twist on Shirley's experience at the mill: there, she saw "without being seen" and thus also without being misconstrued. In this instance she avoids misconstruction and, in addition, represents her feelings without actually making them accessible. As in the scene with Robert Moore, *she* is the one who gets to enjoy the moment, and her pleasure derives from the fact that she has an experience, a secret, worth protecting, and that she successfully baffles penetration of it. Yorke seeks to expose the sexual meaning of Shirley's language and, by exposing it, to make her vulnerable. But Shirley turns the sexual accusation back on him: he is the one who is vulnerable and confused, not she.

What makes Shirley's mode of operation in the novel so absorbing is that she consistently finds ways to exercise power, assert her agency, gain access to significant experience, even represent her feelings, while still preserving the distinction between public and private action, protecting herself from taint and misconstruction, conserving (by veiling) her private self. Navigating the territory between constraint and cover on the one hand, and the exercise of her faculties on the other, Shirley seeks action in covered performances, gains public experience through invisibility, finds knowledge in seeing without being seen, and self-expression in speaking without being understood.

Thus, when Robert Moore says about Shirley that she is "jealous of compromising her pride, of relinquishing her power, of sharing her property" (561), he is clearly wrong. Though she has no wish to subject herself to the risks associated with self-exposure, Shirley also rejects the constraint, starvation, repression, and nonrecognition that Gilbert and Gubar describe with such force and insight in their detailed analysis of Caroline Helstone's life.[30] On the odd middle ground that Shirley occupies, experience without exposure is her credo, and private, mutual recognition with another her aim.

Shirley's central desire in the novel is her desire for recognition. In the old French *devoir* that she composed for Louis Moore when she was his pupil and that he recites for her when he comes to Fieldhead, the new Eve of her creation myth is an orphan who fears "burning unmarked to waste in the heart of a black hollow. She asked, was she thus to burn out and perish, her living light doing no good, never seen, never needed,—a star in an else starless firmament,—which nor shepherd, nor wanderer, nor sage, nor priest, tracked as a guide, or read as a prophecy?" (457). Shirley wants to be seen, where seeing is tied to usefulness and to the exercise of one's powers. What she fears is "burning unmarked . . . in the heart of a black hollow." The latter reference is an intriguing one—because of the verbal allusion to the mill hollow and to the scene in which both Shirley and her friend Caroline do "[burn] unmarked." In that scene Shirley acts under cover, baffling and resisting rather than encouraging recognition. In the mill scene she *prizes* the "mute stars" and the darkness of night that protect her and her companion from taunt, molestation, misconstruction—much as her other fictions do. But this only makes the point that the sort of recognition she writes about is unavailable in the public sphere; it must not be sought in the public sphere, where exposure inevitably means public spectacle, and public spectacle leads not to recognition but to misconstruction. The public exercise of faculties is associated with knowledge and power but not with recognition. Quite the contrary: those who exercise their faculties at all do so under cover. Recognition, if it is sought, is sought separately and elsewhere—as a psychological matter, and in private.[31]

V.

This view perhaps explains why the novel appears to desert its political interests and to move so dramatically from public to private concerns (as well as from outdoor to indoor scenes) in its second half.[32] The only real opportunities for authentic recognition, for mutual beholding, occur in the psychological or psychosexual realms, where the spectacle at hand is the spectacle of interiority.

Mrs. Pryor moves from behind her "screen" and reveals herself to be Caroline's mother—telling her story and offering up the terrifying picture of the hidden interior life of her former spouse—and Caroline engineers an illicit visit to Robert's bedside—all for the purpose of revealing love in private.

The novel's most suggestive, if also its most disturbing, private scenes are those that involve Shirley and Louis Moore—though curiously these often take place when the two are not together. Here, the controlled, guarded, covered self that Shirley manifests in public disappears as she leaves behind evidence of her person and access to her most (symbolically) private places. When Shirley is absent from Fieldhead and Louis wanders about its rooms, he "makes discoveries. A bag, a small satin bag, hangs on the chair-back. The desk is open, the keys are in the lock; a pretty seal, a silver pen, a crimson berry or two of ripe fruit on a green leaf, a small, clean delicate glove—these trifles at once decorate and disarrange the stand they strew" (486). In language that recalls Shirley's French *devoir,* Moore refers to these evidences of Shirley's person as her "mark[s]," or alternatively her "foot-prints," and they do function as representations of her self, as exposing signs. But what Louis sees is manifestly an interior display—the inside of a desk, the inside of a purse—the contents of which are not designed to be seen but are nonetheless (or perhaps therefore) most revealing. The materials in the desk are provocatively intimate too—a seal and a pen, ripe berries, a glove (absent the hand, but standing in for it)—the objects, and the pretty disarray, evoking a sexual vulnerability and openness rarely associated with Shirley's person. Later, Louis notes that the keys are those to her "jewel casket" and that inside the little satin bag lies yet another purse whose "tassel of silver beads hanging out" invites exploration. What Louis examines are Shirley's private places and possessions—he "occup[ies] her room," then examines her desk, then inside that desk her purse, and inside the purse another purse. He refers to all of this as a "spectacle"—a noteworthy choice of words, since after all he is wandering about in Shirley's private rooms. If this is spectacle, however, it is the spectacle of interiority, available to him only because, in private, Shirley relaxes precisely that control over her person that she so vigorously maintains elsewhere. Louis calls this Shirley's "loophole of character" (489), and the phrase is apt because it suggests a point of exit (where she lets evidence of interiority slip out) as well as a point of entry (that permits Louis to gain access to her).

Louis's investigation of Shirley's private places is really a *violation* of her private places—he records in his journal, in surprisingly rough language, that "a whole garment sometimes covers meagerness and malformation; through a rent sleeve, a fair round arm may be revealed," and he makes it clear that he has "seen and handled" her possessions before "because they are frequently astray"

(490). And yet it is evident in Brontë's presentation of this charged material, that Louis's penetration of Shirley's private world would satisfy the desire for intimate recognition and revelation expressed in that early essay of hers and available in the novel in no other way. Furthermore, Louis's invasion of Shirley's privacy is mirrored, and its problematic features partially neutralized, by the reader's invasion of Louis's privacy: as he sits in Shirley's parlor and writes in his journal, Brontë invites the reader to approach and read: "Come near, by all means, reader: do not be shy: stoop over his shoulder fearlessly, and read as he scribbles" (487).

Brontë's sexualizing of the scene is particularly arresting for combining sexual violation with sexual innocence—as, in a different manner, George Meredith will do in *Diana of the Crossways* when he describes his heroine as "spotted but not guilty." What Louis keeps finding as he investigates the desk, or the pouch, or the rent sleeve, is Shirley's unsullied innocence: "I never saw anything that did not proclaim the lady: nothing sordid, nothing soiled; in one sense, she is as scrupulous as, in another, she is unthinking" (490). For all of its provocative language (and there is more to come), the spectacle of interiority is, it seems, a clean spectacle, and this is important because it means that when Shirley does reveal herself, she is not subject to the "taunt and misconstruction" characteristic of public spectacles. The spectacle of interiority, with its audience of one, privatizes display, allows it to remain pure, makes it acceptable.

This is, in my view, stunning, especially because, from this point forward, the language of sexuality—in everyone's description of it—is the language either of sadomasochism or, more specifically, of bondage and mastery:

> My *sweetheart . . . must bear nearer affinity to the rose: a sweet, lively delight guarded with prickly peril.* My *wife . . . must stir my great frame with a sting now and then . . . I was not made so enduring to be mated with a lamb: I should find more congenial responsibility in the charge of a young lioness or leopardess. I like few things sweet, but what are likewise pungent;*
(490)   *few things bright but what are likewise hot. . . . Beauty is never so beautiful as when, if I tease it, it wreathes back on me with spirit. Fascination is never so imperial as when, roused and half-ireful, she threatens transformation to fierceness. . . . my patience would exult in stilling the flutterings and training the energies of the restless merlin. In managing the wild instincts of the scarce manageable "bête fauve," my powers would revel.*

Louis's instinct for mastery, containment, and teacherly correction, combined with his predisposition to violation, are often hard to take—especially as they are exercised in relation to the masterful, contained, and empowered figure of Shirley Keeldar. But this passage and others like it also suggest that Louis appreciates Shirley's playful, mutinous, oppositional energy. The language of sexual mastery is also a language of sexual play, what Louis calls "pleasurable vexation" (489). The question of who is master and who is slave is left open. Shirley says of herself that "she will accept no hand which cannot hold me in check" (513), and Caroline will later say of Shirley, "Whatever I am, Shirley is a bondswoman. Lioness! She has found her captor" (560); but Louis says of himself, at the end of the chapter I have been discussing, that his ability to make Shirley perform for him, to display herself to him, actually makes him *her* slave: "Every feature of her face, her bright eyes, her lips, shall go through each change they know, for my pleasure: display each exquisite variety of glance and curve, to delight— thrill—perhaps, more hopelessly to enchain me. If I *must* be her slave, I will not lose my freedom for nothing" (492).

A similar oscillation between assertions of one's mastery and the other's bondage emerges in the final scene in which Shirley and Louis reveal their love for each other. When Louis playfully imagines marrying a penniless orphan girl—"Oh! could I find her such as I imagine her. Something to tame first, and teach afterwards: to break in, and then to fondle. To lift the destitute proud thing out of poverty; to establish power over, and then to be indulgent to" (576), his fantasy emphasizes his mastery and her objecthood. But when he finally ad-dresses Shirley, he calls her "my pupil, my sovereign" (578). And when she asks, "Will you be good to me, and never tyrannize?" he asks, "Will you let me breathe, and not bewilder me?" (579). It is Shirley who proposes to Louis—an unusual turn of events for a Victorian novel: "I do not ask you to take off my shoulders all the cares and duties of property; but I ask you to share the burden, and to show me how to sustain my part well. . . . Be my companion through life; be my guide where I am ignorant: be my master where I am faulty; be my friend always!" He replies, "So help me God, I will" (580). The emphasis is on the mutuality of relations, not on the mastery of one or of the other.[33]

It thus seems inappropriately disapproving to conclude about Shirley and Louis that their relationship reveals, in the words of one scholar, the "sad in-evitability of female oppression," that it "marks [Shirley] as society's ritual vic-tim," and that it "exhausts itself in resignation . . . personal confusion and dis-illusionment."[34] Brontë combines this extraordinary master/slave language with insistent descriptions of Shirley's "maiden modesty" and "stainless virgin[ity]" (487). She both describes the pleasures of private sexual display and insists on their purity at the same time. In this context, it seems, Louis's display of his most intimate feelings, like Shirley's display of her interior life, is desirable and even proper. Sexual self-representation is an occasion for spectacle and display, but it is permitted and affirmed when it occurs in private and when everyone concerned assiduously preserves the distinction between public and private exposure. (In a later scene, Caroline will insist to an unbelieving Robert that she has privately seen Shirley's true feelings, and Robert will reply, "You saw this spectacle? . . . Her heart's core? Do you think she showed you that?" Caroline will reply in the affirmative and declare that it was "like a shrine, for it was holy; like snow,—for it was pure" (559–60). Shirley's insistence on the screening of the private self in public—in the mill scene and elsewhere—is not, in Brontë's way of imagining it, a relinquishment of the right to appear but, rather, a means to guarantee the separateness of the private self, safeguarding its right to intimate, private exposure and recognition that is free of the dangers of taint and misconstruction.

Shirley's complaint about Robert Moore's earlier, unsuccessful marriage proposal to her emerges both as a complaint about *his* confusion of public and private matters and about the misreading of her character that ensues. Brontë has Robert report on the event much after the fact, almost as though she wants no *direct* representation of his defective proposal and its consequences. Robert describes Shirley's "shocked" and "indignant" response: "You spoke like a brigand who demanded my purse, rather than like a lover who asked my heart. . . . *you* want to make a speculation of me. You would immolate me to that mill— your Moloch!" (498, 499). Robert's purely financial interest in Shirley's purse is differentiated from Louis's sexual interest in it, as Robert's tainting conflation of economic with romantic matters is differentiated from Louis's clean exploration of Shirley's interior life. The conflation of public and private realms brings with it what Brontë always assumes it will bring—the misreading and misinterpretation of what Shirley calls the "possession of all I value most"—namely her character.

The novel's logic demands that Robert will eventually propose to his proper mate, Caroline—not only because she has always loved him, but because he has learned to value *as distinct from himself* the virtues associated with domesticity and privacy. When he comes back to the cottage after his convalescence, Moore announces, "I am pleased to come home." Brontë comments that his sister Hortense "did not feel the peculiar novelty of this expression coming from her brother, who had never before called the cottage his home"—but she should have (555). Acknowledging a home separate from the mill and countinghouse is in effect the same thing as acknowledging Caroline, whose life is transformed when Robert stops appropriating its contents and grants her sphere, seeking first to distinguish public from private, and then to value both.

As different as their stories are, then, Caroline and Shirley affirm in their lives the centrality of maintaining separate spheres and of investing private life with meaning. Brontë does not here imagine, as Elizabeth Gaskell will later do, that public experience is the stage of female self-discovery, including sexual self-discovery. The desire for access to public life—to great endeavors, to consuming occupations and deeds—is very much present in Brontë's, as it is in Gaskell's, novel, but Brontë knows that women cannot survive intact in the public realm. Shirley's undercover operations are efforts fully to exercise her faculties and powers without risking misconstruction of her character. She challenges boundaries, baffles interpreters, gains knowledge that redresses the imbalance of power between men and women, and penetrates the meaning of central events. She also forestalls unmediated self-exhibition and self-display (her own and Caroline's) with the intention of saving them, and the recognition they confer, for a reinvigorated and sexualized private sphere.

The rootedness in social circumstance that is at the heart of the public to private conversion I have described has its context not only in the discourse of paternalism that Bodenheimer analyzes but also in the emerging—if transitional—discourse on the "woman question" in the 1840s. It may be true, as Inga-Stina Ewbank points out, that "the central preoccupation" of this decade "is with the woman as an influence on others within her domestic and social circle,"[35] but it is also true that the debate about woman's influence inevitably became a debate about her power within that circle and, inevitably, about the real meaning of female moral power and its extensions outward into the public realm. As Brontë construed it, the private/public debate was also an occasion to meditate on the meaning of female public life, to affirm its importance, doubt its possibility, and imagine alternatives that made some access to it possible.

Brontë's women gain unmediated knowledge of the public sphere, even though they do not engage directly in its battles, "neither deal nor . . . receive blows" (336), do not *emerge*. Brontë is highly conscious of the instinct toward, and potential excitement associated with, life in the public sphere at the same time that she is acutely knowledgeable about the risks that are still attached to such excitement and about the alternative pleasures of intimacy and privacy protected from public exposure. The world of sexual intimacy that Brontë's language suggests, a combative world of perpetually reversible bondage and mastery that is, at the same time, miraculously free of contamination or taint, transforms political combat into sexual combat, and public spectacle into private, sexual spectacle. Reinvigorating the public/private distinction, while also transposing public terms into private scenes, Brontë affirms and denies the traditional meanings usually associated with the distinction. It is, in the end, the spectacle of intimacy—and not of publicity—that provides the true scene of recognition and emergence for Brontë's extraordinary heroine. But the surprising continuity of public and private terms suggests how closely allied—if still finally separated—the desire for publicity and the desire for intimacy prove to be.

II

Woman's Work in
North and South

I.

Writing to her friend Lady Kay-Shuttleworth after the publication of *Ruth* (1853), Elizabeth Gaskell distinguishes herself from her friend Charlotte Brontë, defending Brontë's person (as she would do on a grander scale in *The Life of Charlotte Brontë*, 1857) by pointing out the "difference between Miss Brontë and me": "she puts all her naughtiness into her books, and I put all my goodness. I am sure she works off a great deal that is morbid *into* her writing, and *out* of her life; and my books are so far better than I am that I often feel ashamed of having written them and as if I were a hypocrite."[1] Gaskell's purpose here is to defend Charlotte by suggesting that the morbidity of *Villette* is "work[ed] off" from her character and in addition that it is an old morbidity ("all the passions & suffering, & deep despondency of that old time"), quite separate from her virtuous, "present self." In contrasting Brontë's character with her own by suggesting that "my books are so much better than I am," Gaskell makes a different kind of distinction between character and text—here reflecting, to the discredit of her own character, that her novels are braver, more courageous, than she feels herself to be. Her shame is a function of the distance she feels between their goodness and her own indifferent selfhood.

What is interesting about these remarks is that Gaskell did not always distinguish her (better) books from her (worse) character in this fashion. Earlier in the same letter, in fact, she noted that *Ruth* would occasion "great difference of opinion" about whether or not her "subject was a fit one for fiction." She did feel that *Ruth* had "made them talk and think a little on a subject which is so painful that it requires all one's bravery not to hide one's head like an ostrich and try by doing so to forget that evil exists." But Gaskell's remarks hint both at her courage and her shame: she is the brave writer who has invited readers to think about the shameful subject of the fallen woman.[2]

Two months earlier than this, in a letter to her friend Eliza Fox, she described herself as suffering from " 'Ruth' fever" in response to the "hard things people had said" about her novel. Then she added, "I think I must be a very improper woman without knowing it. I do so manage to shock people. Now *should* you have burnt the 1st vol. of Ruth as so *very* bad? even if you had been a very anxious father of a family? Yet *two* men have; and a third has forbidden his wife to read it; they sit next to us in Chapel and you can't think how 'improper' I feel under their eyes."[3] Ruth fever indeed! Gaskell's response recalls a variety of scenes in the novel, often in public settings, in which Ruth senses the possible impropriety of her situation by perceiving others' perceptions of it—Mrs. Mason's when she first sees Ruth on a walking expedition with Bellingham in the fields near her old home; Bellingham's mother's when she encounters Ruth during her son's illness at the inn where he and Ruth are vacationing. In this reading of the situation, *the novel's* impropriety is what stands out—though of course it taints the writer (she feels " 'improper' . . . under their eyes") if it does not actually reveal an unconscious, *prior* taint in her character ("I must be a very improper woman without knowing it"). Gaskell suggests here not that her "goodness" has crept into her novels but rather (like Brontë) that her unseemliness has. Even her amusing figure of speech—she has " 'Ruth' fever"—suggests an infectious relation between the person and the text rather than a clear distinction between them.

Still, it would be wrong to dismiss Gaskell's assertion that her novels are "better" than she is. She believed both things: that they were better, more courageous, more philanthropic than she felt herself to be and also that her "goodness" expressed itself in ways others considered venturesome and indecorous—which in turn made her feel "improper." In her breezy, voluble letters to friends and family about all manner of household matters, as in her self-deprecatory remarks about her capacity to discuss social and political issues, it is sometimes hard to discern the strong author of *Mary Barton, Ruth,* and *North and South.* But Gaskell's own complex self-analysis helps us to do so.

In reading her correspondence and in reading about her life, one is repeatedly struck by the mixed tone of her reactions toward the great women's issues of the day—work, property rights, education, philanthropy. Gaskell's relationship to the campaign for reform of the married women's property laws offers an especially interesting example of her complex positions. There is every reason to believe that she would have read Barbara Leigh Smith's "A Brief Summary, in Plain Language, of the Most Important Laws Concerning Women" (1854), which Smith assembled as part of her work on the campaign. Gaskell's signature was actively solicited, and she did sign the petition that was presented to Parliament on 14 March 1856, a document that many of her current and future friends and acquaintances signed as well—the early feminists Anna Jameson, Harriet Martineau, and Mary Howitt; a younger generation of activists including Bessie Rayner Parkes and Barbara Smith (both members of the Langham Place Group; Smith was also the petition's author); and writers like Geraldine Jewsbury, Elizabeth Barrett Browning, and George Eliot.[4]

The petition does not propose the uprooting of familiar social relations or unmask, as Smith's pamphlet certainly did, the elaborate ways in which women were rendered nonexistent under the law. In the pamphlet, Smith wrote that under the present law of coverture "a woman's body belongs to her husband; she is in his custody"; she "acts under the command and control of her husband"; she is "absorbed, and can hold nothing of herself." But the petition argues, in much more moderate terms, that "the custom of the country has greatly changed" already: "That since modern civilization, in extending the sphere of occupation for women, has in some measure broken down their pecuniary dependence upon men, it is time that legal protection be thrown over the produce of their labour, and that in entering the state of marriage, they no longer pass from freedom into the condition of a slave, all of whose earnings belong to his master and not to himself." Gaskell, one suspects, would have appreciated the first part of the sentence for its suggestion that no fundamental changes in social conditions were being urged, though it is easy to imagine her shrinking from the second part's assertion that married women are slaves: as we have seen, this is the sort of language that irritated Brontë in Harriet Taylor's essay and would likely have made Gaskell uncomfortable as well.[5]

Despite her now famous and often quoted comment that her husband "composedly buttoned . . . up in his pocket" the twenty pounds that she earned for "Lizzie Leigh" (a short story that Gaskell published in the first number of Dickens's *Household Words*), there is no evidence that she was dominated by him, financially or otherwise. Gaskell commented that she was sometimes "coward enough to wish that we were back in the darkness where obedience was the only duty of women," but she didn't "believe William would ever have *commanded* me." She traveled—frequently, widely, often without her husband—purchased a house, apparently without his involvement, and in general behaved like a woman who was superintending, and spending, her own income. Her letters to Edward Chapman about the timing of the publication of *Mary Barton*, and then about payment for her work, indicate that she was in charge of her publishing life. She and her friends were among the "married women of education" to whom the married women's property petition referred, women who were already, as the petition put it, "entering on every side the fields of literature and art" and who were asking that legal protection be thrown over their labor. Gaskell did not feel herself enslaved, and would likely have been more comfortable with the petition than with Barbara Smith's pamphlet.[6]

Gaskell would have agreed with the notion that "the sphere of occupation for women" had enlarged—and also that it should continue to do so. She was an ardent admirer of F. D. Maurice, one of the founders of Queen's College for Women (1848), and she was both personally, and on principle, a defender of women's education.[7] She complained about schoolmistresses who would not let their pupils attend the lectures at Queen's, objecting on the grounds that "the difficulty of sending them under proper escort to and fro is very heavy and loses a great deal of time"; she sought out for her daughter Marianne schools in which this was not thought to be a problem. She also envisioned, for her daughter Meta, a career in nursing well before Florence Nightingale made such careers respectable. Equally, she would have chafed at the fact that "women protected by the forethought of their relatives, the social training of their husbands, and the refined customs of the rank to which they belong" had, even under the current property laws (however defective they might be), a measure of protection denied to "women in the lower classes, for whom no such provision can be made."[8]

Sheila Herstein contends that Gaskell's commitment to Barbara Smith's petition could only have been slight, and Jenny Uglow has judged that Gaskell gave the women of the Langham Place Group her "qualified support"—that she "signed the petition for the amendment of the married woman's property laws," sanctioned "their campaigns for education and employment," but was "disturbed as well as attracted by their radicalism." Uglow cites in confirmation of this view the ambivalent feelings toward Barbara Smith Bodichon expressed some years later in a letter that Gaskell wrote to the American art historian and Harvard professor Charles Eliot Norton: "She is—I think in consequence of her birth, a strong fighter against the established opinions of the world,—which goes against my—what shall I call it?—*taste*—(that is not the word,) but I can't help admiring her noble bravery, and respecting, while I don't personally *like* her." Uglow does not mention (though it strengthens her argument) that earlier in the letter Gaskell identifies Smith Bodichon not as the illegitimate child of her parents, but the "illegitimate cousin of Hilary Carter, F[lorence] Nightingale,—& has their nature in her." She seems to want to attach Nightingale's and Carter's unconventionality to the illegitimacy that belongs to Bodichon in relation to her parents' refusal to marry. Gaskell also describes to Norton a portrait that she once saw of Bodichon painted during the latter's honeymoon in America, "in some wild, luxuriant terrific part of Virginia? in a gorge full of rich rank tropical vegetation,—her husband keeping watch over her with loaded pistols because of the alligators infesting the stream." Even married, Gaskell's sense of Bodichon's exoticism is vivid—her daring adventurousness, her placement amidst rank foliage and dangerous reptiles, the image of her at once protected and, by implication, associated with, the loaded pistols ready to go off. And yet, as her letter states, Gaskell finds Bodichon brave, noble, admirable— even though she doesn't "like" her.[9]

Gaskell's attitude toward women's work is, in her letters, equally complex. In a letter to Lady Kay-Shuttleworth she reflects on Charlotte Brontë in particular and "single women" more generally—women "deprived of their natural duties as wives and mothers." Gaskell moves from her sympathetic comments about Brontë to admiring ones about Priscilla Lydia Sellon's community, the Sisters of Mercy, even as she also says that she does not think women "need to be banded together, or even to take a name" in order to do good work. What she laments is "the feeling of *purposelessness*" in single women's lives, though she also agrees with Maurice's notion that it is a false religious spirit that leads people to "disregard those nearest to them . . . in search of some new sphere of action." If Gaskell's comments seem self-contradictory—they move from a consideration of Charlotte Brontë to the Sisters of Mercy; they praise that community but then deny that such communities are necessary; they lament purposelessness but worry about the abandonment of home duties—that is because, as she articulates them here, they are. Gaskell herself notes as she often does in letters that explore social or political views, that she "feel[s] in such a mist" about the question of where one's duties and sense of purpose ought to lie. In a similar letter to Tottie Fox earlier in the year, she explored the same issue and characterized her grammar as "all at sixes and sevens."[10]

Almost four years later, in a long letter to Emily Shaen during the writing of *North and South* (composed, interestingly, on a visit to the Nightingales' house) Gaskell's position remains complicated but her grammar is clear and she doesn't sound lost. The letter—about Florence Nightingale—is at once admiring and critical. She tells Shaen that "one person may act on some and not on others— it's no cause for despair because, darling, you can't work on everybody; very few *can*—only such people as F. N." Gaskell continues, "She and I had a great quarrel one day. She is, I think, too much for institutions, sisterhoods and associations, and she said if she had influence enough not a mother should bring up a child herself; there should be crêches for the rich as well as the poor. . . . That exactly tells of what seems to me *the* want—but then this want of love for individuals becomes a gift and a very rare one." Gaskell understands that Nightingale's "love" is really commitment to a cause, to "institutions, sisterhoods . . .

associations" rather than to individual persons. Strachey notes that "in her absorption in her own work [Nightingale] judged the men and women she lived among almost wholly by their usefulness or uselessness to it." Gaskell perceives that her love for causes, her extremism in a way, is a rare "gift." But she also knows that very few persons have this gift and that, in any case, it is a gift whose price is the "want of love for individuals"—a price Gaskell herself would have been unwilling to pay. If, in the earlier letter, Gaskell seems confused about what she values, here she seems merely divided: Nightingale's gift is admirable, but it is different from her own (and her correspondent's); it can be admired but need not be emulated. At the same time, the love of individuals, she argues, need not be separated from work on their behalf. One person "may act on some and not on others"; action is still possible, work still imaginable, purposelessness avoidable.[11]

Gaskell ends her letter to Shaen with the comment that she is about to return to Margaret Hale and to the conclusion of Margaret's novel—an appropriate and interesting remark in many ways, not least because Gaskell was writing her letter and working out at the same time in the final pages of her novel "that most difficult problem for women, how much was to be merged in obedience to authority, and how much must be set aside for freedom in working."[12] Perhaps the novel lent clarity to the letter. In any case, *North and South* would fearlessly explore the moral role of women in men's lives, the broader question of women's roles in their own public lives, the association between private and public spheres, the dangers and powers affiliated with female public exposure, even the meaning of public shame—with a sense of purposefulness and confidence that would stand in relation to the complex, and sometimes contradictory positions expressed in her letters.

If Gaskell's novels were more forceful than she was, they were also, often, more radical and "improper": *North and South* suggests, among other unusual things, how difficult it is to keep private meanings out of public spaces and how complex the relations are between private and public life. The public realm in *North and South* is associated not merely with industrial and political action but also with female self-manifestation and self-display—and thus at the same time with the intimacy and illicit sexuality that might otherwise be thought to be properties of the private realm. Indeed, it is hard not to feel that Ruth's fall reemerges in Margaret Hale's public and private disgrace (in the strike scene, and in the lie), though of course in the latter case the "fall" occurs metaphorically and by imputation rather than in fact. Still, that Gaskell handles this matter at all—and that she rethinks the whole question of female publicity and sexuality—is one of the most extraordinary and powerful features of *North and South.*

Early critics of Gaskell's novels, however, consistently read them as an expression of her traditional and conservative views. She is identified as a novelist interested in public issues—that is, as a "social problem" novelist—by Louis Cazamian, Kathleen Tillotson, Raymond Williams, and others—but at the same time her investigation of social problems is seen as marginal or subordinate to her "real," that is, personal, concerns. Williams, for example, while sympathetic to her project, comments that in *North and South*'s conclusion Gaskell "once again . . . works out her reaction to the insupportable [social] situation by going—in part adventitiously, outside it." Somewhat more promisingly, Arthur Pollard begins by arguing that Gaskell's is "a more complex achievement than it is often thought to be," and with the claim that *North and South* achieves a "coalescence of personal and public stories in the relations of the two major characters." But in his final estimate the coalescence of public and private inevitably means the disappearance of the public into the personal story: "Before this novel," he declares, "Gaskell had been interested mainly in individuals as they were affected by social and economic forces. This interest is still important, but she has now found that what one person means to another is the novel's supreme concern."[13]

Edgar Wright takes a similar tack: Gaskell is a serious "social novelist," but only in that she is a keen observer of "the individual and his relationships." "If there is a tug between theme and characters," Wright says, "it will be the characters who win." Martin Dodsworth echoes this view: "Critics have spoken of the great sympathy and insight with which Mrs. Gaskell handles the whole business of industrial conflict in *North and South*, and they are right to do so." But it is "a human understanding, rather than a political or economic understanding, that informs the whole novel." As Barbara Hardy concludes, summarizing in my view the essential thrust of earlier Gaskell criticism, "Mrs. Gaskell is never a propagandist; or if she is, she is only a propagandist for sympathy."[14]

More recent critics perceive Gaskell handling in a serious way the integration of industrial and female issues in *North and South*. Rosemarie Bodenheimer is particularly astute in describing Margaret's participation in the strike scene as an experience of "unwomanly publicity." But for the most part contemporary critics come to the same conclusion as their predecessors. Deirdre David takes seriously Gaskell's political agenda in *North and South*, yet she maintains that what Gaskell really does is to convert a public into a private problem—transforming an explosive political situation into a romantic one by diverting attention from the crisis of class relations to the romantic marriage plot with which the novel concludes: "Gaskell symbolically displaces political incursion into sexual violation, and also begins the process of converting the relationship of political opposition between her lovers into one of their conscious recognition of the sexual feelings which they have for each other." David perceives the crucial association not just between the political and the personal but between politics and sexuality in the nineteenth-century novel, but she does not see the public realm of politics as inevitably connected to the private realm of sexuality or recognize the political importance of representing female sexuality and giving it a public incarnation.[15]

Catherine Gallagher finds Gaskell's solution an "unstable" and "ambiguous" one. She argues that Gaskell's ostensible project is to reveal the private realm's "metonymic link" to the public, to see "the moral influence women indirectly exert on men" as the source of the public realm's regeneration. But, says Gallagher, Margaret's compromised moral position (the result of lying to protect her brother) undermines this project and disturbs the metonymic relation between public and private that the novel appears to affirm. Gallagher declares that while trying to "obliterate the separation" between public and private, the novels she studies actually "reinforce" it. More recently, Deborah Nord has argued, from a different perspective, that Gaskell explores "the [private] risks of public exposure for a woman in the city," but she too says that Gaskell "does not—cannot—resist the interpretation of public gestures as private ones, even though she does demonstrate the unfairness and painfulness of the community's . . . sexualization of Margaret's public actions."[16]

As David suggests, *North and South* diverts attention from a narrative of class conflict, but I will maintain that it does so in order to treat, instead, a narrative of gender conflict and to resolve it by refashioning its central terms. This strategy does not substitute private concerns for more important public and political ones, nor, in combining them, does it undermine its own political authority. In merging private with public matters—displaying on a public stage the very private body that Brontë was so careful to obscure in *Shirley* and internalizing in Margaret's "lie" the taint of a public shame—Gaskell both challenges conventional boundaries between private and public life and legitimizes in a new way public action for women.

North and South powerfully demonstrates the risks Gaskell was willing to take in her novels and the unconventional affiliations she was willing to forge in the lives of her novelistic heroines—affiliations that suggest how dramatic a departure from the traditional representation of female lives Gaskell would make in *North and South* and even how dramatic a departure from the representation of female *public* lives the novel would finally offer.

Gaskell's self-contradictory self-criticism emerges frequently in her private correspondence, but in her public role as author and authority she was, I believe, more daring. As Gaskell herself put the matter: "It is different when speaking as the character in a story—or even the author of a book. Do you think I cd say or write in a letter (except one that I was sure wd be regarded as private by some dear friend) what I have said both in MB & Ruth? It may seem strange & I can't myself account for it,—but it *is* so." Gaskell found it easier to express strong views in her fiction, to say there what might later make her feel improper; she wrote in her novels what she could not say, or could say only hesitantly, in her letters.[17]

II.

In the first chapter of *North and South* (1854–55), as her cousin Edith lies sleeping on the sofa—an example of femininity and unconsciousness combined—Margaret Hale complies with her aunt's request and stands as a "lay figure" on which to display the exotic Indian shawls that are part of her cousin's trousseau. The scene is a curious one, for Margaret already seems acutely conscious and thus more appropriately an agent than a mere body emptied of power, a "block" or inert mold (35). Yet Gaskell stations her between the about-to-be married Edith (dead to the world in the back parlor) and Henry Lennox (who enters rather suddenly from without), and intimates, in the language of lay figures and blocks, the transitional and even hypothetical character of Margaret's condition. Margaret is not a woman like Edith—not sleeping, not dressed in "white muslin and blue ribbons" (35), not about to be married, not the owner of the Indian shawls—and yet at the same time she stands in the position of a woman. Not coming in from the outside like Henry Lennox, she is associated, if not precisely in her own person, with what Lennox calls "ladies' business. . . . Very different to my business, which is the real true law business. Playing with shawls is very different work to drawing up settlements" (40–41).

Gaskell's point in this opening scene, however, is that Margaret's position is not as clearly established as Lennox would like to think. Margaret stands in for Edith, but she is not Edith. She participates in "ladies' business" only as her cousin's substitute or proxy. At the same time, it isn't at all clear what Margaret will be and do in her own right. To be not-Edith, or to be between Edith and Henry—between the back parlor and the out-of-doors, between private and public life—is still to be insufficiently defined. Even Henry, not always particularly perceptive about interpersonal matters, notes that whenever he sees Margaret she seems "carried away by a whirlwind of some other person's making" (41).

The conditional and hypothetical nature of Margaret's situation in the world repeats itself in the Helstone episode of the novel, as Margaret returns to the home of her girlhood only to discover that she and her family must leave it. But Helstone is also significant because it represents to Margaret everything that she values in home as a place—even though, as her responses to Henry Lennox's questions suggest, she is unable to generate any language about it. "Oh, I can't describe my home," she declares. "It is home, and I can't put its charm into words" (43). And Lennox himself comments, as he gives up questioning her, "I see, you won't tell me anything. You will only tell me that you are not going to do this and that" (43). What Margaret's refusal and Henry's response both show is the uncritical nature of Margaret's relationship to "home." She can't put language to it because it simply is what it is: it is not subject to analysis. This nonverbal, Edenic character of Helstone reveals itself again when Henry comes south to pay Margaret a visit. Like Adam and Eve in Milton's garden, who eat their fruit and use the rind to "scoop the brimming stream," Margaret and Henry eat pears on a plate made "out of a beet-root leaf" and wander in a garden shut in, like Milton's Paradise, by "great forest trees . . . as if it were a nest" (59, 60).[18]

To Margaret, "home" is "paradise"—by definition, a protected universe of harmonious relations. As Gallagher has suggested, Helstone "represents not only the rural south, with its mixture of quaintness and poverty, but also an enclave where all social relations are personal: a large, isolated family."[19] Helstone is also, not surprisingly, tied to a rigid vision of class relations, as Margaret first reveals in a conversation with her mother. When Mrs. Hale complains about Helstone's isolation from other parishes, Margaret remarks that she has no wish to see the tradesmen her mother would like to visit. "I don't like shoppy people. . . . I'm sure you don't want me to admire butchers and bakers, and candlestick-makers, do you mamma?" (50). Margaret wishes not to know about the world of "made" things. Cottagers and labourers, in Margaret's sentimental view, need not leave home—Helstone, the family—in order to work, and they do not trade away the products they have produced. This distinguishes them from the "vulgarity and commonness" of those who "have something tangible to sell," who have concrete dealings with goods, money, and the marketplace (102). Margaret's unwillingness to associate with "shoppy people" distances her from the rough-and-tumble world of work. But it also reflects an anxiety about the loss of social caste that would figure so prominently in discussions about women in the work-place later in the decade.

As Gaskell's friend Bessie Rayner Parkes would observe in "What Can Educated Women Do?"—one of a series of articles on women and work that she wrote at the end of the 1850s and beginning of the 1860s—"The idea that a young lady cannot engage in business without losing caste must be conquered if any real way is to be made." Parkes was writing in much more practical terms than Gaskell about the need to find avenues of employment for women, and she had specific ideas about how women could be protected in the marketplace (she imagined "efficient female superintendance of all those trades and offices in which women might otherwise be employed"). But her comments help to explain Gaskell's rendering of Margaret's situation as well. *North and South* begins by associating its heroine with an uncritical, Edenic vision of home and, simultaneously, with a gentlewoman's notion of social caste that makes even *associations* with persons who engage in trade unimaginable. Parkes's notion that "the idea . . . [of] losing caste must be conquered" is an idea with which *North and South* must grapple.[20]

Helstone is also, and most crucially, bound up with Margaret's maiden innocence. This becomes evident when Henry Lennox proposes to her and is rejected, not because he is an inappropriate mate (though he does propose, as he puts it, "almost in spite of myself"—rather like Darcy in Jane Austen's *Pride and Prejudice*), but because, as Margaret says, "I don't like to be spoken to as you have been doing" (61).[21] If home excludes the disorder and chaos of the fallen world and the coarse commercialism and loss of caste associated with the marketplace, it also excludes sexuality. Listening to Henry's proposal, Margaret "wishe[s] herself back with her mother—her father—anywhere away from him" (60). She realizes that "it was poor and despicable of her to shrink from hearing any speech, as if she had not power to put an end to it with her high maidenly dignity," but she continues to feel "guilty and ashamed of having grown so much into a woman as to be thought of in marriage" (60–61, 65).

The guilt that Lennox's proposal both assumes and produces is reiterated in and confirmed by Mr. Hale's confession that, because he cannot make a "fresh declaration of conformity to the Liturgy," he is "going to leave Helstone!" (68, 65). The penetration into Eden of sexual love and religious dissent (and, in the persons of Margaret's parents, of marital discord) puts an end to Margaret's vision of home as paradise. It is thus no accident that on the eve of her family's departure from Helstone, Margaret finds herself thinking about Henry Lennox and recalling, in particular, his descriptions of walking in the city at the end of a busy day's work, "freshening himself up, as he had told her he often did, by a run in the Temple gardens, taking in the while the grand inarticulate mighty roar of tens of thousands of busy men, nigh at hand, but not seen, and catching ever, at his quick turns, glimpses of the lights of the city coming up out of the depths of the river" (90). Standing in her own garden, Margaret imagines Henry's physical freedom as he runs at night, and she relates it both to the world of work and to the impressive, impersonal life of the city—its "mighty roar" and its weirdly disembodied lights rising from the river. Helstone, by contrast, seems quiet, human, and knowable, at least until Margaret hears a "stealthy, creeping, crunching sound," which she identifies with poachers. In the past, Margaret remembers, the "wild adventurous freedom of their life had taken her fancy; she felt inclined to wish them success; she had no fear of them. But to-night she was afraid, she knew not why" (90).

Margaret fails to make the association between Henry Lennox—the real poacher in her garden—and the sense of danger she suddenly feels. But her invocation of Lennox is unsettling, reminding Margaret that she has "grown so much into a woman as to be thought of in marriage." That being the case, adventurous violators of the law and of others' property seem more frightening now than they might once have done. This scene ties Margaret's sense of herself as a woman (however dimly conceived) to Lennox's physical freedom in the city. Dreaming about his participation in the world of work and his access to "mighty" London somehow makes Margaret feel at risk herself—as though the physical freedom she here imagines so vividly (as if it were her own) combines with her sense of his interest in her as a woman to render Margaret fearful of penetration from without. A sudden sense that her garden is not safe sets Margaret rapping at the window, begging to be admitted to her own home. She does not feel calm again until she is "safe in the drawing-room, with the windows fastened and bolted, and the familiar walls hemming her round, and shutting her in" (90–91). The harmony and familiarity that has hitherto characterized Helstone disappears in this scene as the safety of the world outside the windows can no longer be assumed. Margaret closes herself into the drawing room as protection both against the danger of the public realm with which, through Henry, she associates herself and the danger of sexual intrusion which that association brings.[22]

The separation of inside from outside for which the final scene in Helstone prepares us reappears as an opposition between domestic gentlewoman and public manufacturer in Margaret's early encounters with John Thornton. Margaret's haughtiness and distance are a function of her sense of superior rank (she is a gentleman's daughter), but they also separate her (she does no work in the world) from a man whose "rough encounter with Milton streets and crowds" is a literal sign of his participation in public industry (100). In addition, Margaret generates distance from Thornton by addressing him with that blend of sexual reserve and sexual defiance that characterized her dealings with Henry Lennox and that here and elsewhere will go by the name of "maiden freedom" (100)—a consciousness of herself as a woman free of compromising dealings with men. Maidenly freedom gives Margaret a power to defy that no married woman would be free to assert and yet, or so she thinks, it acts as a shield to prevent unwanted incursions from without.

In her dealings both with Thornton and with the town of Milton, however, Margaret is remarkably unsuccessful in maintaining her distance. At first, Thornton's earnest discussions with Mr. Hale about "this imagination of power, this practical realization of a gigantic thought" that the invention of the steam hammer embodied, and then about "the war which compels, and shall compel, all material power to yield to science," catch Margaret's attention because her father makes an analogy between Thornton's language and the lines of an old English ballad—leading Margaret to wonder how "they had got from cog-wheels to Chevy Chace." When she enters the conversation she does so in order to disagree with Thornton about the value he attributes to "adventure," "progress," and "the gambling spirit of trade" (122). Only two pages later Margaret is transfixed by Thornton's description of the recent history of industrial transformation: "Seventy years ago what was it? And now what is it not? Raw, crude materials came together; men of the same level, as regarded education and station, took suddenly . . . different positions. . . . The rapid development of what might be called a new trade gave those early masters enormous power of wealth and command . . . over the whole world's market" (124). Gaskell notes that Margaret's "lip curled"—this is her characteristic gesture of disapproval and disdain—but she also comments that Margaret "was compelled to listen; she could no longer abstract herself in her own thoughts" (124).

What is notable about Thornton's descriptions here—and this is true of what Margaret will hear later at the Thornton dinner party—is that he is captivated by the association between industrial activity and power. The language of "wealth and command," of the "almost unlimited power the manufacturers had about the beginning of this century," and, then, of "the power and position of a master," emerges everywhere in his descriptions—and draws Margaret out of herself in a way that suggests she is intrigued too (124, 125). The only real disagreement they will have in this scene is about "caste": he values the mobile quality of class position in a society that allows "mother wit" to distinguish from each other men otherwise equal in station (124); she clearly does not. But there is no indication that Margaret is offended by Thornton's descriptions of the life in Milton-Northern, even though he still perceives her as disdainful.

Margaret's interest in Milton reemerges at the Thornton's dinner party where there "was a very animated conversation going on among the gentlemen; the ladies, for the most part, were silent, employing themselves in taking notes of the dinner and criticizing each other's dresses" (215). But Margaret "caught the clue to the general conversation, grew interested and listened attentively" (215–16). She notices, first, that Thornton is perceived by others as "a man of great force of character; of power in many ways," and although she is not part of the general discussion, Gaskell makes the point that Margaret now "knew enough . . . to understand many local interests—nay, even some of the technical words employed by the eager mill-owners" and was able "silently [to take] a very decided part in the question they were discussing" (216).

By the time dinner is over, and the company reassembles after the men's departure, Margaret is eager for their return: she enjoys listening to their conversation. Gaskell now says openly what she was beginning to suggest earlier in the discussion at the Hale's house, namely, that Margaret "liked the exultation in the sense of power which these Milton men had. It might be rather rampant in its display, and savour of boasting; but still they seemed to defy the old limits of possibility. . . . there was much to admire in their forgetfulness of themselves and the present, in their anticipated triumphs over all inanimate matter at some future time which none of them should live to see" (217). Margaret's preference for the men's conversation, her interest in this historic venture larger than the men themselves, her pleasure in their "sense of power," is emphasized without qualification—and it is surprising for the defiance of limits that it represents. Though interest and participation are surely not identical, Gaskell clearly means to distinguish Margaret from the other women at the party and to demonstrate her unusual curiosity about, admiration for, and desire to engage in, a universe conventionally understood to be without interest for gentlewomen and in any case inaccessible to them.

The disagreement that Margaret and Thornton have about "men" and "gentlemen" at the end of the party indicates an ongoing difference of opinion between them and clarifies (without entirely resolving) the class implications of Margaret's growing interest in public industry. Margaret declares that one of the men in the conversation to which she has been listening, and with whom she disagrees, "cannot be a gentleman." Thornton challenges her use of "gentleman," wishing to substitute the idea that he cannot be a "true man." When Margaret suggests that "my 'gentleman' includes your 'true man,' " Thornton disagrees: "A man is to me a higher and a completer being than a gentleman" (217). Margaret is surprised by their failure to understand each other, and by Thornton's assertion that the term *gentleman* "describes a person in his relation to others," whereas "when we speak of him as 'a man,' we consider him not merely with regard to his fellow-men, but in relation to himself,—to life—to time—to eternity" (218).

Margaret is puzzled by Thornton's comments, for good reason. To begin with, the "Men and Gentlemen" debate (after which the chapter is named) is three discussions in one, two explicit, and one barely implicit. First, it is a discussion about whether the language of class should have priority over—really, whether it should even be allowed in the same linguistic room as—the language of personal merit (Thornton thinks not). Second, it is a discussion about whether community, the concept of a person "in his relation to others," should have priority over individuality, the concept of a person in his relation to himself (Margaret thinks it should). Of course what complicates this part of the debate is that the woman who uses what might be called the separatist language of class is herself the proponent of community; and the man who uses the separatist language of individuality is himself a man of the people. Third, the debate points to a discussion that might be happening but is not: a conversation about whether women have any place in the conversation. Margaret, after all, finds herself in a debate about gentlemen and men, about "the full simplicity of the noun 'man,' and the adjective 'manly'" (218)—but Thornton is not asked to think about Margaret's complex situation as a woman either in a man's or a gentleman's world, even though Margaret's relation to the men's world at the dinner party is in many ways the central subject of the chapter.

It is not surprising that Gaskell cuts the conversation off in the middle. Neither Margaret nor Thornton is yet ready to resolve the questions it raises: Can Margaret's terminology of class be abandoned? Must it be abandoned if Margaret is to enter Milton as a full citizen? If it is left behind, must the language of stark individuality displace all languages of community? If it is forsaken, must it be replaced by a language that inevitably excludes Margaret herself? Margaret is thinking, and about to "speak her slow conviction" when Thornton is called away for what Margaret guesses is a more important conversation about the strike. But in the latter part of this discussion, when Mr. Horsfall takes Thornton "a little on one side" (Margaret conjectures that he is asking Thornton another question about the strike) he does so in order to ask not about the strike but about the woman, to find out "who she herself was"—an interesting, and not irrelevant, exchange of subjects. Moreover, Horsfall wonders whether Margaret is "a Milton lady" and Thornton replies "No! from the south of England" (219). Thornton is answering directly the question he has been asked (about Margaret's place of origin) but it does not occur to him to engage with Horsfall in a debate about the appropriateness of his interlocutor's language, a debate about whether Margaret is a lady (i.e., a gentlewoman) or a woman "in relation to [herself],—to life, to time—to eternity" (218).

As Margaret becomes interested in Thornton's world, her connection to it dramatizes other questions as well—questions about the meaning of caste (as

Parkes calls it) and about the associations that collect around caste for men like Thornton and women like Margaret. Margaret's connection to Thornton's world triggers questions about one set of political relationships (masters and men) and another (men and women)—as the almost too easy transition from the strike to Margaret herself, suggests. Finally, though this is merely a latent subject in the dinner party conversation, Margaret's presence and her intense conversation with Thornton immediately call attention to her, as Horsfall's question implies. He wants to know "who she herself was—so quiet, so stately, and so beautiful" (219).

Margaret's walks through the town of Milton are equally resonant of the impossibility she will experience in maintaining the separation of private from public life and of one class from another as she becomes engaged in the life of the city. The question of class boundaries, and also of sexual boundaries, emerges too in the wonderful scene in which Margaret walks alone through the streets of Milton. She is regularly disturbed by the factory people, whose "ingress and egress" at first upset her:

> *They came rushing along, with bold, fearless faces, and loud laughs and jests,*
> *particularly aimed at all those who appeared to be above them in rank or*
> *station. The tones of their unrestrained voices, and their carelessness of all*
> *common rules of street politeness, frightened Margaret a little at first. The*
> *girls, with their rough, but not unfriendly freedom, would comment on her*   (110)
> *dress, even touch her shawl or gown. . . . But she alternately dreaded and*
> *fired up against the workmen, who commented not on her dress, but on her*
> *looks, in the same open, fearless manner. She, who had hitherto felt that even*
> *the most refined remark on her personal appearance was an impertinence, had*
> *to endure undisguised admiration from these out-spoken men.*

Walking unaccompanied and unprotected in the streets of Milton, Margaret finds herself oddly vulnerable both to what feels like excessive notice and excessive violation. She recalls her Aunt Shaw's idea of propriety, which had made her send a footman to accompany Margaret and Edith on their walks, an insistence that had "circumscribed Margaret's independence" and against which she had "silently rebelled" (109). Now, walking alone in the city streets, Margaret finds herself subjected to indiscriminate notice, unable to guard herself against women who would touch her clothing and men who would comment on her appearance, unable in general to manage or control her intercourse with others.

Gaskell's vision of public life on the busy streets of the city is both engaging and alarming: those who travel there do not walk but rather "rush along"; their expressions, gestures, modes of speech and patterns of behavior are aggressive and even intrusive; there is no way of maintaining either one's physical boundaries or one's sense of privacy in their midst. The rough ways of the street are made particularly so for a woman above the factory workers in station. Verbal and physical invasions are meant to disrupt the class distinction that Margaret, for one, has been so eager in the past to maintain and that Gaskell has associated both with Margaret's maiden innocence and with her wish to preserve home as Eden.

Margaret's initial reaction to this experience of "disorderly tumult" is just what one would expect—"a flash of indignation which made her face scarlet, and her dark eyes gather flame" (110–11). But Gaskell also makes the point, even in this early scene, that although some of the workers' speeches angered and embarrassed her, "yet there were other sayings of theirs, which, when she reached the quiet safety of home, amused her even while they irritated her" (111). Margaret's ability to be "amused" once she reaches the safety of home quickly translates itself into an ability to appreciate the men's compliments when she is out in the street again—and eventually an ability to strike up an acquaintance with one of the workers, Nicholas Higgins. Gaskell indicates in this Margaret's increasing willingness to mix with the world and to accommodate herself to the complicated class relations that, at least in Gaskell's vision, life in the public realm entails.

In "The Condition of Working Women in England and France," Bessie Rayner Parkes remarks, "I was told in Manchester, by one of the most eminent and thoughtful women in England, that the outpouring of a mill in full work at the hour of dinner was such a torrent of living humanity that a lady could not walk against the stream." Parkes adds that she was told the same thing by a friend in another industrial town: "In both instances the quitting of the mill seemed to have struck their imaginations as a typical moment, and they spoke of it as something which once seen could not be forgotten."[23] While Gaskell describes exactly such a scene in *North and South* (surely she is Parkes's eminent Manchester source), she actually portrays her heroine as someone who *does* manage to "walk against the stream" and who, in a later chapter, can "thread her way through the irregular stream of human beings that flowed through Milton streets" with no difficulty at all (226).

III.

Revealing as these scenes are for suggesting the gradual disintegration of Margaret's initial resistances to Milton, its people, and its world of work, the central event for my purposes is Margaret's emergence into the public arena during the strike at Thornton's mill. She goes to the mill on an errand from home—to fetch a water bed for her ailing mother—and finds herself when she gets there in the midst of a crisis.

Margaret is asked to help secure the house against strikers—to "shut down the windows" and stay inside—as the bolted gates are repeatedly attacked. This time, it seems, the intruders will not be kept out, and the language of sexual violation in the scene is almost egregiously clear: "They could all hear the one great straining breath; the creak of wood slowly yielding; the wrench of iron; the mighty fall of the ponderous gates" (231). But instead of defending herself even further against what amounts to a serious threat of intrusion, Margaret first challenges Thornton to face the angry strikers and then, fearful of the consequences of her challenge, moves to face them herself. In a scene that revises and then reverses Margaret's panicky self-enclosure in the Helstone drawing room (when she thinks she hears poachers), she "threw the window wide open," then "tore her bonnet off; and bent forwards to hear," and finally "rushed out of the room, down-stairs,—she had lifted the great iron bar of the door with an imperious force—had thrown the door open wide—and was there, in face of that angry sea of men, her eyes smiting them with flaming arrows of reproach" (233).[24]

John Pikoulis has justly described this scene as "one of the most thrilling moments in Victorian literature, representing, as it does, the first time that a woman has convincingly established herself on the public stage in her own right."[25] The scene is, indeed, both thrilling and unprecedented, describing in a way quite unlike that of any previous novel, a woman who steps dramatically and fearlessly into the political turmoil of a chaotic strike, unprotected and unmediated by the presence of others. It is also crucial to read Gaskell's scene in relation to that of her friend and predecessor Charlotte Brontë, especially because Gaskell told Lady Kay-Shuttleworth that she "disliked a good deal in the plot of *Shirley*"—a significant remark in light of the fact that the strike scene in *North and South* could easily be read as a revision of Brontë's riot at the mill.[26] Brontë's Shirley finds herself in circumstances not entirely unlike Margaret's—presented with a situation in which she thinks she can prevent a violent attack.

In Margaret's appearance before the angry crowd in *North and South* Gaskell rewrites Shirley's restraint and highlights the physical conspicuousness, and surprising bodily openness, of Margaret's action. The strikers themselves are stopped in their tracks, "arrested" by her appearance (233). At first, she is unable to speak and can only stand and "[hold] out her arms towards them." But perhaps most significantly, Margaret stations herself "between [the strikers] and their enemy," covering Thornton, at least partially, with her own body. Thornton stands "a little on one side . . . away from behind her," not wanting her protection and seeking to recover his own proper place, "jealous of anything that should come between him and danger" (234). The movement is a slight one, but it betokens the rivalry here between Thornton and Margaret: Who shall occupy the public stage? Who shall take command? Who shall protect whom? Who shall speak? Who shall act? Who shall really "appear"?

Margaret, whose voice had earlier lacked "tone," speaks first. Her voice rings out, though her assurances to the crowd are empty ones ("you shall have relief from your complaints, whatever they are") and in that sense only incite the strikers. But when the crowd erupts and Margaret sees a group of young men about to take aim at "he whom she had urged and goaded to come to this perilous place," she acts again: "She only thought how she could save him. She threw her arms around him; she made her body into a shield from the fierce people beyond. Still, with his arms folded, he shook her off. 'Go away,' said he, in his deep voice. 'This is no place for you.' 'It is!' said she" (234).

Gaskell returns here to Margaret's conspicuous presence, to her willingness to use her body and to her sense of its powerful instrumentality. When Margaret makes "her body into a shield" to protect Thornton, her action suggests that she is willing to risk exposure; she believes she can manage and control her intercourse with others—even in the public realm—and is willing to risk unwanted intrusion even while she feels she can deflect it. That she should associate this power with her body seems especially intriguing since it confirms the physical and even sexual significance of female public appearance to which Margaret's earlier responses to life in the out-of-doors (at Helstone) and life in the city streets (of Milton) have already pointed.

As it turns out, however, Margaret overestimates the power of the maiden to deflect assault, for as Gaskell remarks, "If she thought her sex would be a protection,—if, with shrinking eyes she had turned away from the terrible anger of these men, in any hope that ere she looked again they would have paused and reflected, and slunk away, and vanished,—she was wrong" (234). The assertion that Gaskell wants to make is that "if she thought her sex would be a protection . . . she was wrong." But she makes it both more difficult to detect, and at the same time even stronger, by inserting the parenthetical "if": if Margaret imagines that she can turn away "with shrinking eyes"—in other words, turn away in maiden shame—in the hope of recovering the protection that maidenly innocence provides, she will learn that it is too late to do so. Gaskell notes that the strikers' "reckless passion had carried them too far," but Margaret's has too (234). She has crossed a sequence of boundaries—opened the windows, torn off the (protecting) bonnet, flung wide the doors, stepped outside, and placed herself between Thornton and the crowd. This insertion of herself into public space and into the great struggle between masters and men challenges the notion that she will be granted the chivalric protection upon which she depends.

The insistently violating sexual language of the strike scene emerges with greater power in the following passage as Margaret suffers her first actual injury: "A sharp pebble flew by her, grazing forehead and cheek, and drawing a blinding sheet of light before her eyes. . . . [The strikers] were watching, open-eyed, and open-mouthed, the thread of dark-red blood which wakened them up from their trance of passion. Those nearest the gate stole out ashamed" (235). The language of this passage shows that the real risk of public exposure is sexual violation, and even though Margaret is only "symbolically" deflowered,[27] the complications that attend her public appearance all serve to intensify its sexual meanings. As Margaret remembers her action at home, in its aftermath, she thinks both of the shame associated with involving herself in a public distur-bance—"I, who hate scenes . . . I went down and must needs throw myself into the mêlée, like a romantic fool!" (247)—and the shame associated with courting a man in public as others, it turns out, think she has done.

Margaret thus suffers, as Bodenheimer points out, "exactly the conse-quences that Shirley foresees for Caroline,"[28] and I would argue, foresees for herself—namely, the misconstruction of character from which both Shirley and Caroline are protected by Shirley's restraint. Margaret enters public space with-out cover (Shirley and Caroline do not: Brontë declares, in language that Gaskell uses almost verbatim, that "they both knew they would do no good by rushing down into the mêlée") and the meaning of her act is, for those who witness it, genuinely difficult to interpret. This difficulty is acute because in one sense Margaret reverses the conventional understanding of gender relations (in which men take public stands on behalf of women, not women on behalf of men) and in another she seems to reinstate it (women convert even political events into romantic ones, public events into private ones). Thornton himself is struck by the first reading: once the strike scene is over he openly asserts, "I don't know where I should have been but for her . . . Not many girls would have taken the blows on herself which were meant for me" (242–43)—a statement that again recalls, in comparison, Brontë's assertion that Shirley and Caroline "desired nei-ther to deal nor to receive blows."[29]

But the second reading is powerful too: everyone (including Thornton himself) sees Margaret's act as a sexual one. The servants have watched the mêlée from "the front garret" where they "could see it all, out of harm's way" (again, like Shirley and Caroline). They describe the scene to Thornton's sister, Fanny, who has fainted and missed the entire event; and what they report is a romantic encounter: "Miss Hale with her arms about Master's neck" (239). The servants regard Margaret's action not merely as sexual in its meaning but as sexual self-display in action ("hugging him before the people," 239). Margaret's own language illustrates how difficult it is to keep sexual innuendo out of an account of the strike scene: she remembers "throw[ing] myself into the mêlée, like a romantic fool" (247).

This, however, is a sign not that women contain, or are used to contain, politically explosive scenes by reducing them to romantic encounters but, rather, that female participation in public life and female public appearance itself are both politically and sexually explosive. Margaret interprets the strike scene by attempting to refute its sexual meaning and by claiming its collective, and thoroughly conventional, character. Hers was not "a personal act between you and me," she tells Thornton when he later proposes marriage to her, but, rather, an act consistent with her membership in the female sex as a whole and, in some sense, an impersonal class action (253). "We all feel the sanctity of our sex as a high privilege when we see danger," she declares, and "any woman, worthy of the name of woman, would come forward to shield, with her reverenced helplessness, a man in danger of the violence of numbers" (252, 253). Margaret invokes here—though in a revised form—the "woman's mission" argument about women's helplessness when she suggests that female passivity is so revered by men that it literally suppresses their desire to injure and calls up, instead, their wish to conserve and protect. She should have been able, Margaret implies, to shield Thornton from the rioters precisely because of her inability to shield herself. Her extreme vulnerability should have arrested the violent activity that threatened them both as the strikers joined with her to confirm the vision of womanhood to which everyone collectively subscribed.

What Margaret fails to appreciate, of course, is the way in which her appearance on a public stage revokes the very protection that she wished to elicit. For as T. H. Lister commented in the 1841 review article to which I referred in a somewhat different context in chapter 1:

> The deference, the tenderness, the courtesy of man towards the other sex, are
> founded principally on the feeling that they need his protection, and can never
> question his power. But let women be made ostensibly powerful; let a sense of
> competition be introduced; let man be made to feel that he must stand on the
> defensive—and the spirit of chivalry . . . will speedily cease; and it will be
> useless to expect a continuance of that feeling, to which women can now ap-
> peal with confidence, and which lends the most essential charms to the ordi-

nary intercourse of civilized society. Women, as a class, cannot enjoy, at the same time, the immunities of weakness and the advantages of power.[30]

Lister makes his claim in relation to arguments about the suffrage, but it is a claim that repeats itself frequently in debates about women's access to public life throughout the nineteenth century. What Margaret does not fully realize is that she has made herself "ostensibly" and conspicuously powerful, and in so doing she has relinquished the female "immunity" she might otherwise have enjoyed. In one sense, her debate with Thornton about men and gentlemen, and more prominently the implicit debate about men and women, reemerges here too. Chivalric relations do not govern the intercourse of men and women in public space—at least not if those women insert themselves into the public domain. Margaret's old insistence on the language of class, and on class separation, disintegrates in this scene. If Lister is right, the class to which Margaret really belongs is the class of women, and she has relinquished that class's right to protection from the other class—from the class of men.

Margaret's defense of herself is interesting for its insistent conservatism in the face of what is clearly an unconventional act on her part. No one, it seems, reveres her helplessness (Thornton certainly doesn't). Everyone is astounded either by the courage, or by the presumptuousness, of her act. Thornton is alternately proud of her bravery and jealous of the way *she* appropriates *his* role as protector. And Margaret's own insistence on her purity is given the lie both by her symbolic defloration and by the "deep sense of shame" she feels whenever she contemplates her own actions (249).

This sense of shame is linked to what Margaret calls "be[ing] the object of universal regard" (249)—a phrase that evokes the identification between publicity and sexuality to which the opponents of legal reform, the expansion of female employment opportunities, and female suffrage regularly referred. To be universally regarded is to be seen by anyone—to have no control over those who do the looking, over the mere fact that they look, or over the kind of looking they might do. Margaret's painful self-consciousness is a self-consciousness both about indiscriminate or, to use a loaded term, promiscuous, regard and also about the very fact of regard pure and simple. As Victorians were only too aware, when a middle-class woman took to the public stage she brought her body, ordinarily confined to the drawing room, before the eyes of others. This meant that her appearance virtually always had both class and sexual implications—unless special steps were taken to "cover" and block her from regard (this is why Shirley always "screens" herself in Brontë's novel). In Margaret's case no such steps are taken. Fanny faints and is carried upstairs; the servants watch from the garret; but Margaret stands before the striking workers and covers Thornton—not the other way around. The related ideas of class erosion and sexual tainting that get bonded to her act by the plot and language of *North and South* are affiliated with Margaret's crossing of boundaries and her entrance into the public realm—and they are, in a variety of forms, persistent features of female public appearance both here and elsewhere in Victorian writing.

In the courtroom scene of her earlier novel *Mary Barton* (1848), Gaskell invoked the association between female publicity and female sexuality and yet went to significant lengths to de-emphasize the impropriety that might be thought to attach to it. Mary's great—and effective—act of courage actually precedes the courtroom scene. It is embodied in the wild errand of mercy on which she goes in advance of her appearance there: she races through the streets of Liverpool, hires a boat at the dock where "the cries of the sailors, the variety of languages used by the passers-by, and the entire novelty of the sight" make her feel "helpless and forlorn"—not excited, as they might make Margaret feel.[31] Mary's intention is to stop the ship that is bearing away the man who might provide an alibi for her lover, Jem Wilson, and in a scene that anticipates Margaret's own first gesture before the striking workers, she "stood up, steadying herself by the mast, and stretched out her arms, imploring the flying vessel to stay its course by that mute action, while the tears streamed down her cheeks. The men caught up their oars, and hoisted them in the air, and shouted to arrest attention" (357). Like Margaret's cry at the beginning of the strike scene, Mary's too lacks tone: "Her throat was dry; all the musical sound had gone out of her voice; but in a loud harsh whisper she told the men her errand of life and death, and they hailed the ship" (358). Though the captain refuses to release the sailor who can prove the alibi, Mary's effort will eventually bear fruit: the young man will emerge later at the trial and his testimony will exculpate Jem.

Mary's own public appearance at the trial, however, will have little bearing on the outcome: the evidence she has to give is not decisive. Still, like Margaret, Mary looks out on a "sea of faces, misty and swimming before her eyes" and sees the "hundreds [who] were looking at her" (388, 389), just as Margaret remembers afterwards "a sea of men," "a cloud of faces," and the "unwinking glare of many eyes" (233, 248, 249). But what is strikingly different about the two scenes is that although the trial is actually the scene of Mary's sexual self-representation—she confesses her love for Jem in public when a lawyer asks her "to tell, before that multitude assembled there, what woman usually whispers with blushes and tears, and many hesitations, to one ear alone" (390)—her appearance in court does not bring with it any sense of sexual impropriety at all. Indeed, Gaskell seems determined in this earlier novel *not* to associate Mary's courtroom appearance with the sort of taint that publicity carries in *North and South* and she accomplishes this in a variety of ways: by separating Mary's public appearance from her earlier heroic act (Margaret's public appearance *is* her heroic act), by having her confess to a love that others would be loathe to acknowledge (she loves a man on trial for murder, a man "abhorred of men," 390), and by having her "los[e] all command over herself" after her testimony ends (392).

In other words, Mary's public appearance lacks the agency that Gaskell attributes to Margaret's. That agency is reserved for the earlier, heroic scenes in Liverpool. By the time Mary gets to the courtroom she is able to speak with clarity and composure, but she can only do so while averting her eyes and, when she is done speaking, covering her face with her hands. Those who watch her are struck by the "higher and stranger kind of beauty" that her face suggests (389), not by the "conspicuous notice" that Sally Leadbitter, at the dress shop where Mary had been working, associates in advance with Mary's court appearance. Mary will prove "quite an attraction to customers," Sally says. "Many a one would come and have their gowns made by Miss Simmonds just to catch a glimpse at you, after the trial's over. Really, Mary, you'll turn out quite a heroine" (335).

Mary does turn out a heroine, but not in the way Sally thinks. Gaskell imagines publicity and heroism separately in *Mary Barton,* and she explores public sexual self-representation hemmed round with self-undermining protections. In *North and South* Gaskell confronts the risks of a bold, and boundary-crossing heroism and, building on the earlier book's innovations, explores much more openly the sexual taint to which female publicity would increasingly find itself attached.

IV.

Sexual tainting is also, I would like to suggest, one of the central themes of the second half of *North and South,* though here it is associated not with publicity but rather with secrecy, concealment, and lying. Virtually everyone in the second half of *North and South* practices concealment of some sort: the Hales, and even the Higginses, cover for Margaret's brother, Frederick, during his secret return to England (he is accused of a mutiny and goes into hiding in his home country); Margaret lies about her presence at the scene of the train station scuffle with Leonards, the man who recognizes her brother; Frederick travels to London under cover; and Thornton himself, without Margaret's knowledge, suppresses the information he has about her presence at the train station and protects her from exposure when he decides not to hold an inquest into Leonards's death.

Yet the focus of attention is really on Margaret herself—on the particular nature of what she hides and on the guilt attached to its concealment. In Margaret's view, she protects an innocent brother from discovery, but Frederick is connected throughout the novel to reckless, traitorous, and illegal activity—a mutiny, a secret visit, accidental involvement in a death, and even, by the end, exile to Spain and marriage to a Spanish Catholic. By protecting Frederick, Margaret traffics with what is dangerous, illicit, even violent, and this fact is re-emphasized when she herself commits a "crime": she lies to the authorities about her brother's whereabouts. Frederick is Margaret's alter ego, not a madwoman in the attic but a mad brother in the wings whose story, and then whose physical presence, are concealed from sight for the better part of the novel. When Frederick goes back into exile, his criminality gets transferred to Margaret, who then spends the second half of the novel guiltily repenting her own violation of the (moral) law.

Margaret's obsession with lying has a variety of sources. Perhaps most obviously, lying deals a fatal blow to her vision of herself as a maidenly center of moral purity—the vision she had of herself at Helstone, and a vision central to the "woman's mission" ideology so familiar in this period. If Margaret is a liar, then she cannot occupy the gentlewoman's private sphere, as Sarah Ellis and Sarah Lewis imagined it; she cannot function as the "moral agent" or as the "representative of moral purity" to whom men appeal because they know her "purity of motive [is] unquestioned"; and she cannot, thus, argue that what others perceived as transgressive behavior in the strike scene was really "woman's work."[32]

Margaret's view is further complicated by Thornton's reading of her actions, which implicates her (unfairly as it turns out) not merely in the crime of lying but also in the more serious crime of being a fallen woman. Thornton believes that Margaret's lie hides a guilty secret, that it suggests "some terrible shame in the background, to be kept from the light in which I thought she lived perpetually" (391). And his suspicions derive both from the compromising situation in which he sees her "at such an hour—in such a place" (351; he means the train station, at dusk)—and then from her lie about where she has been. That Margaret's lie somehow partakes of sexual taint is certainly on Thornton's mind when he says that it "showed a fatal consciousness of something wrong, and to be concealed" (386), and when he refers, more than once, to the way she has "stained her whiteness by a falsehood" (351; see also 386).

Margaret's lie seems, at times, to be just another name for illicit sexuality itself—as her language implies when she realizes that "she stood as a liar in [Thornton's] eyes. She was a liar. But she had no thought of penitence before God: nothing but chaos and night surrounded the one lurid fact that, in Mr. Thornton's eyes, she was degraded. . . . 'Oh, Frederick! Frederick!' she cried, 'what have I not sacrificed for you!' " (355). The "lurid" fact to which Margaret ostensibly refers, the thing "sacrifice[d]" to Frederick, is her moral purity, which Thornton believes is the sacrifice of sexual purity. Although Margaret remains mysteriously unaware of his assumption, the language she uses affirms the connection she denies. This is also true later on when Margaret remembers an earlier conversation with Thornton: "Her cheeks burnt as she recollected how proudly she had implied an objection to trade (in the early days of their acquaintance), because it too often led to the deceit of passing off inferior for superior goods, in the one branch; of assuming credit for wealth and resources not possessed, in the other. . . . No more contempt for her! . . . Henceforward she must feel humiliated and disgraced in his sight" (378). Margaret's view of herself as damaged goods is very powerful: what really seems to be at issue is not just her moral transgression but rather the sexual transgression of which Thornton (incorrectly) assumes Margaret is guilty.[33]

If lying (and secrecy) in the second half of *North and South* has similar associations to female publicity in the first half of the novel—connected as both are with illicit sexuality unprotected by marriage and ungoverned by the constraints of domestic life—that is because Gaskell is suggesting that the two are remarkably alike. We have already seen in Margaret's emergence onto the public stage that female public appearance intimates sexual promiscuity: the willingness or even the wish to appear unscreened, to circulate freely, to be the object of indiscriminate regard, to engage with others in mixed, or what Victorians more meaningfully called promiscuous, company. But in Margaret's relationship to her brother Frederick, Gaskell imagines an alternative realm that is equally charged and dangerous—secretive, violent, devious in its actions, and unrestrained in its intimacy. In this realm—or so Thornton thinks, at any rate—the appearance of a woman before a man is unmediated, action is unguarded, intimacy is unprotected and ungovernable. Under the cover of secrecy, as in the glare of public life, women become the agents of unmanageable desire, so that either to have a secret life, or to have a public life, is to be sexually tainted—even though the sexual involvement may be purely by imputation and association.[34]

But when Gaskell equates secrecy with publicity she confirms what Victorians always seemed to fear—that the private/public distinction was insupportable and could not be maintained. Unable to imagine a woman leaving her private self behind when she entered the public domain, Victorians generally imagined her bringing it inappropriately with her—imagined cradles in the House of Parliament and sexual self-display at the polls or on the city streets. And yet while Gaskell's repeated identification of private with public life, and political with intimate life, confirms the fear that led Victorians strictly to separate the two and to punish transgressions between them, Gaskell's own response to the erosion of distinctions is, extraordinarily, not punitive at all, but celebratory.

It is precisely the fact that Margaret does feel damaged—"degraded and abased in [his] sight"—that makes her come to the realization that she is in love with Thornton: "What strong feeling," she wonders, knowing the answer, "had overtaken her at last?" (358). To Gaskell, the experience of being tainted is oddly beneficial; it is in fact positive and educative. It reduces Margaret's excessive sense of moral superiority, eradicates her snobbishness (class and otherwise), and makes her able truly to connect with others. Moreover, Margaret may castigate herself for her moral failure but she pays no real price for the adulterous aura that surrounds her actions. Quite the contrary, she reaps its rewards. Margaret's shame is transformed into an acknowledgment of her sexual maturity, as though Gaskell meant first to suggest the explosiveness of female sexuality and then to purge it of its taint.[35]

This is also, I would argue, Gaskell's intention in her last novel, *Wives and Daughters* (1865), where she gives her female characters access to unprotected intimacy, argues that it is unacceptably perilous, and finally converts unprotected into protected intimacy in the marriages of Molly Gibson and her half sister Cynthia Kirkpatrick. Just as she ties Margaret to Frederick's illicit activities, Gaskell ties Molly Gibson first to Osmond Hamley's guilty marriage and then to Cynthia's indiscretions with Mr. Preston, and here too the involvement first educates the heroine in the ways of intimate life and then gets dissociated from her so that Molly can be cleared of its contamination.[36]

Much as in the second half of *North and South*, virtually everyone in *Wives and Daughters* is directly or indirectly associated with secrecy and concealment. Most significantly, Molly covers for Cynthia when she meets the latter's former lover in secret. She intends to return to Preston the money that Cynthia has borrowed and retrieve Cynthia's love letters in an effort to terminate their connection. Molly finally completes her assignment in Grinstead's store in town: she "ran in; he was at the counter now, talking to Grinstead himself; Molly put the letter into his hand, to his surprise, and almost against his will, and turned round to go back" (548). Molly operates as Cynthia's proxy (and her go-between) in a public place. She puts money into a man's hand, and finds herself discovered in the act.

Like Margaret, Molly becomes the unknowing object of scandal; her meetings with Preston are perceived to be "clandestine," and "without proper sanction of parents" (550, 551). As the scandal spreads, the stories elaborate themselves: "Why, that Molly and Mr Preston were . . . meeting at all sorts of
improper times and places, and [she] fainting away in his arms, and out at night
together and writing to each other and slipping their letters into each other's
hands" (561; see also 564, 567, 581). Like Margaret, Molly won't justify her
behavior by revealing her sibling's secret. And also like Margaret, Molly is initiated by implication into the mysteries of sexual relations through the fiction
of her involvement in unsanctioned intimacy.

When the honorable Lady Harriet decides to be Molly's champion, she
effects her cleansing in a way that oddly mirrors Molly's tainting. She "so con-
trived that they twice passed through all the length of the principal street of the
town" and even "loitered at Grinstead's for half-an-hour" (584). Lady Harriet's
parading of Molly through the town streets confers upon her innocence by
association, but Molly is still dogged by her own fears of impropriety. As Gaskell
puts it, in words that mirror Margaret's own coming to acknowledgment of her
love for Thornton, Molly "could never be the first to suggest the notion of
impropriety" in her upcoming visit to Roger Hamley's house, "which pre-
supposed what she blushed to think of" (682–83). The suggestion of "impropriety" presupposes the very connection to Roger that Molly is beginning to
contemplate—and that Gaskell had planned for the celebratory conclusion of
her novel.

V.

What I would call the generosity of Gaskell's vision of sexual impropriety extends
itself beyond her rendering of Margaret and Thornton's relationship and into
her treatment of Margaret's role in the social world of London where she plans
to "set apart for freedom in working" a portion of her own life (508). Instead
of abandoning, as she might have done, Margaret's interest in public causes,
Gaskell refashions her vision of female publicity, suggesting—in an admittedly
reticent portrait—that Margaret will become a nineteenth-century lady visitor,
wearing, as Edith humorously remarks, "brown and dust-coloured" dresses to
avoid showing "the dirt you'll pick up in all those places" (509). The critic
Dorice Williams Elliott states that Margaret differs from the traditional Lady
Bountiful, supported by the landed gentry or the church, and even from the
lady visitor who is "emissary for a philanthropic association," because Gaskell
intimates that she will operate independently and on her own authority.[37] But

of course Margaret has been operating independently for much of the novel in her home visits to the Higginses and their neighbors. Gaskell suggests at the end that Margaret will professionalize her independent visiting in London (where she would be unlikely to go visiting on her own), committing herself to it in a way that implies she will join a visiting society.

It would be easy to see such work as part of a project of containment in which Margaret is transformed from a potent strike scene participant into a fledgling lady visitor, a woman who extends the domestic sphere outward into the homes of the poor. In this reading the emergence of a woman onto the public stage somehow becomes the feminization, and thus the conversion and reduction, of a literally explosive relation to the public realm. But as Anne Summers points out in her analysis of women's philanthropic work, "treating social problems on an individualistic basis rather than subjecting them to a structural analysis" did not make women's work "reactionary." Although Summers acknowledges the conservative features of visiting (especially as it bears on the poor themselves), she clearly sees it as providing middle-class women with access to "power outside their homes."[38]

The implication that such work brought one into the "glare of publicity" and that it might even be attached to some undefined "opprobrium" intimates that Margaret has not entirely altered her instinct to strike out on her own potentially dangerous path.[39] She will follow her own authority and "her own ideas of duty" by committing herself more fully to the tasks, and the risks, of nineteenth-century female visiting. Gaskell treats lightly and humorously the scene in which Margaret discusses her plans with Edith, and Edith warns her against becoming "strong-minded," but the indication that Margaret's work will be perilous is nonetheless unmistakable (508).[40]

Gaskell's representation of Margaret's complex circumstances reveals her serious interest in refashioning the meaning of female publicity and reconceiving the relations between private and public life. Unlike the domestic ideologists upon whose thinking she initially draws, Gaskell does not finally portray her heroine as a woman who feminizes the public realm by extending domestic life outward (Margaret crosses the boundary between private and public and relinquishes the immunities associated with private life) nor as a woman who purifies public life of its taint by conserving her own private principles as a sustaining resource (the lie, I have argued, makes this stance impossible). Gaskell abandons both of these visions and focuses first on what happens when a woman enters an unreconstructed and unpurifiable public realm: she is penetrated by it and initiated into it, where penetration consists in physical violation and initiation consists both in enduring public exposure and in suffering the shame of an implied promiscuity. Gaskell also imagines her way beyond her heroine's public initiation and into a new version of public endeavor—even though public space is promiscuous space in Gaskell's novel and entry into it both risky and potentially compromising.

To say this might appear to suggest that Gaskell rejected one set of Victorian conventions (those identifying female domesticity with moral power) only to adopt another (those defining public life as sexually compromising)—and in one sense this is indeed the case. But what makes *North and South* interesting and surprising is that Gaskell neither saw the danger of public life as a reason to exclude women from it nor sought to imagine entry into that realm as an opportunity to domesticate it. The sexualization of public life can only be seen as an effort to imagine its domestication if femininity is really felt to be benign— if a woman's entrance onto the public stage might be seen as an opportunity to neutralize a dangerous world. But Gaskell suggests here both that female sexuality is potent—affiliated with exposure, criminality, indiscretion, and immoral secrecy—and, at the same time, that this is emphatically not stigmatizing. She never reduces our sense that public life is dangerously thrilling: Margaret's excitement about the universe of power and accomplishment in Milton and her determined authority about "freedom in working" emphasize this point. Nor does Gaskell seek entirely to eliminate the sexual shame that gets attached first to Margaret's public appearance and later to her supposed relation with a secret lover. Instead, she converts public into private shame, and private shame into the acknowledgment of mature sexuality, thus affirming rather than condemning the inevitable connectedness of public and private life and imagining a world in which their explosive union might actually be accommodated—as it is in the marriage of Thornton and Margaret, which begins as a business proposition (on Margaret's part) and ends as an intensely erotic proposal of marriage (on Thornton's).

Many critics have seen Gaskell's ending as a conservative project of accommodation.[11] In my view it is the opposite. *North and South* does equate public with private life by equating female publicity with female sexuality, and it transforms private sexual shame into an opportunity for sexual self-recognition, a new form of female public appearance, and, of course, public marriage. But its equations never appear in the service of exclusion, neutralization, containment, or even romantic reduction. The novel confirms what critics of female emancipation tended to fear—that access to public life means access to potentially dangerous kinds of sexual intimacy for women—and it does so while affirming, and hence finally legitimizing, both female public action and female sexuality. This double affirmation does not narrow, but rather expands, the range of possibilities. It does not convert and thus reduce the public into the private, but grants the private its disturbingly public dimension.

III

Rectitude and Larceny in
Diana of the Crossways

I.

WHEN GEORGE MEREDITH published *Diana of the Crossways* (1885), and even earlier when he wrote *Beauchamp's Career* (1875) and *The Egoist* (1879), the British women's movement was well established. The first petition for Woman Suffrage was presented to Parliament in 1866 and was followed by decades of debate in Parliament on the "Electoral Disabilities of Women." The 1870s and 1880s witnessed the agitation for repeal of the Contagious Diseases Acts and debates about the double standard that the repeal effort brought forward. They also saw, among other important educational advances for women, the founding of Girton College in 1869, and passage of the Enabling Act in 1875 (permitting universities to admit women if they so wished). By 1882, after almost thirty years of agitation, the Married Women's Property Act, on whose behalf Elizabeth Gaskell had signed the first petition in 1856, finally became law.

When Meredith published *Diana of the Crossways* he became, as Lionel Stevenson has suggested, the "chosen novelist of the 'emancipated' woman," and there is reason to believe that he would have sympathized with the above efforts, even if he did not always agree with the language, style, or timing of their proponents. In 1876 he corresponded with the feminist and poet Louisa Shore, later inviting both her and her sister (also an essayist and poet) to his home at Box Hill. Shore seems to have initiated the correspondence out of interest in and admiration for Meredith's work, and he in turn wrote to her thanking her for her praise and asking, "Now of you. I gather that you write. Will you oblige me with an indication of what and where it is to be seen?"[1]

Shore had published a book of poetry in 1871 (*Fra Dolcino, and Other Poems*). Then, in July 1874, she wrote an unsigned review article for the *Westminster Review* entitled "The Emancipation of Women" and no doubt would have "obliged" Meredith with information about her authorship of the essay and its place and date of publication. What would Meredith have read in Shore's article?

He would have read a wide-ranging response to the controversy about women's emancipation that was carried on in essays, books, speeches, and parliamentary debates in the late 1860s and 1870s—materials with which Meredith would have been familiar. Shore's subjects include property rights, the suffrage, marriage, women's education, the double standard, and even (although it goes unnamed) prostitution. It is no wonder that the *Dictionary of National Biography* would later declare that the essay "contains the gist of the whole subsequent movement in this direction [of women's emancipation] at a time when it was imperfectly understood."[2]

Shore begins by asking "What is the position of women in England at this day?" and she invokes the similarity between their rights and those of "criminals, lunatics, and idiots." The placement of women in this group was much discussed in the popular press, especially in relation to efforts to reform the laws governing married women's property. The *Times* described the association as an appropriate one in an 1868 article, and Frances Power Cobbe wrote a humorous and mocking reply for *Fraser's Magazine* in which she exposed the "incongruity" of the association and contested the view that women were properly "excluded from many civil and all political rights in England."[3]

Perhaps more significantly, Shore's essay, especially in the beginning, directly echoes John Stuart Mill's *On the Subjection of Women*, which, as J. S. Stone notes, Meredith had read with excitement in 1869 (the year of its publication) on the recommendation of his friend John Morley. Morley later reported that Meredith "could not be torn from it all day." Mill had argued that current social and legal arrangements "arose simply from the fact that from the very earliest twilight of human society, every woman . . . was found in a state of bondage to some man"; Shore starts with the idea that "the position of women in England at this day" is merely "a modification of ancient barbarism," and she too invokes "the early ages of the human race" in which "advantage was taken of woman's physical weakness to make her literally a slave." The advantage, she argues, continues in "the domination of one sex over the other—that is, of one half the mature human race over the other half . . . because the physical force is permanently on the side of the first." Like Mill, who had earlier put the question, "Was there ever any domination which did not appear natural to those who possessed it?" Shore suggests that the results of domination are "so deep-seated and complex" that they "have escaped [the] notice" and "blinded [the] eyes" of those who perpetuate them.[4]

Shore is also interested, as was Mill, in the ways in which revolt is suppressed, and collusion generated, in women who inevitably feel "tenderness for the prejudices of those with whom they live" and an "intense shrinking from masculine sarcasm and mockery." This "moral coercion," as she calls it, has been "lavishly employed to supplement the legal subjection of women" and to produce their acquiescence. In Mill's reading, coercion is viewed from the other side; it expresses itself as the ability of men to create in women the desire to please those with whom they live: "Men do not want solely the obedience of women, they want their sentiments. All men, except the most brutish, desire to have, in the woman most nearly connected to them, not a forced slave but a willing one, not a slave merely, but a favourite."[5]

Shore's analysis, like Mill's before it, imagines, in effect, *The Egoist*'s Sir Willoughby Patterne, whose power is exercised through his excessive, supervisory sensitivity to the intentions of "eyes and tones," who wishes to exercise his control not through dictation but through the subtle management of others' feelings, and who, in the midst of powerful verbal manipulation, can also assert that "I do not claim servitude. I stipulate for affection."[6] Like Sir Willoughby, Mill's patriarch wants power "most over those who are nearest to him, with whom his life is passed, with whom he has most concerns in common, and in whom any independence of his authority is oftenest likely to interfere with his individual preferences."[7] It is to this subtle form of subjection that Shore turns her attention in the early pages of her text and that Meredith explores so brilliantly in his novel.

Taking up the implications of her opponents' arguments and seeking to counter them, Shore addresses the "special unfitnesses urged against women" by such opponents of the suffrage as Edward Pleydell Bouverie, whose remarks in parliamentary debate suggest, as Shore points out, that their "chronic state of blushing and fear . . . would make it improper for [women] to face the bustle of polling-places." Bouverie declares that "the great English divine of two hundred years ago was right when he said that 'fear and blushing were the girdle of virtue.' In the polling booths and in the House of Commons, in the market and in the Exchange, women, if they engaged in an equal struggle with men, must go to the wall. They were the weaker part of the human race, and in competition with men they must be worsted." Shore is contemptuous of the notion that civil rights depend upon physical prowess and will not even "condescend to dwell" on the argument that polling places cannot be made fit for women. Nor can she sympathize with Bouverie's assertion (and his fear) that the entire institution of marriage was "to come to an end, and that women were to engage in men's pursuits—to be politicians, to become Members of that House, and to take part in the administration of the country." She merely notes in passing that "the objection that women, when once admitted to the vote, will (logically) be eligible to a seat in Parliament," can be "decided on its own merits by some future generation." She does not take up, though clearly she sees, the larger implications for female public life that the suffrage implies.[8]

When Shore considers the social and cultural implications of refusing women the vote, she argues that, in the guise of noninterference, this refusal serves to guarantee women's continued performance of domestic responsibilities. Parliament sees its "business" as "to provide more rigorously for the performance of women's private duties than men's," and this interference is expressed as well in what looks like the reluctance of legislators to cause marital strife by creating argumentative household partners (who would quarrel about parties and candidates). Again, however, Shore points out that what looks like a refusal to interfere is really an excessive concern by the State "to provide against these little domestic difficulties of married life (but only of course by laying restrictions on the wife)."[9]

Shore identifies a common strain in debates about women's suffrage, namely, the argument by suffragists that what looks like the refusal to interfere in the realm of domestic freedom is interference of another kind—the active, partisan legislation of female domestic privacy where no comparable legislation of male privacy exists and the commitment to maintain, through the active instrument of the law, existing marital relations, especially those that limit female access to power and confine women to the home.[10]

As I hope to indicate when I turn to Meredith's *Diana of the Crossways,* the author's sympathy with the above positions reveals itself throughout this novel. He exposes domestic privacy as a violation, rather than a preserve, of personal liberty; he provides release both from the "little domestic difficulties of married life," and from its more powerful restrictions and partisan legislation in Diana's separation from her husband; he grants his heroine an extraordinary measure of public freedom after her liberation and places her in the midst of the very public settings that, according to Bouverie, ought to make her blush—but do not. As Meredith's letters over several decades demonstrate, he saw the confinement of women to domestic life as impeding their essential growth and their development toward full citizenship. In Diana he creates a woman who leaves home and, despite her many mistakes, flourishes.

One of the most interesting arguments that Shore takes up—and Meredith addresses it too—has to do with the understanding of "chivalrous homage" that appears frequently in debates about the suffrage and that Shore seeks to unmask in her article. In the 1871 debate to which Shore's language again refers, Alexander James Beresford Hope asserts that "the very nature of women called for sympathy and protection, and for the highest and most chivalrous treatment on the part of men; but instead of this being accorded for the future, it was now proposed to thrust them into a position which they were by their sex, by their condition in life, and by their previous training totally unqualified to grapple with." Shore's counterpoint is that chivalric "sympathy and protection" are offered to women by men in compensation for "every disadvantage and every humiliation attending the whole sex, in and out of drawing-rooms, and which they think women cannot reasonably look for except as a tribute to their legal inferiority and helplessness. . . . How is this? Is the spirit of 'chivalry' a spirit of bargain? and a very one-sided bargain?" Shore views chivalry as a bad transaction in which women exchange honor and power for protection. Those who purport to offer protection in the spirit of loyalty and respect, however, offer it in what Shore considers the spirit of extortion: "We are not going to quarrel with it for thus seeking its reward—only it must not boast itself too much. . . . Such objectors, however 'chivalrous,' however kind-hearted . . . *have no faith* in woman, no faith in the goddess they worship with flattery, incense and gay pageantry; and it would be well if they would frankly confess this. Then we should know exactly where to meet them." We shall see again in later debates about the suffrage and in Elizabeth Robins's novel *The Convert* a similar effort to deconstruct chivalry—to challenge the idea that relations between men and women are based on respect for the objects of chivalry's protection and to disclose the bargain that underlies the "pageantry": women retain men's respect as long as they neither exercise power nor move into the public sphere; if they do so move they forfeit the respect (which is in any case a mere fiction) and also the protection of their male counterparts. In short, as Bouverie had put it, "they must be worsted." Chivalry "must not boast itself," then, because it is tendered on false pretenses. It is offered only on conditions, and in exchange for "every disadvantage and every humiliation"—social, legal, and economic—under which women suffer.[11]

Meredith's critique of chivalry emerges in his characterization of Sir Willoughby Patterne, whose aristocratic protection of women (lightly) covers his own egotism and spectacular self-interest; in his sympathy for but criticism of Nevil Beauchamp, whose chivalric relations with women are at odds with his democratic instincts; and, more openly, in *Diana of the Crossways,* where the faithlessness and sexual rapaciousness of men (Redworth notwithstanding) rises up in sharp contrast to their supposed protectiveness and where chivalric metaphors regularly contend with metaphors of the primitive hunt.

Meredith would also, one suspects, have agreed with Shore's critique of female purity and would have opposed the view of woman as "a glorified, but well-educated invalid, who is to influence man for his good by her physical imperfections, as much as by her ethereal and intuitive morality and docile affections. She is to guard this physical incapacity as well as her supposed incapability of sharing in the highest national concerns, and her unfitness for any social business beyond the precincts of home, as sacred treasures, because man, it is said, requires this contrast to himself as a moralizing element in his life." Shore's description, which echoes the "woman's mission" debates of the 1840s, anticipates Meredith's rendition of Diana's friend Emma Dunstane, whose "physical imperfections" and "intuitive morality" stand in opposition to, but also oddly enable, her husband's infidelity because they guarantee him a place of safe return, an affiliation with the just and pure. Diana, as we shall see, offers no such safe haven, and yet she seeks, in an unusual effort, to maintain sexual purity while "sharing in the highest national concerns" and engaging in "social business beyond the precincts of home." Her challenge to the view that these cannot coexist, or that participation in the world inevitably brings sexual taint, is one of the most interesting features of Meredith's novel. Shore finds "the whole theory" described above "a morbid one"; she longs to "turn the ethereal prisoner into free fresh air, to develop her moral and intellectual muscle and stature at her will." In Shore's view freedom is simply not incompatible with "moral . . . stature," though her instinct is to de-etherealize morality, to give it "intellectual muscle." This is Meredith's intention as well.[12]

On 11 August 1876 Meredith wrote to Shore again. His response seems to have been aimed both at comments she must have made about his "Ballad of Fair Ladies in Revolt" and her own writing about women's emancipation. The ballad seems disturbingly conventional in its critique of rebellious women, though Meredith insists that he has "not assumed the present situation." He focuses on the "claim for justice" that his fair ladies make so vigorously in the poem and that Shore presents in her essay—and his response is at once sympathetic and cautionary:

> As to the claim for justice, it is, I repeat, waste of force to cry for it. Convenience, or in other words, the good of all, is all that is recognized by the judicial mind; and it must be proved that this movement is for the good of all. This I am of opinion will be done with time. . . . But it is not yet time for active measures. By spreading instruction among women, as you do, far more is accomplished than by besieging Parliament. This is a movement that, when general enough to command respect, will knock away obstruction as the lid of a pot. . . . I hope for the advancement of the race, and conceive that there can be none till women walk freely with men.[13]

Meredith's belief that more is accomplished by "spreading instruction" than by "active measures" (like "besieging Parliament") is a moderate one, but his confidence that the obstruction *will* be dislodged, along with his forceful imagination of the day when "women walk freely with men," is moving testimony to his vision of future equality. Like the "professedly temperate" Seymour Austin in *Beauchamp's Career*, who favors "opening avenues to the means of livelihood for [women] and leaving it to their strength to conquer the position they might wish to win," it could be said of Meredith that "his belief that they would do so was the revolutionary sign."[14] It is striking, in fact, that while Meredith opposed aggressive action ("besieging Parliament"), he favored "spreading instruction"—even when the instruction was as subversive as Shore's.

Meredith's preferred method of subversion is evident in "On the Idea of Comedy and the Uses of the Comic Spirit" (1877). Here he suggests that he yearns for a future of equality, a society of "cultivated men and women . . . wherein ideas are current and perceptions quick"—a society of equals without which, he asserts, comedy itself is impossible. Meredith describes comedy as "an exhibition of [women's] battle with men, and that of men with them"—but his is a spirited sparring in which "the two, however divergent, both look on one object, namely, Life, [and] the gradual similarity of their impressions must bring them to some resemblance." It is easy to see in a statement like this why Meredith would both admire Shore and find her mode of operation at least somewhat alien to his own. "The Comic poet dares to show us men and women coming to this mutual likeness," while the feminist essayist unmasks their differences in a stroke. And while Shore beckons men to reveal themselves so that "then we should know exactly where to meet them," the comic poet imagines a world in which "pure Comedy flourishes, and is, as it would help [women] to be, the sweetest of diversions, the wisest of delightful companions."[15]

Carolyn Williams has proposed that Meredith's assertions about male and female equality stand in a strange relation to this assertion that comedy is, and would help women to be, "diversions" and "delightful companions." But while it is true that his conception of equality seems to assign women a surprisingly conventional set of roles, it isn't clear that men would occupy different roles themselves. Man and woman—each would be the other's delightful companion, the other's diversion. In other words, while comedy (and its absence) has political origins, its resolutions are interestingly apolitical: equality once reached, the comic perception governs interpersonal relations and their tone: "You may estimate your capacity for Comic perception by being able to detect the ridicule of them you love, without loving them less: and more by being able to see yourself somewhat ridiculous in their eyes, and accepting the correction their image of you proposes." Derision, as Meredith notes, is "foiled by the play of intellect," and "the test of true comedy is that it shall awaken thoughtful laughter." Like the "intercommunicative daylight" in which Meredith's Diana hopes eventually to live, Meredith's universe of sexual equality is a world of active, mobile human exchange.[16]

This is not to say that Meredith invoked feminist ideas only to move away from them; it is to argue, rather, that he believed in gradual changes that would inevitably lead to emancipation. His letters reveal that he favored opening the professions to women; educating daughters so that they would "not be instructed to think themselves naturally inferior to men"; encouraging women to "state publicly what has long been confined to the domestic circle—consequently a wasted force"; providing women with access to "the business of the world." Though some letters express antipathy toward "the [loud] shrieks for the Suffrage," Meredith's letters generally attest that he became a constitutional suffragist—someone who, along with Millicent Garrett Fawcett and Elizabeth Garrett Anderson, believed in seeking the suffrage through gradual legislative, and not militant, means.[17]

The most consistent feature of Meredith's position on women's emancipation lies in his belief that women must grow into the role that they wish to occupy—gaining strength through education, through work, through exposure to public life—until their manifest strength makes it impossible not to grant them the equality they have already demonstrated. It is for this reason that Meredith engages the central issues of the emancipation debate and at the same time focuses on the growth of his heroine and not on her legislative activity.

II.

In *Diana of the Crossways* Meredith models his heroine on a woman who occupied a key place in the history of the agitation on behalf of women's rights—an unwilling participant, perhaps, but a significant one. The novel was based on the life of Caroline Norton (1808–1857), granddaughter of the playwright Richard Brinsley Sheridan. Caroline married George Norton when she was nineteen and then, like Diana, separated from her husband—though in Caroline's case after years of marital incompatibility, and spurred by George's refusal to allow her sons a visit to their uncle. George moved the boys to an undisclosed location and Caroline refused to return home. Her husband responded by publicly declaring himself not liable for her debts and then by suing her friend Prime Minister Lord Melbourne for "criminal conversation" (adultery). The suit was unsuccessful and the case, whose political implications were not easy to disentangle from its personal and sexual ones, reappears in Meredith's text, though the element of party politics is there downplayed.

Unlike Meredith's Diana, however, Norton's response to her husband's actions was to turn directly to political advocacy. In her efforts to change the laws regulating the custody of minor children, she wrote (and published privately) a pamphlet entitled *Separation of Mother and Child by the Law of Custody of Infants Considered* (1837), and later a *Plain Letter to the Lord Chancellor* (under the pseudonym Pearce Stevenson, 1839). Eventually, the Infant's Custody Act of 1839 was passed, giving women limited rights of access to children under seven years old. Caroline Norton's *English Laws for Women in the Nineteenth Century* (1854), an exposé of the laws governing married women's property rights (or lack thereof), grew from many years of personal and legal wrangling with her husband. *A Letter to the Queen on Lord Cranworth's Marriage and Divorce Bill* (1855) followed—a study of the divorce laws that had an important impact on the 1857 Matrimonial Causes Acts.[18]

But Meredith's Diana is childless: the removal of Caroline Norton's children (the precipitating incident in her separation from her husband) and the subsequent loss of their custody (which allegedly contributed to the death of one of her sons while in his father's care) are thus not reflected in Meredith's novel. Meredith chooses to stress Diana's romantic and political interests and engagements (Caroline Norton had these too), rather than the legislative initiatives that arose from Norton's personal circumstances.

Though more of a political activist than her novelistic counterpart—because she found herself to be, in matters of custody and property rights, " 'non-existent' except for the purpose of suffering"—Norton never identified herself with the cause of women's rights, nor did she believe, as Joan Huddlestone has noted, either in the "advocacy of equality . . . or the equality of men and women at all." Instead, she "sought to improve the methods by which men could protect women, and to establish legal remedies if this protection should fail."[19]

While Meredith eliminates, in Diana, both Caroline Norton's children and thus her contribution to a female legislative agenda, he also affiliates Diana more openly with the cause of women. The repeal of the 1834 Corn Laws is the political issue most immediately at hand in the novel, but Meredith obscures the details of the Corn Law debate. Diana has no direct "feminist" legislative agenda, yet she nevertheless has elaborate public work. Most centrally, her public life emerges in the offering up of political advice and counsel and the making of political relationships and reputations. She is at once more explicitly feminist in her self-identification than Caroline Norton, less identifiable with feminism's legislative agenda, and more actively involved in the creation of a female political life.

Meredith begins, however, with Diana as a woman who is parentless and homeless, "constantly wandering, like a leaf off a tree," an "unprotected beautiful girl" (43), and a "waif" (54)—a woman without parents or husband who is both literally and figuratively vulnerable. Diana Merion senses her danger, especially when her best friend's husband makes advances to her. She does "the wisest thing a waif can do" (54): she marries, and marries the man to whom she has rented her property. She returns to live in her old home—as she puts it, "my old home for my new one" (54). This odd reacquisition, or rather reoccupation, of the family property suggests the direct association for Diana between marriage and housing, or marriage and (literal) coverage—an association that seems particularly pertinent in a novel concerned, as this one is, with problematic exposures of various kinds. Diana's desire for cover highlights her sense of dangerous homelessness in that odd space between parental and marital protection.

Diana's marriage to Augustus Warwick turns out to offer false cover, and its failure is attributed to the fact that, as Diana's friend Emma Dunstane notes, "the house [was] locked up and empty . . . empty of inhabitants, even to a ghost" (61). Emma's point, as she merges husband and house, is that Diana's husband is himself vacant. Diana marries a man who is a house, because men, like houses, provide necessary protection; but this house/man lacks even a ghost, even a sign of having ever been occupied by an authentic human person. (Hence, one suspects, the radical underrepresentation of the marriage and the husband.) Indeed, Diana's husband turns out to embody not protection but its opposite: the regulation of intimacy, the imposition of "constraint"; not freedom from feared violation, but rather subjection—"a leash, a muzzle, harness, a hood, whatever is detestable to the free limbs and senses" (45). When he accuses her of adultery, brings a suit for criminal conversation against her friend Lord Dannisburgh and then loses, the marriage effectively comes to an end, though of course the loss of the suit means that there is no divorce.

This puts Diana in an extraordinary situation for the remainder of the novel. In the introductory chapter, when the breakup of her marriage is noted, she is described as entering a dinner party late: "Just before starting from home she had broken loose from her husband for good, and she entered the room absolutely houseless" (4). The statement emphasizes Diana's vulnerability, her sudden and radical change of position: she "start[s] from home" in the colloquial sense, but this local gesture becomes an absolute, ontological fact. It is also oxymoronic: she enters someone else's house "houseless." It's hard not to feel that Diana is at once situated (she's at a dinner party, among friends) and desituated (practically, she has no home of her own to which she can return).

From this point forward Diana is a woman in transition. Percy Dacier will later call her a woman "in . . . miserable suspension, neither maid nor wife, woman nor stockfish" (238). Meredith, it seems, marries and "unmarries" his heroine in order to think about the situation of a woman *at once* single and married, innocent and experienced, liberated and constrained by the marital contexts from which she is partially, but not wholly, free. In writing about Diana Warwick, Meredith explores the very condition of constrained liberty. Like Clara Middleton in *The Egoist*, who is betrothed to Sir Willoughby Patterne but not yet committed to him, and in a different way like Cecilia Halkett in *Beauchamp's Career*, who gives her heart to Nevil Beauchamp but never marries him (she is "conquered but unclaimed," 381), Diana hovers between states in a manner that Meredith finds compelling.

Examined from one perspective, Diana's transitional identity means that she lives in lodgings, travels, entertains, works, earns money, and conducts her life under the "cover" of marriage. She has the freedom of movement that comes with her status as a matron, but she has shed the muzzling confinement and regulation of her private life that is attached to a relationship with Augustus Warwick. At the same time, her constrained behavior has consequences. To look at the matter from another perspective, as Lois Josephs Fowler has done, is to see Caroline Norton (and by implication, Diana) as a woman whose "struggle for independence kept her in precarious balance. . . . She lived with none of the advantages of marriage, yet without the freedom of divorce." These opposing points of view lead Penny Boumehla to describe Diana as a woman "in a vertiginous state of sexual-categorical suspension . . . she is allowed—or forced—to escape those categories that had encompassed the narratives of femininity in the mid-century. But to stand outside the categories is not to be free." Fowler's point is that Diana's uncertain status permits Meredith to face "squarely the growing conflict over sexual freedom." Diana is not free, when living with her husband, to conduct with impunity a friendship with Lord Dannisburgh; but although she is free, when she has stopped living with her husband, to attach herself to the young statesman, Percy Dacier, she is not free to do so with impunity. According to her friends, she isn't even able to conduct with impunity an innocent relationship with Dacier: her reputation is, as Meredith likes to say, "spotted"—regardless of what she does (98, 112, 150, 237). In the uncharted space between marriage and sexual freedom Meredith will stake out his claim for his heroine.[20]

Diana's friendship with Lord Dannisburgh, which she undertakes while still married, combines virtually all of the characteristics associated with female publicity in the novels we have examined so far: Diana is not at first a political agent herself; Dannisburgh provides her with an entrance into the world of politics, which she then experiences through him; and her association with him is immediately considered scandalous by others: their "names were openly spoken and swept from mouth to mouth of the scandalmongers, gathering matter as they flew" (70). Nevertheless, Meredith alters this familiar configuration in a critical fashion when Diana asserts that she could "say [their friendship] in the streets without shame" (65). Meredith asserts, in other words, that Diana's relationship with her parliamentary friend is, despite appearances, innocent and that Diana experiences it this way herself. She has no disguise and "he has no disguise": "as long as he does me the honor to esteem my poor portion of brains by coming to me for what he is good enough to call my counsel, I shall let the world wag its tongue. . . . I know I am of use in various ways. . . . He can favor me with no more than an hour in the afternoon, or a few minutes at night. Or I get a pencilled note from the benches of the House, with an anecdote, or news of a Division. I am sure to be enlivened" (65–66). Diana values her own sense that she is "of use in various ways," and she is willing to be talked about if that is the price she must pay—an interesting development that advances the issue beyond the stage at which Brontë and Gaskell explored it.

What is equally unusual in the text is the specificity of Diana's experience of parliamentary politics. Unlike Gaskell's veiled references to Margaret "taking her life into her own hands" to perform philanthropic work among the poor, Meredith identifies openly Diana's receipt of information about parliamentary votes and about political stories that circulate in the House—and these suggest a palpable connection with the daily business of the House of Commons, a connection that the formerly "houseless" Diana wants and that Meredith will develop more fully in later chapters.

But the novel also escalates the sense of risk attached to this sort of experience. If Margaret Hale's political interests (and intrusions) impel others to imagine a romantic connection between herself and Thornton, Diana's political interests bring a legal suit for divorce. Moreover, Meredith's language shows that the suspicions that attach to Diana multiply her fault, that publicity of one kind brings publicity of another: "A woman doubted by her husband, is always . . . a creature of the wilds, marked for our ancient running. . . . The doubt casts her forth, the general yelp drags her down; she runs like the prey of the forest under spotting branches. . . . her character is abroad" (89). The sense of exposure that is so central a feature of the strike scene in *North and South* is here intensified, and in two ways. First, Meredith uses again the language of the hunt, which stands in sharp contrast to the language of chivalric protection that he associates with the relation of the sexes. Diana's local present is really an ancient past in which men and women revert to predator and prey. Suspicion "casts her forth" and the mass hunt is launched. Second, Meredith suggests that the punishment for her interest in and association with political life is inevitably the loss of character (a familiar notion)—except that now the emphasis is not so much on misconstruction as distribution: her character is "abroad," the subject of endless inappropriate handling.

Diana, however, has a complex response to the accusations. She does feel exposed—"Wherever I go now, in all weathers, I am perfectly naked!"(101)—and her first thought certainly is to run away and hide herself. But unlike Gaskell's Margaret Hale, Meredith does not suggest that what Diana feels is shame. At times he associates her response with her wish to preserve distance from, and thus dignity in relation to, her accusers; at times to "an odd apathy as to my character; rather like death. . . . What does it matter? I should have left the flies and wasps to worry a corpse" (109).

Between these divergent responses, Diana comes, over the course of a long self-examination, to a complex understanding of her own engagement in what she calls "the world of facts" (98). She asserts her innocence of the charges against her, but she doesn't confuse this with a more general innocence about the operations of her world. She knows that she is not "this utterly simple person," that she takes "pride in her power of fencing with evil." But she also knows that "such are men in the world of facts, that when a woman steps out of her domestic tangle to assert, because it is a tangle, her rights to partial independence, they sight her for their prey, or at least they complacently suppose her accessible. Wretched at home, a woman ought to bury herself in her wretchedness, else may she be assured that not the cleverest wariest, guard will cover her character" (98).

Meredith presents Diana as a knowing person: she is among that group of the "cleverest, [the] wariest," who, despite her cleverness, cannot "cover" herself. She realizes how little protection from others she can expect. Still, Meredith suggests that "Diana had not the heart to hate her kind, so she resigned herself to pardon, and to the recognition of the state of duel between the sexes." This is a striking remark, especially in the context of her husband's punishing behavior. But Meredith's point is that Diana is a keen reader (at least here) of her social universe—not a "ninny" young woman, "purely innocent" (98)—and her admission that she is neither surprised at nor ignorant of the complex way her world operates is her most significant response to the charges against her. At one juncture she even imagines herself unmasking her world: "The first martyr of the modern woman's cause . . . this martyr, a woman capable of telling the world she knew it, and of confessing that she had behaved in disdain of its rigider rules, according to her own ideas of her immunities" (99). The combination of knowledge and rebellious defiance undoes her earlier notion of distance and detached dignity, but the truth is that neither position carries the day. Diana follows "the road recommended by friends" (100), and remains to face her accuser. She resists "telling the world she knew it"(99). Meredith comments that "the night's red vision of martyrdom was reserved to console her secretly, among the unopened lockers in her treasury of thoughts" (100).

What Diana faces is public ridicule for a sin she didn't commit: "It is a singular fact, I have not known what this love is, that they talk about. And behold me marched into Smithfield!—society's heretic" (111). She also experiences a sense of being "branded" by her husband, marked with an "immovable patch—attractive to male idiots . . . and a mark of scorn to females. Between the two the remainder of my days will be lively" (112). Her brand (like Hester Prynne's scarlet letter in Hawthorne's 1850 novel) makes her even more vulnerable to men who think a guilty woman easy prey and makes her less acceptable to the women who might befriend and protect her. Diana is "spotted" (98, 112), but not guilty—and this, despite the fact that the "damned spot" (an ironic allusion to Lady Macbeth's "Out, damned spot, I say!") is "not on the hand" either, but "on the forehead" (112), for all to see.[21]

Diana then awaits the trial of her friend, which is, by implication, her trial, though she cannot be sued. (In trials for criminal conversation the husband sued the purported lover for loss of his wife's company, or "consortium.") Her field becomes London, and she experiences a "savage exultation in passing through the streets on foot and unknown" (116). Meredith allows us to imagine for a moment that Diana actually experiences freedom in the streets of London, whether she walks eastward toward her lawyers' offices or westward "against smoky sunsets, or in welcome fogs, an atom of the crowd!" (116). Sounding surprisingly like Henry Lennox in *North and South,* she enjoys her walks, her work, her independent life, and her anonymity: "I can eat when I like, walk, work—and I am working! My legs and my pen demand it. Let me be independent! Besides, I begin to learn something of the bigger world outside the one I know" (117). Diana describes to Emma her sense of being "generally protected" by the crowds—a "delightful" feeling to her, since it suggests the possibility of a protection not associated with marriage and privacy but, rather, with freedom and publicity. This feeling doesn't last, however, and Diana must eventually tell Emma of scenes in which the "English gentleman trad[ing] on his reputation" annoys her in the streets, making her a prisoner again, or a woman in need of a chaperon (119).

When Diana is exonerated at the end of the trial, the irony of her situation and its familiar categorical suspension is palpable: "she was exonerated" but "not free" because the failure to prove adultery also means the failure to produce evidence that would constitute grounds for divorce (134). Fleeing to the Mediterranean with friends "to escape the meshes of the terrific net of the marital law brutally whirled to capture her by the man her husband" (135), Diana yearns for England:

(139)

> She had been flattered by her friend, her "wedded martyr at the stake," as she named him, to believe that she could exercise a judgement in politics—could think, even speak acutely, on public affairs. The reports of speeches delivered by the men she knew or knew of, set her thrilling; and she fancied the sensibility to be as independent of her sympathy with the orators as her political notions were sovereignly above a sex devoted to trifles, and the feelings of a woman who had gone through fire. She fancied it confidently, notwithstanding a peculiar intuition that the plunge into the nobler business of the world would be a haven of safety for a woman with blood and imagination.

Diana also comments, in a letter to Emma, on her friend Thomas Redworth's success in Parliament and on Percy Dacier's as well (though she hasn't met him yet). She thinks of the possibility that one of them might some day have "power in striking at unjust laws, which keep the really numerically better-half of the population in a state of slavery" (139).[22] Meredith repeats that imagining the "happy championship of the cause of her sex" by one or another of her political acquaintances helps Diana to think of herself as "a contemplative, simply speculative political spirit" when it is clear to others that "her possession of a disengaged intellect" is a "fancy" (140).

Diana's interest in politics is itself interested, though she likes to imagine herself independent and objective. But an interest in "the cause of her sex," though perhaps not disinterested, is nonetheless political, rather than personal, in nature. Moreover, the notion that she is more interested in her political acquaintances than in their subjects—a familiar assertion about women and politics—is undermined by Meredith's larger point: that a "plunge into the nobler business of the world" would mean security, not danger, for someone like Diana because it would satisfy the demands of her "blood and imagination" that otherwise remain unsatisfied. Meredith senses that the public arena has its noble business to do (not something to take for granted, as we shall see in George Gissing's novels) and also that, instead of being a dangerous realm for women, it is potentially a "haven of safety." If he undermines Diana's vision of her disinterestedness here, he does so in order to emphasize that her interested perspective, her combination of self-interest and political interest, is a central feature of her character.

III.

Soon after this, Diana meets Percy Dacier in Lugano and writes to Emma that he seems a promising candidate: he "may be of use to our cause" (144). But her own attention to politics seems quickly to move into the background, as Meredith describes in her a different kind of awakening:

> *All her nature flew and bloomed; she was bird, flower, flowing river, a quivering sensibility unweighted, unshrouded. . . . Freedom to breathe, gaze, climb, grow with the grasses, fly with the clouds, to muse, to sing, to be an unclaimed self, dispersed upon earth, air, sky, to find a keener transfigured self in that radiation—she craved no more.* (145–46)
>
> > *Bear in mind her beauty, her charm of tongue, her present state of white simplicity in fervour.*

Throughout the novel Diana refers back to Lugano as a time of freedom and simplicity, but Meredith suggests that this is the wrong reading. The language of the passage mimics—in part duplicates, in part reverses—the language of gossip associated with Diana's relationship with Dannisburgh. There she was uncovered and thus vulnerable, her name in many mouths, her character abroad. Here too she is uncovered—she says unclaimed—and she experiences what we might call good dispersion: a sense of freedom, transfiguration, radiation. But Meredith suggests that her feelings do not emerge exclusively from a sense of independence; they are too closely associated with her experience of meeting Percy Dacier for that. Instead, they seem to grow out of her sense of freedom from the husband whom she has earlier described as "stifler, lung-contractor, iron mask, inquisitor, everything anti-natural" (132). The language of freedom that is also the language of nature makes sense if marriage is antinatural, but the language of the natural is tied to sexuality and sexual awakening as well.

The difference between Dacier's sense of Diana and Diana's own sense of herself is illuminating. Comparing her with his fiancée-of-sorts, Constance Asper, Dacier notes to himself that Constance "struck him cold. He fancied her transparent, only Arctic. Her transparency displayed to him all the common virtues" including "the inestimable and eminent one outweighing all [presumably chastity]; but charm, wit, ardour, intercommunicative quickness, and kindling beauty, airy grace, were qualities that a man, it seemed, had to look for in women spotted by a doubt of their having the chief and priceless" (150). Still, Meredith states that at Lugano, Diana "had not a spot of secrecy" and even describes hers as a "state of white simplicity" (145, 146). Dacier's sense that "intercommunicative quickness" and "kindling beauty" are inevitably associated with spottedness, with a doubt as to the woman's chastity, implies a notable discrepancy between his view of Diana and Meredith's, though Meredith comments that Dacier must "distinguish within himself the aspect he preferred" (150)—as though he might prefer a guilty to an innocent woman, despite his pretensions.

The confusions about Diana's innocence are also tied to her anomalous, hybrid social position. As Meredith reminds us here, she is "a wife and no wife, a prisoner in liberty, a blooming woman imagining herself restored to transcendent maiden ecstasies" (160). Her relationship with Dacier is a mixed one from the start—part writing, part love, part politics, part protection, part exposure. At Lugano she responds to him both as a politician and as a possible lover. She exhorts him to leave his holiday behind and return to his party, mentioning specifically the agitation about the Corn Laws. Dacier wants to keep politics out of Lugano and presumably out of his relationship with Diana ("Ah, but no politics here!") yet Diana insists from the start, "Politics everywhere!—in the Courts of Faery! They are not discord to me." In addition, she reminds Dacier not to "forget your assurance to me that you would give some thoughts to Ireland—and the cause of women" (156).

It is not long after this that Diana receives a commission to write "leading articles for the paper [Mr. Whitmonby] is going to conduct! 'Write as you talk and it will do,' he says. I am choosing my themes" (172). Diana complains, at first, that writing as she talks is "like an effort to jump away from my shadow. The black dog of consciousness declines to be shaken off," a comment that suggests her lack of ease at the prospect. But several pages later, when Diana tells Emma that "society is the best thing we have, but it is a crazy vessel worked by a crew that formerly practised piracy, and now, in expiation, professes piety" (175), Emma responds, "Have you not got into a trick of composing in speaking at times?" (176). Diana confesses: "Perhaps the daily writing of all kinds and the nightly talking . . . I may be getting strained. . . . I wonder whether [London] is affecting me! . . . A metropolitan hack!" (176). Diana's speech is permeated by her work, her scintillating talk now become crafted writing, as she feels her transformation into a newspaperwoman.

Despite his initial reluctance about mixing politics and romance at Lugano, Dacier finds Diana "a Lady Egeria, helpful in counsel, prompting, inspiriting" (183–84).[23] He tells himself that Diana's attractions are "chiefly mental" (186), but the description of their activities together already suggests more: "To see her, hear, exchange ideas with her; and to talk of new books, try to listen to music at the opera and at concerts, and admire her playing of hostess, were novel pleasures, giving him fresh notions of life, and strengthening rather than disturbing the course of life's business" (184). Dacier challenges his own more conventional views about women in his relationship with Diana. Not only does he enjoy the exchange of ideas with a woman and the receipt of her counsel, but he even tries social and cultural experiences that are part of her world, and not his (he isn't by nature appreciative of music). Meredith makes this point in the context of a description of Dacier's supposed fiancée, who, he declares, is "still more [Dacier's] type." Constance offers a potential husband "a casket of all the trusty virtues as well as the security of frigidity in the casket. Such was Dacier's native taste" (187).

The contrast is unnerving. Constance's virtues are presented in a casket, which suggests that they are bound up and contained, but also, obviously, dead. And yet Meredith declares them to be "the trusty virtues"—known and tested. Of course they offer, in addition, the "security of frigidity," that is, the security of what is entirely reliable because it is coldly invulnerable to feeling; and, because it offers its frigidity as a fixed, dead thing, becomes utterly so. And yet Constance (her name repeats the point) represents and confirms Dacier's native taste—a taste denied and from which he is enticed away by a woman at once less contained, infinitely more vivid, much more emphatically hybrid in her nature.

The mixture of politics and what will turn out to be, indeed, romance, in the relationship of Diana and Percy Dacier, is represented in another interesting mixture, the writing of Diana's novel, *The Young Minister of State*, which is a book about Dacier himself. The problem that arises when Diana is identified as the author is that the relationship is played out in an even more public—or at least a different public—realm than Diana's earlier relation with Dannisburgh. At first, the assumption is that Diana is writing about her husband: "The signature of the authoress was now known; and from this resurgence of her name in public, suddenly a radiation of tongues from the circle of Lady Wathin declared that the repentant Mrs Warwick *had* gone back to her husband's bosom and forgiveness! The rumor spread in spite of sturdy denials" (199). Then, the novel's hero is identified as Dacier:

> *The Young Minister of State could be he only who was now at all her parties, always meeting her; had been spied walking with her daily in the park near her house, on his march down to Westminster during the session; and who positively went to concerts and sat under fiddlers to be near her. It accounted moreover for his treatment of Constance Asper. What effrontery of the authoress, to placard herself with him in a book! The likeness of the hero*

(200)

to Percy Dacier once established became striking to glaringness—a proof of her ability, and more of her audacity; still more of her intention to flatter him up to his perdition. By the things written of him, one would imagine the conversations going on behind the scenes.

In this passage Meredith merges Diana's writing and its attendant publicity with the public actions of the author and her hero. He is seen with her in public places, on daily walks, at concerts, "on his march down to Westminster during the session." She "placards" herself with him in a double exposure by linking her name as author with his as hero, thus exhibiting him in a way that becomes "striking to glaringness" and exposing her own desire for him in her flattery of him (or so her critics say). Finally, the novel she writes exposes their lives "behind the scenes"—lives composed, as the book would suggest, of conversations about politics, conversations that (again, according to public opinion as here reported) inappropriately mix personal knowledge with political knowledge.

If it is hard to disentangle the real complaints here—are they complaints about inappropriate forms of public exposure (walking in public? writing about one's lover? exposing one's relationship?) or are they complaints about inappropriate mergers (placarding oneself with another? flattering a man in the guise of writing about him? speaking in private about public matters?) —that is because the nature of the complaints is double. Diana regularly mixes private with public experience in her writing and in her relationships, and her sense of the permeability of the public/private boundary embodies itself as a disinclination to acknowledge exposure, since seeing publicity as exposure would mean believing that private life doesn't belong in public or that public matters don't belong in the private realm. It is thus a common, repeating feature of Meredith's representation of Diana that she seeks hybrid experiences (romance and politics, for example) and that she either acts in defiance of rules of self-exposure or seems oddly oblivious to them.

The intensity with which Meredith explores the blending of Diana's experiences, and the repeated ways in which he merges private and public realms in his representation of her, is more extensive and more open than the mergers we have examined so far. Unlike Brontë's Shirley, for whom man's work must be a form of play and who may witness but not participate in life's battles, Meredith's Diana gives and receives counsel, participates in the making of parliamentary careers, and is herself engaged in a writing career that, for good and for ill, mirrors the life she leads. Even Margaret Hale, who resembles Diana (though she is perhaps closer to Jenny Denham in *Beauchamp's Career*) is at first a hesitant participant in public affairs. Gaskell does connect Margaret's public exposure and her growing interest in public affairs and makes a similar connection between her interest in Milton-Northern and her eventual love of the manufacturer John Thornton, but these are connections that Margaret must spend virtually the entire novel discovering.

Like Gaskell, Meredith is interested in exploring the relationship between publicity and sexuality. But he goes a step further: he invokes (in the scandal-mongers) and invites (in Diana's near escape with Percy) the association of publicity and illicit sexuality, but in the end he *uncouples* the association and derails political relationships that move in this direction. While he continues to emphasize the hybridity of Diana's person, her open courting of self-exposure, and the complexity with which she intentionally mixes the personal and the political, Meredith begins to accent Diana's chastity—a chastity that sits in an intriguing, uneasy relation to her growing passionateness.

When Percy Dacier finally proposes to Diana that they "cut the knot" (233), telling her "I thirst for you; I look to you for aid and counsel; I want my mate" (237), Diana is well aware of the dangers of her position. She reminds Dacier that she has barely "lived down" a buried fever, and "instantly I am covered with spots. The old false charges and this plain offence make a monster of me" (237). Diana is nonetheless moved to follow her passionate longings—until she is saved from running away with Dacier by the miraculous coincidence of Emma Dunstane's illness. When Diana doesn't show up at the train station—that paradigmatic location for dangerous meetings in Victorian novels (in *The Egoist* Clara Middleton gets into trouble at the train station, as does Jessica Morgan in Gissing's *In the Year of Jubilee*), Dacier, who had earlier reviewed Diana's strengths—"womanly, yet quite unlike the womanish women, unlike the semi-males. . . . She had brains and ardour, she had grace and sweetness" (242)—now begins

> abusing her for her inveterate attachment to the regions of Westminster. There
> she used to receive Lord Dannisburgh; innocently, no doubt—assuredly quite
> innocently; and her husband had quitted the district. Still it was rather child-
> ish for a woman to be always haunting the seats of Parliament. Her disposi-
> tion to imagine that she was able to inspire statesmen came in for a share of
> ridicule; for when we know ourselves to be ridiculous, a retort in kind, unjust   (244)
> upon consideration, is balm. The woman dragged him down to the level of
> common men; that was the peculiar injury, and it swept her undistinguished
> into the stream of women. . . . She had not merely disappointed, she had
> slashed his high conceit of himself, curbed him at the first animal dash for-
> ward, and he champed the bit with the fury of a thwarted racer.

When Dacier feels ill-used he immediately thinks of Diana's old relationship with Dannisburgh, ties it to her "attachment to the regions of Westminster," and questions her innocence (in the guise of not questioning it). He criticizes her political investments ("childish . . . to be always haunting the seats of Parliament"), and sweeps her into the "stream of women," blurring into nothingness her distinction from others. Dacier behaves as he does because his own (unfamiliar) passion has been thwarted—which suggests that his generosity toward Diana is dependent on her fulfilling his sexual needs.

When he discovers that Diana has gone to attend her friend during a dangerous operation, Dacier becomes forgiving. Meredith offers up her attendance on Emma during surgery as a counter to her willingness to run away with Dacier. At the least, her devotion, courage, and passionate loyalty to her friend are placed next to her devotion to Dacier. As Sir Lukin declares: "And that's the woman the world attacks for want of virtue! Why, a fellow hasn't a chance with her, not a chance. She comes out in blazing armour if you unmask a battery. I don't know how it might be if she were in love with a fellow. I doubt her thinking men worth the trouble. I never met the man. But if she *were* to take fire, Troy'd be nothing to it" (251). Sir Lukin's point is that Diana's courage is incompatible with "want of virtue"—though he does note that, were she truly to love, she would love with all the intensity that she shows in attending her friend and perhaps would kindle great strife (as the illusion to Helen of Troy implies). He also emphasizes Diana's hybridity in emphasizing her power in this trying situation: "She's all around you; she's man and woman in brains; and legged like a deer, and breasted like a swan, and a regular sheaf of arrows in her eyes" (251). Sir Lukin praises these qualities in Diana, a surprising reversal of the standard criticism of sexual indeterminacy in women, here a sexual and species hybridity that at the same time identifies her with her mythological namesake's innocence.[24]

As Diana reviews the past in the aftermath of Emma's crisis, she recalls Emma's view—reversing the roles of Samson and Delilah—that "women who sap the moral laws pull down the pillars of the temple on their sex" (265). This is Meredith's point as well. Diana is passionately attached to Dacier, and capable, as Sir Lukin suggests, of "tak[ing] fire." But she doesn't act on this capacity. Meredith's intention is to disrupt the connection between publicity and illicit sexuality, to remove sex from the mix—not by creating a character incapable of fire but, rather, by creating one who does "take fire" yet finally resists the inevitable association in the very process of merging the other traditional ingredients.

Meredith subtly describes the sort of moral integrity he cares about. He hints that Diana's sexual restraint (initiated by the accident of her friend's illness but later sustained by her own intentions) is not tantamount to a new narrowness or even purity of character. He suggests this in his exploration of Dacier's view of Diana in the aftermath of their balked elopement—a view that Meredith treats as suspect, suggesting how easy it would be to mistake her sexual reserve for something it is not: "He had a head for high politics and the management of men; the feminine half of the world was a confusion and a vexation to his intelligence, characterless; and one woman at last appearing decipherable, he fancied it must be owing to her possession of character, a thing prized the more in women because of his latent doubt of its existence. Character, that was the mark he aimed at; that moved him to homage as neither sparkling wit nor incomparable beauty, nor the unusual combination, did" (279). Dacier's view of "character" is something we have already met up with in his admiration for Constance Asper. Character is "reserved," "composed," "capable of holding him in . . . awe." His admiration for Diana's character was "imperilled by her consent to fly with him," even though he initiated it; now it is restored, and her "subsequent reserve . . . proved the quality positively" (279).

Dacier's creation of Diana's unassailable character is in part a creation of his own character: "Where he respected, he was a governed man." What he doesn't want to realize is that his own desires are unacceptable to him and that he needs her restraint to be "governed" himself, as he needs to respect her in order to refrain from "the common masculine craze" to seduce and violate women (279). As to Diana's other traits, Dacier claims to be moved neither by her intelligence, nor attractiveness, nor the rare mix of both; these are not the "mark he aimed at," and her "mental attributes" are mere "satellites" (279). He values in a woman her capacity to constitute *his* character in constituting her own impenetrability. The rest is "refreshing"—though even the essentially superfluous performances (like Diana's letters to him) are expected to maintain "their integrity under critical analysis" (280).

In *The Egoist*, Meredith describes in the attitude of Sir Willoughby Patterne what he calls the "infinite grossness of the demand for purity" in women, a demand that he attributes to the "greed of possession" (115) In *Diana of the Crossways* Meredith both values Diana's decision not to engage in illicit sexual relations and at the same time disrespects the inclination to fetishize her chastity, to turn her pure character into a thing that might be possessed.[25] That is, clearly, what Dacier is doing here. Diana's character is, to him, an object of integrity that, like her collection of letters, is subject to scrutiny. One of the intriguing things about Dacier is that despite (or perhaps because of) his instinct to restrain and to admire restraint, to separate out and admire what is separate, he nevertheless mixes worlds in his encounters with Diana. In their meetings and exchanges of letters, Percy's "manner of opening his heart in amatory correspondence was to confide important secret matters, up to which mark [Diana] sprang to reply in counsel. He proved his affection by trusting her; his respect by his tempered style:—'a Greenland style of writing' . . . [that] was to her mind Italianly rich; it called forth such volumes" (281). Like Dorothea Brooke in George Eliot's *Middlemarch*, who reads into Casaubon depths that aren't there, Diana fills out the spare, cool language of Percy's letters until his pages are volumes.

More importantly, Meredith demonstrates that Percy's "manner of opening his heart" provides Diana with secret political knowledge—knowledge that she wants and to which she springs "to reply in counsel." In discussions with Redworth, she is a woman "surprisingly athirst, curious for every scrap of intelligence relating to the power, organization, and schemes of the [Corn Law] League" (286)—though this thirst for political information is in good measure a desire to provide substance for her political writing. She writes for "the savour of Percy's praise, which none could share with her" and also "to strengthen him; she naturally laid her friends and the world under contribution; and no other sort of writing was possible" (287–88). All of this political labor on Percy's behalf is the work of what Meredith terms "the slave of passion" (289)—a phrase that indicates in advance the problems that this relationship entails—a slave whose means of expression and communication with her lover is not sex but politics. If one faults her belief that "whether anything she wrote was her own, mattered little" (287), one must also realize that, like Percy himself, there is nothing that the law permits her to give him but her political knowledge.

Indeed it is quite extraordinary to note—before the critical scene of Diana's political betrayal—how frequently love slides into politics, and politics into love. After one of Percy's renewed overtures, Diana insists:

> "Now let this pass. . . . All around us it sounds like war. Last night I had Mr. Tonans dining here; he wished to meet you; and you must have a private meeting with Mr. Whitmonby: he will be useful; others as well. You are wrong in affecting contempt of the Press. It perches you on a rock; but the swimmer in politics knows what draws the tides. Your own people, your set, your class, are a drag to you, like inherited superstitions to the wakening brain. The greater glory! For you see the lead you take? You are saving your class. They should lead, and will, if they prove worthy in the crisis. Their curious error is to believe in the stability of a monumental position."
>
> "Perfectly true!" cried Dacier; and the next minute, heated by approbation, was begging for her hand earnestly. She refused it.

(290)

If Meredith has earlier suggested that she appropriates, even plagiarizes, her friends' materials, there is no such suggestion here. Diana counsels Percy both to be practical—not to act contemptuously toward the press—and to resist inherited superstitions—to take the lead, be courageous, and lead his class. Again, however, her attention to him and his political position moves him to beg her "earnestly" for her hand.

IV.

Hence it is not surprising that Meredith probes the complex relationship between sex and politics in the great scene in which Percy comes to Diana late at night, after leaving a political dinner party at her house, to impart to her secret news from his chief. This scene and its aftermath have received more critical analysis than any other in the novel, and for good reason. The scene is powerful in its own right—and it revived a rumor about Caroline Norton that her friends vigorously disputed.[26]

Critics, however, are notoriously divided in their assessments of the reasons for, and the credibility of, the episode. Some make sense of the scene by adding up all of Diana's problems and identifying them as motive. Gayla McGlamery comments: "Her unreasoning distress requires relief in action; her bruised sense of self requires revenge for Dacier's importunities; her independent spirit demands that someone acknowledge her usefulness; her household requires money." Others, like Jane Marcus, for example, have described the episode as "the most difficult problem in the novel for Meredith's contemporaries as well as for students today" because the novelist "fails to convince us . . . that Diana's real or fancied financial difficulties are such as to warrant her action." Still others find Diana's seeming unawareness of the implications of her actions inconsistent with her strength of character and thus a violation and undermining of the novel's purpose. Gillian Beer has even argued that "the novelist's commentary exculpates her even while Diana feels to blame." Meredith, she claims, "shift[s] the blame to Dacier too easily."[27]

Diana's betrayal of Percy's secret, however, matters less for the clarity of motive that it does, or doesn't, reveal than for the way it illuminates Diana's social situation. The incident replicates, albeit at a higher pitch, the complex and problematic slide from sex to politics and back again that has characterized Meredith's writing about Diana and Dacier throughout the novel, *and on both sides.* Dacier brings Diana news about "me, you, the country"—the news that his chief has determined to stand for repeal of the Corn Laws. But instead of actually offering the information to her, he teases her, makes her guess, and asks, "What am I to have for telling it?" She replies, "Put no price. You know my heart" (304).

Dacier's method, as the language of Diana's response shows, is suspect. The stock in trade of his seduction is not romantic talk (he has none) but political coinage. He asks her to pay for the knowledge that he has and that she wants— much as she will later seek payment of a different sort for the same information. Moreover, his entire attitude toward Diana in this scene is manipulative: "Dacier smiled in a way to show the lock without the key; and she was insensibly drawn nearer to him, speculating on the smile." This is Percy's intent: to create in her a curious, open, inquiring attitude that draws her on. Meredith also makes clear that Percy sees "the blindness to his motive of her studious dark eyes, and her open-lipped breathing." When he finally admits that her guess is right, that "he [the chief] has decided!" Diana is

(305)

> *radiant with her dark lightnings, yet visibly subject to him under the spell of the news he had artfully lengthened out to excite and overbalance her:—and her enthusiasm was all pointed to his share in the altered situation, as he well knew and was flattered in knowing.*
>
> *"So Tony is no longer dejected? I thought I could freshen you and get my excuse."*

Dacier's point in this final statement is that, having noticed her dejection during the dinner party (she is plagued with bills that her political entertaining on his behalf generates), he can bring happy news and "get [his] excuse," that is, use the occasion of cheering her up as excuse to reenter her house, throw her off guard, and get his "payment."

Diana resists in the usual fashion—"no softness! no payments! Flatter me by letting me think you came to a head—not a silly woman's heart, with one name on it, as it has not to betray" (305). The use of the word *betray* looks forward to Diana's later actions, but what she means here is, Don't make me betray, that is reveal, the name in my heart. As Diana begs, she leaves herself open: "The supplicating hands left her figure an easy prey to the storm, and were crushed in a knot on her bosom. She could only shrink. 'Ah! Percy . . . you undo my praise of you—my pride in receiving you' " (305). In their subsequent conversation, Diana insists that she is not Percy's "paramour" (as she calls it) and resists his pressure to name a time when she will end his waiting. When she complains that he hurts her hand, he replies "I could crack your knuckles. Promise!" Even after this untoward scene, he "punished her coldness by taking what hastily could be gathered. . . . Her shape was a pained submission" (307).

The scene is unpleasant, though somewhat softened at the end when Dacier apologizes for hurting her and admits to himself that "she was never prudish, only self-respecting." But Meredith's final comment sums up the encounter:

"Although the great news he imparted had roused an ardent thirst for holiday and a dash out of harness, and he could hardly check it, he yielded her the lead" (308). Dacier's passion, his thirst, his wish to break out of constraint, are engendered by political excitement, by his sense of political power. He isn't moved by passion; Meredith remarks that "the little he had was a fitful gust" (307). So his actions in this scene exemplify how he confuses his "own craving for 'incident,' "[28] his excitement about political power, with sexual excitement, and uses his knowledge of Diana's political interest to disarm and excite her with the intention of winning sexual rewards for his political secrets.

As usual, Dacier is relieved when he doesn't succeed because Diana's restraint restores him to himself (something he is incapable of doing on his own): "He resumed his natural soberness . . . whence it ensued . . . that his manly sentiment of revolt in being condemned to play second [to her first], was repressed by the refreshment breathed on him from her lofty character, the pure jewel proferred to his inward ownership" (308–9). Dacier is always relieved when he is returned to himself and when he can perceive Diana's resistance as a sign of her high, immutable, ownable, fetishized character. In the end, he comes away with the jewel anyway. Not, perhaps, the prize he thought he wanted, but a payment nonetheless, and some smaller rewards as well. When he contemplates the scene on the way home, he thinks of his "pardonable cunning," the "dexterous play of his bait on the line," and the "lover's ingenuity and enterprise" he has shown; they illustrate to him that, as he puts it, "love is indeed a fluid mercurial realm, continually shifting the principles of rectitude and larceny" (316).

Diana has a similar mixture of thoughts in the aftermath of this scene. Though she rates herself rather differently from the way Dacier rates her, the language of rectitude and larceny hovers in her thoughts:

> *Oh, she forgave him! But clearly he took her for the same as other women consenting to receive a privileged visitor. And sounding herself to the soul, was she so magnificently better? Her face flamed. She hugged her arms at her breast to quiet the beating, and dropped them when she surprised herself embracing the memory. He had brought political news and treated her as—name the thing! Not designedly, it might be: her position invited it. "The world had given her to him." The world is always a prophet of the mire; but the world is no longer an utterly mistaken world. She shook before it.* (311)

Diana understands that Dacier brought her a gift (political news) and treated her as—his mistress. What's interesting is not simply that she sees it but that she does not weigh her resistance in the same way that he does. She feels at once degraded by his treatment and unable to detach herself from the pleasurable memory of his touch—which is why she drops her arms "when she surprised herself embracing the memory." Diana admits that, in surprising her, Percy "tore away, exposing me to myself, as well as to him" (311). She may be right about the former—as her astonishment above indicates; but she is only partially right about the latter. Percy does not feel that she is degraded. He leaves with a sense of her character "lofty and intact," though he will later think that "she must, and without further hesitation, be steeped, that he might drag her out, washed of the *imputed defilement* and radiant, as she was in character" (317; italics mine). Her sense of degradation, which she connects with keeping "a costly household for the sole purpose of seeing him" (312), suggests she has made herself vulnerable to being treated as a mistress. Though the transaction is reversed—it is not he but she who has bought love with money; he has bought love with political knowledge—she sees that her "position invited" it. In a sense, she has treated him as men treat mistresses; and he has returned the favor.

Diana perceives her love already reduced to a token in a complex transaction that sometimes masquerades as rectitude, sometimes as larceny. Her inclination to blame not only Dacier but herself, and then, feeling tainted, to think it a small matter to do again what he has already done—to seek payment for the secret in other quarters—is at once blameworthy and consistent with prior incidents in the novel. Furthermore, her sense of excitement at the "duel between herself and Mr. Tonans, and she sure of her triumph—Diana victrix!" (312) is akin to Dacier's sense of excitement at having political secrets that will bring him victory over her. Elizabeth J. Deis is thus right to notice that Diana "mirrors [Dacier's] power-play" by proving herself "more powerful, more in control than the newspaper editor, since she knows something he does not," and more powerful than Percy, since she is in a position (unconsciously) to "ruin his reputation." Jane Marcus suggests that Diana wishes to "wield the power of the editor," that she wishes to "act like a man, and . . . does."[29]

The trip to the newspaper office begins as Diana and her maid, Danvers, walk the streets to find a cab, take a carriage (whose occupants are usually parliamentarians heading off to the newspaper office themselves, presumably to tell their tales to the editor), and head down into the city late at night. The actual scene in Tonans's office is not written from Diana's perspective: she enters while Danvers waits outside and observes, noting that "things of more importance were about. . . . Here was manifestly a spot where women had dropped from the secondary to the canceled stage." Diana comes out again and remarks to Danvers, in a statement reminiscent of Shirley's comment to Caroline when they watch the action at the mill from the sidelines ("we are here on the spot, and none know it"), that "you are not an Editor of a paper, but you may boast that you have been near the nest of one" (314–15). Diana has been *in* the nest, the place where, as she earlier puts it "the marrow is manufactured" (314). In that nest she has made a bargain; she has sold Dacier's secret for money and has betrayed her lover.

When Dacier reads his secret in the newspaper and discovers that Diana is the source of its revelation, he focuses on the fact that, as he variously puts it, "you sold me to a journalist!" (325); "you took payment for playing spy"; "then you sold me to a journalist for money?"; "you were to receive money!" (326); and eventually, reduced to exasperated sentence fragments, "Money—women!" (327). What Dacier focuses on is not the betrayal but its form. He invokes the wives of parliamentarians, the wives of ministers, who, he assumes, trade their knowledge for money too, as though their entire intention in connecting themselves to men were to drain them of information and convert the information into cash. The sense of being sold—of being prostituted, really—is what stuns Dacier, and he is right to be stunned. What Meredith suggests, though, is that his own implication in the more general confusion of love and larceny is invisible to him. Recasting his actions "in splendid colours of single-minded, loverlike devotion" (328)—no slippage here—Dacier distinguishes himself from Diana in ways that efface their surprising similarity.[30]

As Dacier leaves Diana's house for good, contemplating the folly of "trusting a secret to a woman . . . none should be trusted," he imagines "the effect of naming her" to his chief and thinks about the way this would doubly placard an already notorious woman (328). In other words, he associates her lack of trustworthiness in this instance with the prior accusation against her (an unproved accusation of infidelity); he associates treachery of one kind with her (already) public notoriety of another kind.[31] His further thoughts are equally unkind: he imagines Diana practicing her tricks on a wide circle of men— "Westlake . . . Redworth . . . old Lord Larrian . . . Lord Dannisburgh . . . Arthur Rhodes, dozens" until treachery slides into promiscuity: "Old and young were alike to her if she saw an end to be gained by keeping them hooked. Tonans too, and Whitmonby" (329). The sense of Diana's wide promiscuity extends to him as well; he is "one of the leaky vessels" (327), a man "duped and squeezable . . . produc[ing] more substantial stuff" (329). To a man for whom integrity of character, in himself and others, is always associated with self-mastery and containment, the vision of Diana's intellectual and sexual promiscuity, combined with his own vulnerability, is inevitably repellent.

As Meredith notes, "The background of ice in Dacier's composition was brought to the front by his righteous contempt of her treachery" (329). And again, "He was icy at an outrage to his principles, and in the dominion of Love a sultan of the bow-string and chopper period, sovereignly endowed to stretch a finger for the scimitared Mesrour to make the erring woman head and trunk with one blow: and away with those remnants! This internally he did. Enough that the brute facts justified him" (329). The invocation of the language of the harem—everywhere present in the novel and always an example, for Meredith and, more generally, for writers about female emancipation, of the unexpected similarity between Eastern forms of the domination of women and English ones—here counters Dacier's feeling that he is a member of Diana's harem.[32] By insisting on *his* role as Sultan, he reasserts dominion over her both by assigning power to himself and by making her one of his collection of lovers. The order to his Mesrour that her body be severed from its trunk reifies her as he feels he has been reified (in one place the leaky vessel, in another the squeezed container) and violates her, as he has been unable to do. Tossing out the "remnants" completes—exceeds—the domination, reification, and elimination of her person. The act is internal, and metaphorical, but stunning in its completeness. Treachery on one side; psychological and metaphorical murder and dismemberment on the other.

Dacier's cool transfer of his affection from Diana to Constance Asper effects the last exchange in a sequence. In Dacier's relationship with Diana, love's coinage is politics ("the frosty cupid striking a bargain for his weighty secret," 368); in Diana's betrayal of Dacier, political knowledge is exchanged for coin (and is experienced as sexual betrayal); and in Dacier's renewed relation to Constance, marriage buys off scandal. Dacier trades his old (political) disgrace for a new (marital) grace: "He was comfortably able to face his Club after the excitement of the proposal, with a bride on his hands" (334). The rapidity with which Dacier effects this last exchange, and its literalization in Meredith's language (Constance is "on his hands"), reveals that the bride is a token; she is the interesting good news he offers up to displace the interesting bad news. That she is accepted in exchange for the political scandal she displaces only shows how closely related sexual relations and politics are. Moreover, in this exchange Dacier is still trading in romance and politics, as he has from the start. It is no accident, either, that Constance's "fortune would be enormous; a speculation merely due to worldly prudence and prospective ambition" (334). It is tempting to declare, "Men—money!"

What Dacier also decides to want in Constance Asper is "the lofty isolation of her head above politics" which gives her "a moral attractiveness in addition to physical beauty." This is exactly what critics of female public life have in mind when they invoke the moral purity that must stand apart from political engagement: " 'It's a dusty game for ladies,' Dacier said. . . . There is a pathos in a man's discovery of the fair young creature undefiled by any interest in public affairs, virginal amid her bower's environments" (330–31). In addition, he glimpses in her what he wanted to see in Diana—that fetishized character that can be possessed.[33] "She . . . is her own: or vowed but to one. She is on all sides impressive in purity" (331). Her character is "guaranteed" (334).

In relation to her, Diana is

> *the flecked heroine of Reality: not always the same; not impeccable; not an*
> *ignorant-innocent, nor a guileless: good under good leading; devoted to the*
> *death in a grave crisis; often wrestling with her terrestrial nature nobly; and a*
> *growing soul; but not one whose purity was carved in marble for the assurance*
> *to an Englishman that his possession of the changeless thing defies time and*   (335–
> *his fellows, is the pillar of his home and universally enviable. . . . On the*   36)
> *contrary, the heroine of Reality . . . [has] in her composition the motive prin-*
> *ciple. . . . Mind and heart must be wide open to excuse her sheer descent*
> *from the pure ideal of man.*

The forgiving language of the above passage is important precisely for the way that it *embraces* a "flecked . . . Reality." As Diana Elam puts it, "The heroine of reality is not constant, is not 'the pure ideal of man' traditionally imagined [Constance occupies that role]. Rather, she is excessive—uncontainable and threatening—and as such not valorized by Dacier."[34] Meredith values Diana's changefulness, her "motive life" (12), the absence of guarantee, the faultiness. Because she grows, she can't be possessed in the way that Dacier has wanted ownership. She is not a changeless "thing," not the "pillar of his home."

The passage intimates that Diana is guilty of many things, she is not innocent, not guileless, not carved in marble. But as she notes later in a conversation with Emma after her illness and recovery: "I dare say I have disgraced my sex, *but not as they suppose.* I feel my new self already, and can make the poor brute go through fire on behalf of the old. . . . Nothing is a secret that has been spoken. It's in the air, and I have to breathe and live by it. And I would rather it were out. 'She betrayed him.' Rather that, than have them think—anything!" (359–60; italics mine). Diana means that she is guilty of betrayal, but not of adultery. She calls herself "a black sheep; a creature with a spotted reputation; I must wash and wash; and not with water" (361); but she also insists, "I have not outraged the world, dear Emmy, whatever certain creatures in it may fancy" (367).

Meredith's distinction is crucial: Diana is spotted but not guilty of sexual taint, not an adulteress. And Meredith values her spottedness, just as he devalues the false purity of a character like Constance Asper and of Dacier in admiring Constance. Robert S. Baker is thus right to remark that "Meredith employs Constance as more than a foil to Diana; her presence in the novel is to illustrate graphically the sentimentalist sensibility of Dacier and its unconscious prurience."[35] Emma calls him the perfect "English gentleman of the higher order [who] seemed the effigy of a tombstone one, fixed upright, and civilly proud of his effigy bride" (372). This damning language—"effigy" gentleman, "effigy bride"—unmasks false purity for what it is: the inability to grow, to move, to live; the failure to distinguish authentic human values from dead ones. Diana, Emma theorizes—invoking the orientalist language so prominent elsewhere— could only have made Dacier happy by self-immolation "in a performance equivalent to Suttee" (372), the Hindu ritual in which a widow cremates herself to fulfill her true role as wife.

The triple action of discrediting (false) purity, accepting spottedness (and the consequent loss of the world's respect), and at the same time distinguishing this decisively from sexual impropriety—is what Meredith examines in his final chapters. Though Diana feels "a burning regret for the loss of the fair fame she had sacrificed to [Dacier] and could not bring to her truer lover," she can declare, when she finally becomes attached to the long-faithful Redworth, "I bring no real disgrace" (408). Unlike Maggie Tulliver in George Eliot's *Mill on the Floss*, for whom the loss of her fair fame is equivalent to sexual impropriety and leaves no choice but exile or death, Meredith's Diana is able to survive "the outer view of herself" (408), and move on to a worthier lover.

IV.

Why this emphasis on Diana's sexual restraint in a novel that breaks so many boundaries and seems willing, even eager, to value erring persons? Meredith criticizes in *Diana of the Crossways* women's status as property and the associated importance of maintaining the privacy of their persons; he disputes the notion that women have neither political knowledge nor the capacity for public engagements; he blurs the boundary between private and public experiences, suggesting that the crossing is at once fascinating and still dangerous; and he challenges the idea that the integrity of female character and its consequent innocence are essential social and human values. Perhaps Diana's sexual restraint represents what is intractable in Meredith's view of women—that conservative residuum, the thing that cannot be given up even when so many things are relinquished. Or, to put it more favorably, as Margaret Conrow has done, perhaps "Meredith really only objected to the notion that purity meant an absence of sexual emotion in women and that making his heroines seduceable but not seduced very well suited his own standards of romance."[36]

This may be so. But Meredith's instinct to dissociate from his heroine that guilty sexuality that her intricate affiliations with the public world inevitably attach to her is an important one. Diana's freedom of movement, and the free conduct of her life, seem to suggest—as they will in many of George Gissing's novels—that sexual license is the consequence of other kinds of public freedom. But Meredith resists what has been a metaphorical association (in Gaskell, as I have noted, it is an association that is both embraced and purged of its taint) and will become, in the novels of the 1890s, an inevitable fact. He writes a novel in which the public heroine is guilty of many things but brings "no real [i.e., no sexual] disgrace" to her new husband. Meredith creates a heroine at once public in her activities and sexually *un*promiscuous at the same time, someone who makes critical errors, but not *that* critical error, someone whose sexual restraint is, moreover, not to be confused with passionlessness.

Robert Baker argues that Diana consistently asserts that she *is* passionless, "that as far as love was concerned 'she did not know it' "—and he connects her passionlessness with "an underlying coldness" that reemerges in her marriage to Redworth and connects her with the (false) sentimental ideal that Meredith also criticizes in Dacier and Constance.[37] But this argument misses the central point made in the final pages of the novel when Diana agrees to marry Redworth. Initially she declares, "I am going into slavery to make amends for presumption. Banality, thy name is marriage!"(402). But Meredith says at the same time that "what she craved, in the absence of the public whiteness which could have caused her to rejoice in herself as a noble gift, was the spring of enthusiasm" (410). Since Diana can't offer public whiteness, she wants to offer emotional ardor; enthusiasm, she thinks, would be an authentic substitute for reputation. At first, this eludes her; but in a scene several days before the marriage, it emerges in a surprising form.

Diana alludes to a speech of Dacier's that Redworth has praised to Emma; she wants to demonstrate that she can speak of her former lover before her new one, and as she does so she realizes that what once seemed to her "paternal benevolence" on Redworth's part was really "the loftiest manliness." The result of this realization is a small act on her part: "she was an impulsive woman . . . she put a kiss upon his arm." This is the first time in the novel that Diana has initiated any sexual expression of her feelings. She has always been the unwilling object of other people's attentions, never the agent. Furthermore, as Meredith notes, "she had omitted to think that she was dealing with a lover[,] a man of smothered fire, who would be electrically alive to the act through a coat-sleeve.

Redworth had his impulse. He kept it under,—she felt the big breath he drew in. Imagination began busily building a nest for him, and enthusiasm was not sluggish to make a home of it. The impulse of each had wedded; in expression and repression; her sensibility told her of the stronger" (411). Meredith's vision of passionate love (in a world in which sexual aggression has been the norm) combines "expression and repression"—here, expression on the woman's side, repression on the man's. This reversal gives Diana the initiating role and also differentiates Redworth from other men—Sir Lukin and Percy Dacier among them.

Moreover, and more importantly, it points in a different way to Meredith's sense that passion and repression are not opposites but vital companions. Redworth "had his impulse. He kept it under"—and Meredith admires him for doing so. Restraint is a sign of passion that can contain itself and whose containment creates energy. Redworth, after all, is "electrically alive to the act through a coat-sleeve." For Diana's part, she reacts to his withheld response (indicated by the taking in of his breath) with the enthusiasm she had before lacked. The two wed "in impulse"—hers to express feeling, his to repress felt desire—and although Meredith records that Diana's "sensibility told her of the stronger," the implication is that this interesting combination of expression and repression is what constitutes authentic passion. Or, as Judith Wilt puts it, "it is time" for Diana to "stand on the real earth, which in Meredith's view exhales Romance enough."[38]

In valuing Diana's earlier repression of desire, Meredith is not undercutting his vision of Diana's emancipation but rewriting it. He separates sex from its conventional association with female publicity and then rewrites repression as passion—and Diana's sensibility knows the difference. Given these complexities, it is not surprising that critics differ about the meaning and import of Meredith's ending—seeing in it the "chosen ending . . . the wine in the bottle of fiction," or, more moderately, "remarkable realism," or, disappointingly, submission and loss of freedom. Diana Elam focuses on the language of possession and absorption that emerges in the scene in which Redworth earlier embraces Diana at the cottage, but she goes on to argue that the narrative's stance is "self-critical" and that Diana illustrates "resistance to conformity by refusing any fixed position of inscription within the romance narrations." Elam relies on the theoretical notion that "woman discloses the *mise en abîme* of representationality," but this is not specific to Meredith's text.[39]

Meredith presents at once a reading of Diana's marriage that is both conventional and subversive—one that parallels his blend of expression and repression above. Diana does seem to lose, as Elam and others argue, her mind and her sense of self-possession in the earlier scene at the cottage—"There," Redworth says, "now you belong to me! I know you from head to foot"—in response to which Diana realizes that she had "not an idea in her head!" (406–7). But Meredith also provides a counternarrative to this one of possession and self-displacement.[40] Diana has been resisting a certain idea of love and tells Redworth as much when he asks her to marry him: "What I cannot do, my best of friends, is to submit to be seated on a throne, with you petitioning" (405). Diana is here resisting the role of pedestaled woman, "glorified . . . ethereal . . . unfit . . . beyond the precincts of the home."[41] And yet after the scene in which she experiences "her loss of self in the man," she admits that "this was not like being seated on a throne" (406). Not at all.

In any case, if Diana loses her ideas as she comes into "some harmony with man's kiss on her mouth" she regains them soon enough. In a conversation about her past, Redworth says Diana "pushed for the best society, like a fish to its native sea." When she parries, "pray say, a salmon to the riverheads," he responds, "Better" (407). "By degrees her apter and neater terms of speech helped her," Meredith writes, "to a notion of regaining some steps of her sunken ascendancy" (407). And later, Emma perceives that "her Tony's mind had resumed its old clear high aiming activity" and had "return[ed] to mental harmony" (413). It is wrong to maintain, as Boumehla does, that, "like Scheherezade, [Diana] will surrender language in exchange for motherhood" (204). True, Diana isn't writing novels at the end, but she has regained both mind and voice—and a husband who admires "the tongue that always outflew him" (407). Moreover, the sexual relation that is reopened is not the one Diana fears.

Meredith does assert that "this union, the return to the wedding yoke, received the sanction of grey-toned reason" (409), and this can hardly be read as an unambiguous, ringing endorsement. But the subtle combination of expression and repression, the resistance offered to the old plot of the pedestaled woman by the new plot of the "kindled" woman, and the acknowledgment that sex temporarily shuts down self and mind while mutuality makes space for their reappearance, captures, I think, Meredith's own mixed sense of the role that marriage plays in the life of this unconventional, public woman.

As *The Egoist* and *Beauchamp's Career* bear witness, Meredith was drawn to mixed visions, to surprising, subtle reversals of familiar conventions, and to what E. M. Forster called (not always positively) "the always unexpected."[42] For example, despite Sir Willoughby Patterne's obsession with the purity and seclusion of his mate (like Dacier, he prefers, finally, a private woman, and one who "had not passed through other hands," 499), he is himself publicly exposed when it becomes clear that he has proposed to one woman after another, and proposed most recently to one while still betrothed to another. He has thus been "cla-mouring about more immodestly than women will bear to hear of" (529–30). It is Willoughby who, at the end, is "discussed in public! Himself unroofed!" (503). *His* (theoretical) infidelity, *his* exposure, is the subject of the novel's con-clusion, as is the reversal of power relations in Laetitia Dale's initial refusal of his belated marriage proposal and her final acceptance of him on the condition that he understand her as "[his] wife, [his] critic" (539–40). Clara Middleton's mar-riage with the (feminist) Vernon Whitford is surprising too, precisely because Meredith attaches the spirited and resisting Clara to a man at once refreshingly unlike Willoughby and yet someone whom Lionel Stevenson aptly characterizes as having "unspectacular merits."[43]

In *Beauchamp's Career*, the woman who finally claims Nevil's hand is not the aristocratic Frenchwoman Renée, the intense eroticism of whose relation-ship with Nevil is described with such power. Nor is it her opposite, the aris-tocratic Englishwoman Cecilia Halkett, whose erotic feelings for Beauchamp emerge, much as Diana's feelings for Dacier do, through political conversations that she properly perceives as "his manner of probing her for sympathy, as other men would have conducted the process preliminary to deadly flattery or to wooing" (204). Instead, Nevil marries the much more marginal Jenny Denham (after losing Renée to a prior engagement and Cecilia to his own distraction and hesitation), and the relationship is described in the same grey tones that characterize the description of Diana's marriage.

Jenny Denham is represented for the better part of the novel as both "pas-sive" (in her quiet devotion to Nevil's mentor, Dr. Schrapnel) and capable of "high courage" (258). She regularly "run[s] the gauntlet beside" Shrapnel when he goes out into the crowd while electioneering and in return gets pelted with bags of flour. Once, in a scene reminiscent of Margaret Hale's in *North and South*, she "saved the doctor from being roughly mobbed." By "simply moving on with an unswerving air of serenity [she] obtained a passage for him," and Mer-edith notes that a stone thrown in her direction "missed its mark" (258). Mer-edith creates in Jenny a female character who can operate in the dangerous public world *and* somehow retain her "unswerving air of serenity." Still, Jenny herself is subject late in the novel to Nevil's extraordinary powers of attraction. And in what can only be described as an unconscious error on Meredith's part—though one that has, I would argue, a potent meaning—Nevil looks at what Meredith calls "the bruise of the old Election missile on her fair arm" (526) and "presse[s] his mouth to the mark of the bruise" (527).

This rewriting of the novel's history—which makes the uninjured Jenny more like the injured Margaret—suggests that she *is* vulnerable, that her womanly dignity was no more proof against attack than Margaret's.[44] Here it exposes a vulnerability of another kind as well, a delayed sexual vulnerability that Meredith seems to have invented in order to permit Nevil to soothe it. Like Cecilia before, and Diana after her (and in language that sounds more like D. H. Lawrence than anything else), Jenny must "grovel to find her diminished self somewhere in the mid-thunder of her amazement . . . the thought—my husband! palpitated, and destroyed and re-made her" (529, 536). But Jenny's sexual vulnerability to Nevil emerges *after*, and at a distance from, her public exposure; Meredith only connects the two events by rewriting his own text.

In a manner similar to Diana's reluctant acceptance of Redworth, Meredith suggests that Nevil marries Jenny without loving her but then "come[s] to be her lover through being her husband" (541). Jenny's surprisingly intense attraction to Nevil disorients and disarranges her and "shut[s] her mouth" (540), but again Meredith remarks that "their conflict will be seasonable"; she would have "as fair play as a woman's lord could give her" (540). Because Nevil's unmanageability is so central a subject of the novel, it is no surprise that Cecilia Halkett's eventual husband, Blackburn Tuckham, declares, in a comment that reverses the notion that men privately manage their wives, "His wife's a prize. . . . If she manages him she'll deserve a monument for doing a public service" (544).

Jenny has no opportunity to perform this public service, as Nevil dies a pointless and brutal death at the novel's conclusion. Meredith brings three intensely erotic relationships to life and allows none of them to survive—thus expressing in another way the balked hope and opportunity that *Beauchamp's Career* explores everywhere in its language and plots. For women as for men, passion flowers only to be curtailed, and marriage, when it finally occurs, never happens where it is expected to happen and often brings love after the fact. It proves a complex contract that promises great advantages as well as inevitable compromises.

Still, in the earlier *Beauchamp's Career* and the later *Diana of the Crossways*, Meredith's women are engaged in public affairs in extraordinary, often courageous, ways, and their engagements are wound up with affairs of the heart (either during or after the fact) from which they are sometimes indistinguishable: Diana's relationship to Dacier and Cecilia's relationship to Nevil are literally composed of political exchange. As David Howard says of *Beauchamp's Career*, "The elaborate presentation of feminine consciousness growing aware of the world of politics and the world of men . . . is one of [the novel's] most unifying elements."[45] Like Margaret Hale in *North and South*, Cecilia gradually "consent[s] to listen to politics" (261), and is interested, if surprised, by Seymour Austin's belief in "new and higher destinies for women . . . at a prospect of women taking council, *in council*, with men upon public affairs" (262). These mergers are both perilous and promising, offering opportunities to confuse "love and larceny" (as Dacier does) or, more hopefully, to experience love "in the councils of humanity."[46]

Politics and sexuality—or, more properly, politics and illicit sexuality—are, however, pressed away from each other and thus avoid the familiar association between the two to which I have already pointed. When sex and romance overtake Meredith's heroines, they do so at a distance from the central, initiating experience of the novel—Diana marries Redworth and not Dacier; Nevil marries Jenny and not Cecilia—so that what looks like a political initiation that is also a sexual initiation simply doesn't take place. Instead, the eventual marriages are secondary to the central public experiences of the novel and have about them that odd greyness of tone, that distinctive sense of merged pleasure and compromise, that makes some critics feel the subjection of Meredith's women to be the note on which he concludes. But in merging and then separating sex and politics, and finally in granting to his women characters complex secondary (or even tertiary) marriages on the other side of political initiation, Meredith affirms their public engagements while distinguishing them from the erotic romances that they both lose and, in another form, regain. The muted relationships at the ends of all of these novels grant the central public experiences of women a life of their own—public experiences that are associated with a sexual initiation that doesn't quite come off—without denying to those women the relationships that hover on the outskirts and then make a subtle, sometimes mournful, peace at the end.

IV

Crowds and Marriage in
In the Year of Jubilee

I.

IMAGINING A WOMAN's revolt in *In the Year of Jubilee* (1894), George Gissing invents a heroine who travels unchaperoned in crowds: "I should like to walk about all night," Nancy Lord boldly asserts, "as lots of people will. The public-houses are going to be kept open till two o'clock. . . . It's horrible to be tied up as we are; we're not children. Why can't we go about as men do?"[1] Nancy's desire to attend the Jubilee celebrations is in part a rebellious one directed at her father. But like other female characters in Gissing's novels—Clara Hewitt in *The Nether World* (1889), who leaves home to become an actress; Marion Yule in *New Grub Street* (1891), who labors in the British Museum library; Alma Rolphe in *The Whirlpool* (1897), who makes her public debut as a violinist—Nancy's attendance at the Jubilee Day celebrations represents her wish to gain access to the wider scope, greater challenges, more complex pleasures and powers of the public sphere.

As the novel unfolds it becomes clear, however, that Gissing is critical of Nancy's public exploits—as he is of the activities of his other public heroines. Nancy's explorations are quickly associated with class confusion, coarse com-mercialism, and sexuality neither controlled nor restrained by moral vision. But Gissing's condemnation of women's lives in the public sphere offers no simple denunciation of women's claims for individuality or equality, no easy argument for the conventional distribution of public and private endeavor. Rather, his critique derives from a complex examination of public life broadly conceived, an investigation of its social, sexual, and economic meanings, and, as it turns out, its surprising relation to intimacy and privacy. Gissing's anxiety about the content of both private and public life and about the ways in which public and private merge inappropriately with each other leads him to conceive of alter-native means by which private persons might structure their relation to the public sphere. In the unusually modern marriage of Nancy Lord and Lionel Tarrant—unusual because husband and wife love each other but maintain separate establishments—he reconfigures the public/private dilemma, offering an intriguing, if unsettling, resolution to the problems that the novel investigates.

Gissing's attitude toward the "woman question" (he used the phrase himself) is difficult to characterize. In a letter to his friend Eduard Bertz Gissing declares:

> *And after all I doubt whether we are greatly at variance in our views on the woman question. My demand for female "equality" simply means that I am convinced there will be no social peace until women are intellectually trained very much as men are. . . . Among our English emancipated women there is a majority of admirable persons; they have lost no single good quality of their sex, & they have gained enormously on the intellectual (& even on the moral) side by the process of enlightenment, that is to say, of brain-development. . . . And I believe that the only way of effecting this is to go through a period of what many people will call sexual anarchy. Nothing good will perish; we can trust the forces of nature, which tend to conservation.*[2]

Written as Gissing was "set to work upon a vigorous book, of which the scene will be in Camberwell" (the setting of *Jubilee*), the letter provides convincing evidence of Gissing's feminism. The campaign for equal intellectual training for men and women, begun when Gissing was a child, became a central feature of the agitation for women's rights and was often placed in parallel relation to the suffrage campaign. As early as 1869—after defeat of the bill for female suffrage first proposed by John Stuart Mill in 1867 and rejected in 1869—the *Times* observed that "intellectual woman ought to derive some consolation for her recent defeat on the female suffrage question from the University Intelligence which we published yesterday. If she cannot establish her right to political equality with her oppressor, man, she is at least to be admitted to a share of certain pleasures and pains hitherto considered exclusively his." The article goes on to describe women's initiation into the various entrance examinations to which only male students had previously been granted access, acknowledging as well that both women's education and women's suffrage raise the issue of female popular notice. The *Times* points out that the results of the women's examinations would not be printed (as results usually were) in the newspaper but would be conveyed by mail to circumvent unwanted publicity.[3]

In 1874, when Gissing was a very young man, the *Daily News* reported the case of a female student, Miss Rogers, who had headed the "first division list in order of merit, at the recent Oxford Local Examinations." The *News* again made the connection between the education and suffrage questions by pointing out that this event virtually coincided with the death of John Stuart Mill, who has "directed public attention to the great question of Women's Rights." Mill had also left a bequest in his will to any university in Great Britain or Ireland that first opened its degrees to women, along with a further sum in scholarship money "for female students exclusively." The *News* raised the possibility that Oxford might be eligible for the first bequest because it already granted associate of arts degrees to women and Miss Rogers for the second bequest because of her standing as senior candidate and as someone to whom the university had thus "offered an exhibition" [i.e., a scholarship]. Her father, however, did not wish to make his daughter's example the test case for women's admission to university degrees. He declined, among other reasons, from "a natural dislike to invite that inevitable publicity to one's daughter which the ventilation of such a case would involve."[4]

By 1873 Emily Davies's school at Hitchin had become Girton College, and in 1875 the Enabling Bill, empowering universities to admit female students if they wished, became law. By 1884, when Gissing was writing regular letters of instruction to his sisters about their education, "most of the honours schools and examinations . . . were open to the women students" at both Oxford and Cambridge. Women would not, however, be granted degrees "on equal terms with men" until the next century—in 1920 at Oxford, in 1948 at Cambridge.[5]

The agitation on behalf of female higher education had made significant advances by the 1890s, but its terms were still a matter of debate. Gissing's forthright position in his letter to Bertz is thus noteworthy—as is his willingness to endure a temporary "sexual anarchy" because of the ultimately positive effect on the culture that female equality would bring. As Elaine Showalter has noted (choosing Gissing's term for the title of her book), social change and turbulent sexual consequence were familiar bedfellows.[6]

Gissing's letters to his sisters, Margaret and Ellen (familiarly Madge and Nelly), reveal that he was an early believer in the value of rigorous intellectual training for women and that his beliefs intensified over the years. Though it excluded Greek and Latin texts in the original, the course of study he recommended to Ellen in 1885 was strenuous: he insisted that "because you are a woman, & living at present in an out of the way corner, that is no reason why you should not keep before your eyes an exalted aim, & should not acquire more of real insight into literature and art than the majority of people ever get." Gissing's comment about Ellen's location suggests one reason why he did not worry about her acquiring the knowledge toward which he directed her: her social marginality was more a protection against the risks of female education than it was a potential reason not to "keep before [her] eyes an exalted aim."[7]

In a later letter to Ellen, Gissing reports on the success in the Cambridge Classical Examination of "Miss [Agnata] Ramsay, a girl of 20, who has only been studying Greek four years. It is scarcely credible. She stands alone in the 1.st class; no man was good enough to get higher than 2.d. . . . They say she is in excellent health and doesn't seem to have worked very hard. She must have a rare brain. Girton is her college." Gissing then modifies his earlier views: "After this, don't despair even of learning Greek. In any case it is clear that you can pursue your Latin with every hope of reading Vergil." The public ordeals to which opponents of women's education often referred (and with which the students themselves were forced to deal) were not issues for Ellen, but Gissing's support of his sister's education and of women's education generally shows his fellowship with the cause of female emancipation.[8]

Nevertheless, critics have found Gissing's attitude toward the "woman question" difficult to identify. He is sometimes portrayed as a writer sympathetic to the movement—as Jacob Korg describes him when he writes, in response to the letter to Bertz quoted above, that "on this subject, at least, Gissing's opinions were clear, consistent, and uncompromising. An enemy of the Victorian myth of the inferiority of women, he believed firmly that women were the intellectual and spiritual equals of men." But Gissing's June 1893 letter to Bertz is just as frequently cited in support of his *anti*feminism: "More than half the misery of life is due to the ignorance and childishness of women. The average woman pretty closely resembles, in all intellectual considerations, the average male *id-iot*—I speak medically. That state of things is traceable to the lack of education, in all intellectual considerations." The hostile, even bitter tone of these remarks stands in a curious relation to the confidence expressed in the section of the letter quoted earlier and to the enthusiasm Gissing voiced about the success of the Girton student and the promise of his own sister. As Lloyd Fernando succinctly puts the negative case against Gissing, he was "the only important novelist of the period whose approach to emancipation looks rather more like resolved animosity."[9]

More frequently, Gissing's critics see him as internally inconsistent. Gissing's prodigious editor and critic, Pierre Coustillas, explains what he calls "one of Gissing's many paradoxes" this way: "He wishes for women's emancipation, but as he realizes that it will be achieved at the expense of her femininity, Gissing stands abashed at the consequences of his own suggestions." John Goode describes *In the Year of Jubilee* as centrally concerned with and sensitive to the problem of "sexual politics," but he too acknowledges that Gissing "retreats into his own churlish ideology at the end . . . because he confronts issues which are not, in his terms, soluble." Gail Cunningham finds Gissing unsympathetic to the female cause, but even she describes him as "opinionated without having consistent views; aggressive without always identifying his target."[10]

In my view, Gissing was sympathetic to the cause, but like other writers in late Victorian England, he was both moved and concerned by what fellow novelist Henry James called in his *Notebooks* "the devouring *publicity* of life, the extinction of all sense between public and private." This concern bore directly on Gissing's complex attitude toward female emancipation. In the admiring letter quoted above about the success of the female student in the Cambridge Classical Examination, Gissing turns to a discussion of Victoria's Jubilee celebration (commemorating the fiftieth year of her reign). The two subjects seem to have little to do with each other apart from their presence in the same letter, but they are intimately connected. Gissing urges his sister to learn Latin and Greek (hitherto decidedly male subjects of study), and then, moving on to the subject of the Jubilee, he remarks:

> *After all it is something to have seen the most gigantic organized exhibition of fatuity, vulgarity & blatant blackguardism on record. Anything more ignoble can scarcely be conceived. Prithee, what is it all about? What has this woman Victoria ever done to be glorified in this manner? The inscriptions hung about the streets turn one's stomach. It is very clear to me that England is very far indeed from the spirit of republicanism. Well, I don't object to that, but it certainly degrades humanity to yell in this way . . . the vulgarity of the mass of mankind passes all utterance.*

What Gissing clearly expresses in this letter, as he does elsewhere, is his loathing for public display (made worse in this instance by its link to English nationalism)—the hugeness of the celebration, the sense of inappropriate exposure attached to it, the paradox of its spectacular organization combined with the emptiness of the thing organized, its failure to represent something of value. Gissing hates the advertisements on the streets, the noise, and the vulgarity (literally the commonness, the lack of distinction) of the crowds. Like James himself, whose antagonism toward the newspaper, the lecture hall, the hotel lobby, and the crowd, both fuel his criticism of Verena Tarrant in *The Bostonians* and make it difficult to distinguish his critique of public movements in general from his critique of feminism in particular, Gissing's antipathy toward public life (which also expressed itself as an antipathy toward newspapers, crowds, advertising, and the increasing commodification of life) collides in his letters, and even more persistently in his novels, with his interest in and representation of the "new woman" of the 1890s, a woman who increasingly described herself, and was described by others, as a traveler in the public realm. Gissing sent his sister the newspaper descriptions of the Jubilee "that you may study the paltriness of mankind" and added: "I hope you are well . . . & that you are able to find peace of thought in your books. I can find it nowhere else."[11]

Gissing's support for female education is, as he perceives it, curiously separate from the access to public life that education usually entailed and also from the vision of life after university education that many women students—newly armed with knowledge from which they had previously been excluded, and newly experienced in the habits of a world away from home—would seek to fulfill when they had completed their schooling. The connection between university education and the phenomenon of the "new woman" of the 1890s is thus particularly interesting in Gissing's case, since his support for education did not imply advocacy of the expanded vision of public life with which it is often connected. Rather, it meant an expanded vision of human potential divorced from what some called public experience but Gissing identified as public spectacle.

II.

The 1890s saw the emergence in periodical literature and fiction of the "new woman"—a phrase used by Sarah Grand in an 1894 article entitled "The New Aspect of the Woman Question" and then employed even more emphatically (and with capital letters) in an article by Ouida entitled "The New Woman" (in the same journal and the same year). The language in which the debate was framed bears crucially on Gissing's representation of the "new woman" in his novels.[12]

In two key essays on this subject (written in the aftermath of Parliament's failure to consent to the second reading of the bill for Extending the Parliamentary Suffrage to Women but before the term *new woman* emerged) Eliza Lynn Linton identified what she called "The Wild Women" and considered them first "As Politicians" and second as "Social Insurgents" in a pair of 1891 articles. Linton was an opponent of the suffrage and more generally of the movement for women's emancipation, and she starts her first essay with the assertion that "the wild women" represent "a curious inversion of sex": they "disdain . . . the duties and limitations imposed on them by nature" and want instead to "do without let or hindrance from outside regulations or the restraints of self-discipline." Linton's essay sets the problem as one of simple choice—between "rampant individualism taught by the insurgent sex" on the one hand and "the sweeter, dearer, tenderer emotions of the true woman" on the other. "Politics or peace, the platform or the home, individualism or love, moral sterility or the rich and full and precious life of the nature we call womanly—they must take their choice which it shall be. They cannot have both." Linton also emphasizes that "the cradle lies across the door of the polling booth and bars the way to the senate." Politics and maternity don't mix; public life and womanhood don't mix; if they do mix the result is "inversion" (or deformity) in the woman and "fuel to the fire of strife" (or sex wars) in the world.[13]

It is hard to imagine Gissing taking such a position: it is too neat in its oppositions. As Gissing's novels—like those of his predecessors in this book— reveal, the distinction between private and public life was never easy either to discriminate or to maintain. The sentimental view of domesticity to which Linton clings would sometimes seem desirable to Gissing, but rarely would it seem viable.

Linton's representation of the "wild women" as "social insurgents" in the second essay focuses on the relationship between what she calls "despising the old distinctions" and a problematic instinct toward exhibition that Gissing too would certainly have disliked: "No barriers restrain. No obstacles prevent. . . . The spirit of the day is both vagrant and self-advertising, both bold and restless, contemptuous of law and disregarding restraint. . . . Everyone who has a 'gift' must make that gift public. . . . Everything is exhibited." When Linton moves from the political to the social—from the polling booth to the place of public congregation—she makes the connection between political rights and cultural consequences that underlies Gissing's divided sentiments: "She smokes after dinner with the men; in railway carriages; in public rooms—when she is allowed. She thinks she is thereby vindicating her independence and honouring her emancipated womanhood" when what she is really doing is unmooring herself from her grounding at home and thus freeing herself for unwomanly self-exhibition.[14]

David Rubinstein has pointed out that "employment and emancipation from family restraint were . . . important objectives" to some women who had completed their formal education and that they "often found themselves pushing at an open door." But Gissing's interest in women's intellectual and cultural development stands in counterrelation to the female publicity that, as Linton's essays negatively portray it, such beliefs frequently imply. These beliefs, in their positive form, reemerge in an important 1894 essay in the *Nineteenth Century*, "The Revolt of the Daughters," by Blanche Althea Crackanthorpe—an essay that inaugurated serious discussion of the issue both in the *Nineteenth Century* and elsewhere. The essay comments on the consequences of higher education for women:

> *We have of late elected to educate everybody, our daughters included. Girton and Newnham, the "halls," and all kinds of minor establishments of a like kind fill the land. . . . The attempt to open wide the doors one side the house, and to hermetically close them the other, is a trifle illogical. . . . Wisely or foolishly—it is yet an open question—we have said that our daughters are to know. They in their turn, insist that they shall be allowed the free use of the weapon with which we ourselves have furnished them. Are they to be blamed for this?*

Once opened, the door to university education reveals on the other side the rest of the world—travel, admission to the professions, and passage to commercial engagement, all of which Gissing's novels so compellingly (and problematically) describe.[15]

While Crackanthorpe defends a right that Gissing, as we shall see, finds troublesome, she also raises a related question that Gissing will confront, albeit with different results, in *In the Year of Jubilee*. Crackanthorpe defends a young woman's right of access to "my bit of world's work" and suggests that the desire for youthful liberty is one that parents (or in this essay, mothers) resist both blindly and inconsistently. Her point is that mothers think about propriety in too limited a way—worrying about latchkeys and access to music halls but allowing their daughters to marry, without concern, men with a " 'past' to bury." These mothers resist the girl's accurate sense that "the 'burying of the past' means the putting aside a woman who has faithfully filled the place of wife and mother for many years." Such a girl "is not far wrong who feels that, under these conditions, she is after all but the lawful mistress, the other remaining the unlawful wife."[16]

Crackanthorpe raises the question of the double standard: mothers think about and protect their daughters' reputations but do not investigate the reputations of their prospective husbands. She considers not only the divergent standards for male and female purity but also the position of the wife who knows that she has supplanted another woman. As Crackanthorpe puts it, the wife becomes the mistress, the mistress the (unlawful) wife. (Gissing connects the "new woman" question with the double standard as well—though he does so in a different fashion, as we shall see.) The issues come together for Crackanthorpe because she wants to argue for a single standard—education, access to public life, and a sexual norm for marriage that doesn't abandon at the altar the principle of female purity that, she argues, can be maintained before marriage even by women who have access to the public arena and should be maintained by men who have always had such access.

As the essay comes to a close, Crackanthorpe's argument takes a surprising turn, however. Speaking of the strike of the daughters, and the big trade strike that has just ended, she declares: "Salvation comes from within always and everywhere. Since the capitalists have failed them, the operatives must work out their own. Then perhaps we shall have the woman of tomorrow, pure of heart and fearless of speech, who demands of herself and of every one else, not a flimsy and superficial 'correctness,' but that inward sincerity which enables her both to say and to hear, 'I have erred,' with equanimity." Here the single measure is not the standard of purity but rather the standard of "inward sincerity" that replaces "superficial correctness."[17] The implication is that both men and women may "err"—but that women, as well as men, should be able both to err and to speak fearlessly about erring in a world where inward sincerity would be constitutive of a different (and better) purity for men and women alike. Sincerity *replaces* purity in this description.

Crackanthorpe proceeds from the assertion that we have "elected to educate everybody," to the understanding that education generates a movement outward into the world, to the judgment that publicity need not be seen as contaminating ("a larger liberty, not license") and then to the assertion that what is really contaminating is not publicity but the double standard.[18] This leads her to argue for a new standard of inward sincerity that proves to be more liberating—and liberal—than the bad faith of the double standard that pretends to preserve female purity but really makes mistresses out of wives.

Gissing's vision of education is complex: he valued it, recommended it, prescribed it in his letters—but when he treated it in *Jubilee* he associated it with contaminating publicity. Jessica Morgan is a caricature of the "new woman" with a college degree who wants nothing more than to see her name in the newspaper. She wastes her health, betrays her friend, becomes mentally unstable, and eventually joins the Salvation Army as a social welfare fanatic. Nancy Lord has also been educated, if not as formally as Jessica, but Gissing cannot imagine for her, as Crackanthorpe does, "a larger liberty" that is not "license." In the world that Gissing's characters inhabit education leads to liberty, liberty to license, and it is license that makes wives into mistresses—not the double standard. Still, Gissing believes, like Crackanthorpe, in a curative inward sincerity that cuts through pretense and creates a new standard—again, a more liberal standard than the text might at first prompt us to expect. In Crackanthorpe's vision the double standard is the vehicle by which hypocrisy and problematic redefinition enter, making wives into unwitting mistresses. In Gissing, publicity itself creates the problem, and something must emerge to undo its damage. A similar curative inward sincerity emerges out of Nancy Lord's self-education, making possible a *theoretical* single standard and a new conception of marriage that is at once open, erring, and fearless, and yet more conservative than Crackanthorpe's because it demands the recreation of privacy in the only place that Gissing can imagine it—in the body of the woman herself.

Gissing's analysis of the education question merges with his analysis of the "woman question" broadly conceived, and both bear on the debate about the double standard with which *Jubilee* concludes. Gissing's complex attitude toward publicity helps to explain his mixed relation to Nancy Lord's predicament in the novel: in this, as in his other "woman question" novels, women represent a special, or heightened, instance of the problems that emerge at the intersection of public and private life, special because their emancipation both foregrounds and exaggerates the very questions about privacy and publicity that always set Gissing's terms turbulently into motion. Furthermore, in the case of Nancy Lord, the theoretical possibility of adultery that emerges at the novel's end (always a feared consequence of female freedom) reflects an anxiety about specifically female publicity that even Gissing's unconventional treatment of marriage cannot fully resolve.

II.

Gissing begins his heroine's story with her emblematic escape from assigned chaperons and her unprotected journey through the streets of London on the night of a national celebration. Nancy Lord's initiation into public life is thus accomplished early in the novel, and its surprising consequences reverberate throughout. But what, precisely, does it mean to be initiated into public life? As Nancy first suggests, it means "go[ing] about as men do," gaining freedom from the constraints of the home, challenging the gender conventions that restrict her.[19] But it also means gaining experience of strangers and participating in a world in which the mutual self-exposure of unsorted persons is the norm. "It'll be wonderful," Nancy declares, "all the traffic stopped, and the streets crammed with people, and blazing with lights" (21).

Nancy seems eager to expose herself to the gaze of others: she likes the idea that the streets will be at once busy, crowded, and illuminated. But Gissing intimates that this desire for freedom and for self-exposure is as much a function of her psychological and social indeterminacy at the beginning of the novel as it is a political statement about women's rights. Her father's house is part of "a neighborhood in decay"; and she is uncertain about the extent of her father's wealth and hence about "her social position." Her education is also described ambiguously: "Her studies at a day-school which was reputed 'modern' terminated only when she herself chose to withdraw in her eighteenth year; and since then she had pursued 'courses' of independent reading, had attended lectures, had thought of preparing for examinations . . . but latterly it had become a question with her how the independence was to be used, and no intelligible aim as yet presented itself to her roving mind. . . . Now there are so many ways of living, and Nancy felt no distinct vocation for any one of them" (16). Gissing suggests that Nancy is a woman between states—neither a newly educated woman who has clearly identified her changed political status nor an uneducated woman who is content with her familiar life.

But instead of seeking direction, either in the course of her education or in some other way, Nancy intentionally abandons it: she affirms and extends her feelings of social and sexual confusion by mixing with what her father calls "the rag-tag and bobtail" (33). Social mixing in a crowd means the indiscriminate mixing of bodies that don't under other circumstances mix at all. In his description of the Jubilee Day masses, Gissing stresses their assault upon the senses and their assault upon the body. At Camberwell Green, Nancy and her companions "mingled with a confused rush of hilarious crowds, amid a clattering of cabs and omnibuses, a jingling of tram-car bells. Public-houses sent forth their alcoholic odours upon the hot air" (52). As they made their "charge" on the Westminster tram car, "a throng of far more resolute and more sinewy people swept them aside, and seized every vacant place on the top of the vehicle. Only with much struggle did they obtain places within. In an ordinary mood, Nancy would have resented this hustling of her person by the profane public; as it was, she half enjoyed the tumult, and looked forward to get more of it along the packed streets, with a sense that she might as well amuse herself in vulgar ways, since nothing better was attainable" (52).

Nancy here takes pleasure in social disorder and especially in the physical experience of confusion. She looks "forward to get more of it along the packed streets" and Gissing confirms that she gets what she wants: "every moment packed her more tightly among the tramping populace" (58). Nancy's affirmation of class confusion results in a sexual abandonment that is made all the more "vulgar" for the largeness and the indiscriminateness of the gesture. Lacking access to refined pleasures, Nancy Lord "amuse[s] herself in vulgar ways," relinquishing all at once her social place, her sexual place, and—symbolically at this point—her claim to female virtue.[20]

When Gissing later evokes the "thud, thud, of footfalls numberless, and the low, unvarying sound that suggested some huge beast purring to itself in stupid contentment," the crowd becomes a vulgar body—a beast's body, purring in its own base pleasure. Nancy is herself part of this animal body. Giving her body to the crowd simply extinguishes her difference from it: "Nancy forgot her identity," the narrator declares, "lost sight of herself as an individual. Her blood was heated by close air and physical contact. She did not think, and her emotions differed little from those of any shop-girl let loose. The 'culture,' to which she laid claim, evanesced in this atmosphere of exhalations. Could she have seen her face, its look of vulgar abandonment would have horrified her" (58). Gissing here combines, in order to reemphasize, the component parts of public exposure: joining the crowd means abdicating one's individuality and, as a consequence, the social status, culture, and sexual purity that distinguish one from others. The horror is not present to Nancy (she cannot see her own face), but it is manifest to observers, like Gissing or us (we can see her face). Nancy permits herself to converse "unrestrainedly" with a young man, and he in turn scrutinizes her "with much freedom" before she heads off to keep an appointment she has made with yet another male acquaintance (59). This new companion is surely right to exclaim that the "big crossings are like whirlpools," but though Gissing comments that "for the first time she understood how perilous such a crowd might be" (61), it isn't at all evident that Nancy has fathomed the full implications of her initiation into public life.

What begins as a political wish to "[set] up [her] standard of revolt" by escaping from her father's home (22) ends in the social, cultural, and sexual degradation of a young woman whose central crime is that she joins in the public celebration of a national holiday. In Gissing's rendering of it, Nancy's self-exposure in, and identification with, the crowd is both the result of the freedom and mobility to which she thinks she has a right and the embodiment of that right. In the scene that immediately follows this one, she will discover that her father has promoted the family servant, Mary Woodruff, to a position of domestic authority in their home. But rather than offending Nancy, the promotion produces in her a sense of relief, because it permits her to cast off what is the mere "show of domestic authority" and to satisfy her desire for "freedom from responsibility,—to be, as it were, a mere lodger in the house, to come and go unquestioned and unrestrained by duties." In Gissing's view, Nancy's wish to be free of "restraint" (we have seen this word before in Brontë's *Shirley*) does not represent a desire for authentic human liberty. Instead, as Linton predicted in "The Wild Women," Nancy has become, however unwittingly, a rootless lodger—anonymous, mobile, unrestrained—for whom the boundary between private and public, pleasure and duty, self and other, has become meaningless.

Gissing even suggests (as Linton also had) that Nancy's "personal demeanor" undergoes a change as she affects "a mannishness of bearing, a bluntness of speech" hitherto uncharacteristic of her. "Thus, by aid of circumstance," Gissing notes, "had she put herself into complete accord with the spirit of her time" (82).

To Gissing, the emergence of private persons free of restraint onto a public stage is a political act with personal consequences because their experiences of the public realm will be experiences of inappropriate intimacy: such free selves, dissociated from origins, "mere lodger[s] in the house," can no more restrain themselves than they can be restrained by the world in which they travel. It is thus oddly appropriate (in this world of spectacle and display) that the man Nancy meets in her travels is himself preeminently a public man. Lacking the sort of private identity that comes from having a family and a family name— his last name is that of an adoptive family, his first name that of a man who was "kind as a father to me" (61)—Luckworth Crewe is the product of his own self-invention. An advertising man who "stick[s] up . . . great big board[s]" everywhere he can, he violates, and is violated by, the public realm: his clothes, Gissing comments, bear "the traces of perpetual hurry and multifarious impact" (85).

When Nancy next joins Luckworth Crewe—they meet at London Bridge for a trip up the Monument and a walk about the city—the complex meanings associated with public life more fully present themselves. The pair climbs the winding monument stairs and steps outside:

> *On issuing into daylight, he became silent, and they stood side by side, mute before the vision of London's immensity. Nancy began to move round the platform. The strong west wind lashed her cheeks to a glowing colour; excitement added brilliancy to her eyes. As soon as she had recovered from the first impression, this spectacle of a world's wonder served only to exhilarate her; she was not awed by what she looked upon. In her conceit of self-importance, she stood there, above the battling millions of men, proof against mystery and dread, untouched by the voices of the past, and in the present seeing only common things, though from an odd point of view. Here her senses seemed to make literal the assumption by which her mind had always been directed: that she—Nancy Lord—was the mid point of the universe. No humility awoke in her; she felt the stirring of envies, avidities, unavowable passions, and let them flourish unrebuked.* (87–88)

Gissing situates his heroine in an emblematic public place—at the top of a historical monument. He also puts her in position to feel the power of the past and to witness the present spread out wonderfully before her. The Monument commemorates the cataclysmic Great Fire that destroyed London in 1666, but it also places the spectator in a position to view the bustling new city and one of its busiest bridges, rebuilt in 1832 but still noted for its "prodigious traffic."[21] And yet Nancy's relation to all this—to history, to public life in the city, and to the spectacle of human suffering and human striving that both embody—is, in Gissing's view, a defective and disqualifying one.

At first he criticizes her for her imperturbability, claiming that she is "untouched" by what she sees. But the feelings he wants her to have are all apprehensions of her own distance from experience. She should feel awe; she should stand in dread; she should revere what she observes. Indeed, Gissing's real criticism of Nancy has to do not with her impenetrability but rather with her refusal to hold experience at a distance. She is exhilarated, and her exhilaration manifests itself in the brilliance of her eyes and glow of her cheek. Gissing intimates that in this sense Nancy may be too vulnerable, too penetrable, too close to what she sees. It is surely right to note in Nancy's response an extraordinary display of narcissism (she is not "the mid point of the universe"). In Gissing's attitude there is also an anxiety about engagement that would make most forms of it suspect. Gissing criticizes Nancy for identifying her own interests and desires with those of the masses below, or, to put the matter more accurately, for identifying their passions as precisely her own. Nancy wishes to participate in the spectacle "of London's immensity" to which this scene gives her access, and in Gissing's view such participation and engagement are inevitably compromising.[22]

When Nancy translates Luckworth Crewe's admiration (stirred up by his perception of her greediness for experience) into a bargain for her body, Gissing's assessment of her comes into focus. Her companion tells her how beautiful she looks ("his lips parted hungrily"), and she declares, "Portraits for the Academy cost a great deal, you know" (88). Crewe has earlier told her that one of his ambitions is to have his wife's portrait painted and to see it hung in the Academy, so Nancy is here both expressing her willingness to be exhibited and suggesting how expensive she will be to buy in marriage. The final condemnation of Nancy's instinct for freedom and self-exposure appears, then, in her wish to participate in the marketplace by making herself into marketable goods. Her beautiful body, she tells Crewe, is to be had for a price—and when it becomes his, he can convert it into a portrait and display it for all to see.

Nancy's participation in her own commodification reflects and anticipates the ultimate critique of life in the public realm that Gissing offers. The bad merging of public and private life is nowhere more apparent than in the commercialization of intimacy that Nancy here encourages. Nancy participates in, and even enjoys, her commodification in this scene. But she will be victimized later by the instincts of all her antagonists to use their intimate knowledge of others as barter in sexual transactions (as both Jessica Morgan and Samuel Barmby will do in scenes we shall shortly examine) or, in reverse, to engage in business transactions for inappropriately personal reasons (as Beatrice French will do when she offers Nancy a job in order to force her to reveal the name of her "lover"). The hazardous merging of the world of commerce and publicity with that of privacy and intimacy represents to Gissing the final example of bad merging that Nancy's life has come to embody.

III.

In the social world, as Gissing describes it, class gradations are unenforceable, sexual propriety is at risk, the proper distances strangers keep from each other are threatened, and (especially in the Monument scene) the social person's proper status as a historical observer disappears as the desire for vulgar participation gains ascendancy. Perhaps the most striking feature of Gissing's representation of public life in these scenes is the danger it poses to boundaries—between classes, between sexes, between bodies, and, in the most general sense, between persons who normally maintain their mutual status as distant observers of, rather than participants in, each other's lives. Nancy takes the idea of participation to an extreme—first appropriating the lives of others and then imagining her own transformation into a commodity exchanged in their marketplace—but her real crime is the crime of participation in a public universe for which her creator feels both contempt and fear.

Gissing's critique of female public experience is part of a larger attack on the vulgarity of public life in which English novels of the 1880s and 1890s often participated. James's *The Bostonians* (an 1886 antisuffrage novel with an American setting) and his *The Reverberator* (an 1888 novella with a European background) are as critical of the culture of newspapers as Gissing's novels are. *In the Year of Jubilee* everywhere manifests this criticism, as do many of Gissing's other works, perhaps most notably *New Grub Street* (1891) and *The Whirlpool* (1897). As *Jubilee* begins, Ada Peachey and her sister, Beatrice French, are reading the newspaper: Ada reads "paragraphs relating to fashion, sport, the theatre, answers to corre-spondents . . . and gossip about notorious people"; her sister Beatrice reads about "law suits, police intelligence, wills, bankruptcies, and any concern, great or small, wherein money played a part. She understood the nature of investments, and liked to talk about stocks and shares with her male acquaintances" (8). Ada, in other words, reads the "women's" pages, and Beatrice the "business" section—but both are associated with a salacious interest in the affairs of the world that engenders the "slovenly housekeeping" that characterizes the Peachey establishment (5).

Moreover, everyone in the novel seems eager for affiliation with the press: Jessica Morgan is studying for her examinations, wasting her health and losing her hair, all to "become B.A., to have her name in the newspapers" (18), and even Samuel Barmby Sr. regularly writes letters to the paper (though under a pseudonym) (179). Samuel Barmby Jr. is obsessed with the press and the publishing industry. He measures the level of a country's culture and civility by the number of daily newspapers it can support (China has only ten), and admires the sheer bulk of writing that the daily paper represents: "printed in another way it would make a volume" (50). Though Jessica Morgan's view that newspapers confer fame differs from Barmby's sense that their power lies in their almost literal weightiness ("a positive volume; packed with thought and information," 50), the two are allied. The newspaper's embeddedness in the world— its factitious nature, its raw bulk, its dailiness—explains why Jessica Morgan's desire for fame in its pages is vulgar. Gissing might have focused on Jessica's pursuit of education, but instead he concentrates on her desire to see her name published in the paper when she passes her examinations and compares her interest in self-publication with Barmby's. The public existence of the self is made possible by a medium that guarantees the loss of privacy, concretizes, reifies, and multiplies the self, dooming it to a life of unregulated exposure, tainted by the political marketplace in which it appears.

In his superb study of the relationship between publicity and privacy, Alexander Welsh points out that "the modern law of privacy is often said to originate not from any legislature or court, but from a famous American essay by Samuel D. Warren and Louis D. Brandeis, who were in fact responding to what they regarded as intolerable encroachments on privacy by Boston newspapers in 1890." Warren and Brandeis's description is one that Gissing would certainly have recognized: "To satisfy a prurient taste the details of sexual relations are spread broadcast in the columns of the daily papers. To occupy the indolent, column after column is filled with idle gossip, which can only be procured by intrusion upon the domestic circle." Warren and Brandeis aver that the need for privacy is a direct result of the increasing publicity of the "new" information age, though Gissing's newspaper readers do not themselves recognize such a need. Quite the contrary, their entire sense of self is dependent upon self-multiplication and self-exposure. They have no domestic circle which they desire to protect.[23]

Not surprisingly, Gissing also associates the political arena with degraded—

indeed criminal—financial dealings. When Nancy Lord asks Luckworth Crewe if he has "any Jubilee speculation on hand," he describes his failed effort to promote a Jubilee Day drink. His business partner in the venture has, he explains, cut his own throat because he was about to be arrested for betting and forgery. "That's the third man I've known go wrong in less than a year," Crewe explains. "Betting and embezzlement; betting and burglary; betting and forgery" (56). Later, when Lionel Tarrant's grandmother dies without leaving him an inheritance, he comments that "the foolish old woman has been muddling her affairs for a long time, speculating here and there without asking any one's advice, and so on; and the result is that she leaves nothing at all" (162). Here, as earlier, the culprit is "speculation" (sophisticated betting), and the effort to magnify or inflate value has as its consequence the wasting and emptying of resources.

Tarrant's grandmother (whose family name directly recalls the publicity-hungry Tarrants of *The Bostonians*) is ruined by an advertising broker too—a man like Luckworth Crewe, advertising man par excellence, and head of the publicity department for Beatrice French's South London Fashionable Dress Supply Association. Though Crewe is never tied to criminal activity of any kind, he is identified as a speculating man who inflates value in one place and empties it out in another. This is also what Beatrice's business means to do: create the desire to own fashionable clothes and waste the resources of its clients. The sham nature of this interesting businesswoman—and she is just that—is reflected in the elaborate marketing schemes she employs: a "Fashion Club" (like a Christmas Club) that permits its members to make deposits for purchases in advance, and a "bonus" scheme (like a frequent-flier card) that pretends to return—in credits good for additional purchases—the profit made on a transaction (200). Both entrap the customer through the elaborateness and showiness of their schemes, whose complication and density bear an inverse relation to the goods they purport to represent. But the bad exchanges upon which Beatrice's business depends are the characteristic exchanges of the marketplace. And their success depends, moreover, on the vendor's ability to advertise her schemes widely in "hand bills, leaflets, nicely printed little pamphlets, gorgeously designed placards." Gissing imagines in Beatrice a woman who actually owns and operates a business, but he associates her venture and her advertising agent with the world of degraded publicity that is itself associated with Victoria's Jubilee (201).

Gissing's condemnation of public life as it is represented in the experiences of Nancy Lord is not limited to her, or even to women as a group. As the above remarks indicate, *Jubilee* panoramically discredits the realm Nancy wishes to enter—identifying it not only with empty political display but also with inappropriate self-exposure, social and sexual confusion, the loss or degradation of self that these entail, and with degraded and even criminally speculative dealings in a marketplace whose exchanges are both corrupt and empty.[24]

IV.

When Nancy Lord goes on vacation in the country, Gissing's novel seems—though only momentarily—to leave its exploration of publicity aside. Gissing describes Teignmouth as a place of "solitude . . . safe from all intrusion," and his vivid descriptions of the natural setting of the place ("the tall foxgloves bending a purple head in the heat of noon") suggest its great distance from Nancy's urban adventures (91). But Nancy quickly discovers that Tarrant has also come to Teignmouth, and in an extraordinary passage—one that editors deleted from American editions of the novel—Gissing makes a direct connection between the "debilitating climate and absolute indolence" of the country and "that impulse of lawless imagination which had first possessed [Nancy] on the evening of Jubilee Day." Gissing's point is clear: the abundant natural privacy of the country shares with the crowded intensity of the city a "luxurious heedlessness" that makes Nancy "cast aside every thought that might have sobered her; even as she at length cast off all her garments, and lay in the warm midnight naked upon her bed" (94). Not only does Nancy herself connect the privacy of Teignmouth with the publicity of the Jubilee celebrations, but she bears witness that what they share is an impulse toward illicit sexuality that makes Nancy abandon not only her sobriety of thought but her garments as well.

When Lionel Tarrant proposes that the two of them take "a country ramble of an hour or two," the prospect of a journey with him makes Nancy think of her comparable engagements with Luckworth Crewe, though she is aware from the start of powerful differences between them: "With [Crewe] she could go anywhere, enjoying a genuine independence, a complete self-confidence, thinking her unconventional behavior merely good fun. Tarrant's proposal startled her. She was not mistress of the situation, as when trifling with Crewe. A sense of peril caused her heart to beat quickly" (98). The differences between the two men appear often to Nancy's consciousness, and the narrator frequently calls his audience's attention to them as well. Luckworth Crewe's "coarse vitality and vigour" are contrasted with Lionel Tarrant's "half-recumbent attitude" and his "posture of languid ease" (95, 103, 105). Moreover, while Luckworth Crewe takes Nancy to London Bridge, Tarrant takes her to a secret country hideaway. First they "left the streets," next "Tarrant led from the beaten road into a lane all but overgrown with grass," next past a broken gate and down a "narrow cartway" (101). From this, they "emerged into a small circular space, where the cartway made a turn at right angles and disappeared behind thickets. They were in the midst of a plantation; on every side trees closed about them, with a low and irregular hedge to mark the borders of the grassy road" (102).

Gissing is at pains here to indicate the deep privacy of the setting. Each stage of the journey involves a greater relinquishment of publicity and community, a deeper turn into privacy, intimacy, and seclusion. From street, to road, to lane, to cartway, the two abandon in successive stages the public setting from which they have come. "Better than the pier or the promenade, don't you think?" Tarrant remarks, highlighting, as if emphasis were necessary, the connection to and the contrast between his walk with Nancy and Luckworth Crewe's. Still, Nancy registers her own sense of the riskiness of privacy when she remarks, just as they are about to arrive, "But we have gone far enough" (102).

Gissing also implies that Tarrant's secluded spot is really a dangerous Garden of Eden—splendidly overgrown, luxuriantly beautiful—in which Nancy's fall will be effected. She peels off her gloves (it is hard not to think here about the warnings Clough issued to her Newnham students about their gloves; see the Introduction) to eat the blackberries Tarrant has offered her and later feeds him some fruit from a plate made out of leaves (103). As Gissing remarks during the interlude between the first and second visits to the spot, Nancy asks her friend Jessica no questions about the latter's upcoming university examinations, for Nancy, "whether consciously or not, was making haste to graduate in quite another school" (106).

What is interesting, then, about the initial distinction between Nancy's public experiences with Luckworth Crewe and her private ones with Lionel Tarrant is that they aren't fully distinguishable after all. Both in Nancy's experiences on Jubilee Day and in her imagination of access to the public realm at the Monument, female public experience is perilously close to sexual promiscuity—to giving oneself to the crowd, either in an act of vulgar self-abandonment, or in narcissistic self-delight, or both. In certain respects this is also the meaning of Nancy's descent into privacy with Lionel Tarrant. The crowd is missing, but the sense of self-exposure is not. When Nancy takes off her gloves in the first scene, Tarrant takes the opportunity to "[touch] the blue veins of her wrist with his lips" (104). And when the two return for their second visit to Tarrant's secluded enclosure, Nancy seems once again to be undressing herself. In order to receive a wreath that Tarrant has made for her, she "unfastened her hat, and stood bareheaded, blushing and laughing" (108). It is not, however, until the two are faced with a pair of hungry donkeys who suggest to them the animal meaning of their own actions (the donkeys are "munching eagerly" on some thistle bushes, and Lionel and Nancy laugh with "something like recklessness" at the sight) that Gissing's assessment of their passionate liaison is disclosed (109, 110). Nancy's "unavowable passions" at the Monument play themselves out in a private encounter with Lionel Tarrant, thus binding the two scenes together.[25]

Nancy's recklessness in both settings is similarly suggestive: "We shall be trespassing," she declares near the end of the scene in the woods. "What do I care," replies Tarrant (110)—and, as Gissing concludes, "he did carry her through the brushwood, away into the shadow of the trees" (111). When Nancy herself later comments to her father (without of course explaining the real significance of her remarks) that she wishes "far, far more sincerely than you think—that I had kept more control upon myself—thought less of myself in every way" (135), she indicates that her sexual fall is significantly preceded by and connected to the abandonment of self in the Jubilee Day episode and to the narcissistic self-absorption at the Monument that led her to embrace the passions of the world as her own.

Gissing's novel moves from the depiction of national publicity to the representation of privacy, but it reveals in the process that the two are images of each other and cannot neatly be distinguished. Going about freely in this public world is equivalent to a failure to keep control of oneself, because the public realm has come to embody the very failure to control: in it the self loses control over itself, the boundaries between self and other are jeopardized, distinctions between classes are lost, and sexual appetite becomes unmanageable. Unlike Meredith's heroine in *Diana of the Crossways*—who experiences a similar slide between public and private life but *not* the sexual fall that others impute to her— Nancy's experiences at Teignmouth suggest that privacy is both charged and sexually dangerous. Inappropriate self-exposure, loss of self-control, unsanctioned intimacy, and sexual impropriety are the content of her experience in the private realm.

The problematic conjunction between public and private is nowhere more apparent than in Gissing's spectacular description of the suburban train station in which Jessica Morgan and Samuel Barmby stand "together upon the platform, among hurrying crowds." Once again Gissing describes how public places assault the senses. Here, "waggons full of people" speed by, and those who wait listen to the "hiss and roar of steam, the bang, clap, bang of carriage-doors, the clatter of feet on wood and stone" (259). But the tumult of the train station—that emblematic public place in which strangers meet and part—is made even more chaotic by its use as advertising space: "High and low, on every available yard of wall, advertisements clamoured to the eye: theatres, journals, soaps, medicines, concerts, furniture, wines, prayer-meetings—all the produce and refuse of civilization announced in staring letters, in daubed effigies, base, paltry, grotesque. A battle-ground of advertisements, fitly chosen amid subterranean din and reek; a symbol to the gaze of that relentless warfare which ceases not, night and day, in the world above" (259). Gissing emphasizes that advertising is political representation in a degraded, debased form: it is a symbol of the "warfare above," and it is degraded because half of what it represents is not produce but refuse— refuse shamelessly displayed. Advertisements solicit the viewer in "staring letters" and "daubed effigies," overrepresenting their case in an effort to outsolicit their competitors. The competition among advertisements that makes one advertiser more aggressive in his publicity than the next merely represents in its turn the brute "warfare" among competitors "in the world above." The hellish underground of the train station is the setting for the most obvious kinds of public competition precisely because it is both part of, and separate from, the public realm it represents. For Gissing, the subterranean world merely exhibits openly what cannot be openly revealed in the world of work above—the gross perversion of the marketplace and its brute reduction to a battleground among chaotic, competitive forces.

The train station also signifies a different, but equally relentless, warfare— not among marketplace competitors for the attention of customers, but among women for the attention of men. In the train station scene, Jessica Morgan fights for the attention of Samuel Barmby, whom she hopes to win away from Nancy Lord. Standing on the crowded train platform after an evening in the lecture hall, Jessica's "thoughts [are] in a tumult like to that about her" (259), and she engages in a competition—a sexual competition—of her own.[26] She tells Barmby the secret that Nancy has been laboring to protect (that Nancy is married and has a child) in exchange for what she hopes will be Barmby's greater "kindness" to her. She uses knowledge of her friend's intimate life as currency with which to purchase the emotional, perhaps even the sexual, favor of the man she loves. Jessica seeks, furthermore, to deepen and extend the taint associated with her friend's action (and thus by comparison improve her own moral stature) by making known that Nancy's illicit sexual act, her subsequent secret marriage, and the birth of her child are tied to an illicit financial one: "You see what she is," Jessica concludes. "She hides it [the child] for the sake of the money" (260).

This scene exemplifies the complex interrelations between the publicity wars and the underlying sex wars. Jessica turns to Barmby because her association with the public realm leaves her starved for intimacy, so that here, surrounded by the most blatant examples of the market economy in which she lives, she is moved to "confide" in Barmby. In this reading the publicity wars generate the sex wars as remedy or antidote. But the remedy is perverse, the antidote another form of poison, and in this sense it must be said that the publicity wars generate the sex wars more as reflection than as remedy.[27] The competition among marketplace producers for the attention of consumers results in the shameless self-display and commodification of prostitution (advertisements are "daubed effigies") and this, in turn, is represented—reflected, imitated, reproduced—in the competition among women for the attention and interest of men.

In Jessica's effort to gain the attention of her lover, she sells her friend rather than herself, revising both the prostitution plot at which Gissing hints and also the blackmail plot that might have ensued (it is, after all, not money from Nancy, but love from Barmby, that Jessica wants). Gissing's variations, however, only amplify, by extending, the theme. Jessica is multiply emboldened by the world in which she lives—to trade for a moment in private rather than in public matters, to transform the private into the public, to convert her intimate knowledge into an exchangeable commodity.

The scene in the train station embodies the brutal conjunction of publicity, sexuality, and degraded financial dealings with which Gissing is so centrally concerned. Jessica cannot distinguish the tumult outside from the tumult inside her head—as though the public representation of marketplace competition served up to her an instance of what private citizens might do if they wished and as though what occurred in public might indeed represent, even serve as a model for, private exchange. Gissing treats "the warfare above" as an analogue for "the warfare below" and describes private matters as reflections—even embodiments—of public ones. Jessica Morgan's transformation of a private romantic encounter into a coarse business deal reiterates and reconfirms the elision of public and private life that is at the heart of Gissing's novel.[28] Like Meredith's rendition of the slide from love to larceny in the scene in which Percy Dacier uses his knowledge of parliamentary affairs to gain sexual advantage over Diana—and then the companion scene in which Diana sells her knowledge to the press—Gissing's episode in the train station suggests the collapse of one world into another. Unlike Meredith, however, who considers Diana "spotted" by her actions but not fatally guilty, Gissing will not excuse Jessica Morgan for her failure but will deepen and extend that failure into fanaticism.

V.

Perhaps the most central, if also the strangest, illustration of the problematic relationship of private and public realms occurs in the marriage of Lionel Tarrant and Nancy Lord. Because marriage traditionally provides a social sanction for private feeling, it holds out at least the possibility that some positive accommodation between public and private might be managed. But in Gissing's novel this possibility is blocked by the circumstances of Nancy's father's will, which disinherits her if she marries before the age of twenty-six. Married already (after her sexual encounter with Tarrant, on the eve of her father's death, and without knowledge of his will), Nancy must keep her marriage a secret if she is to receive her inheritance. In her husband's view this is at first a positive consequence because the obligation to conceal, combined with the financial independence that concealment confers upon Nancy, means that the two can "maintain their mutual independence" (151)—an important notion to Tarrant, himself a liberty-seeker who fears obligation and duty. What Tarrant wants in marriage is to conserve the pleasing illusion that his wife is his mistress—in other words, to participate in the fiction that he is engaged in an illicit relation—all the while being free of the guilt that accompanies true blackguardism.

The irony is striking. Instead of marriage serving as a social sanction for intimacy, as the sign of that proper union of public and private action, marriage here becomes another occasion for secrecy—for concealment and the "dis-honour" that concealment brings (150), for the illusion of illicit relations, for lies, shame, and "vulgar fraud" (167).[29] If the first part of Gissing's novel explores the meaning of female exposure and publicity in a political, urban setting, the second, third, and fourth parts recount the heroine's descent into secrecy as she suffers the consequences of her actions. As the Jubilee Day participant of part 1 becomes "The Veiled Figure" of part 4, and the woman who sought exposure now courts secrecy and fears revelation, the meanings of privacy and conceal-ment begin more and more nearly to resemble those associated with publicity and exposure.

Nancy's experience of the public realm both mirrors and ratifies her sense of social confusion. Mixing with the crowd reduces her sense of social superi-ority and makes her subject to advances by persons of other classes. But Nancy's secret life mimics this confusion about social rank. When Nancy tells Mary Woodruff, the family servant, about the plan to conceal the birth of her child, Mary "looked at me as she had never looked before—as if she were the mistress, and I the servant. But see what I have come to; all I felt was a dread lest she should think it her duty to cast me off. I haven't a bit of pride left. I could have fallen on my knees before her" (169). In fact, in order to prevent her pregnancy from being linked to her name, Nancy switches identities with her servant, thereby embodying the confusion of social class that her earlier experiences had generated (230).

In many respects, Nancy's switching of identities with Mary is benign, since Mary has consistently proved her loyalty and merit as a person. But Nancy experiences more punishing reversals than this. When Beatrice French confronts her with the knowledge that she has borne a child, eager to confirm that Luck-worth Crewe is—or rather isn't—the father, Nancy is placed in the position either of revealing her marriage and exposing her fraud, or concealing her marriage and exposing her shame. She chooses the latter, and suffers the consequences: "A full sense of her humiliation had burst upon her. She, who always condescended to Miss French, now lay smirched before her feet, an object of vulgar contempt" (238).

This reversal of roles repeats itself when Nancy is humiliated by the obviously inferior Jessica Morgan and when Samuel Barmby exacts from her, in return for his willingness to keep Nancy's secret, the pretense of a respect she certainly doesn't feel. In an odd twist on the theme that Crackanthorpe proposes when she refers to the wife of a man with a past as "the lawful mistress," Nancy is also humiliated by her own recognition that she was Lionel Tarrant's "mistress, never his wife" (244). Of course Nancy *is* Lionel's legal wife, but her "confession" to Beatrice, though technically false, has about it, she discovers, the ring of truth. Lionel has configured their relationship so that it mimics the one to which Nancy must here confess. The fact that Nancy recognizes what she has become is an index of her moral growth, but it also confirms what the novel has been professing all along—that Nancy is a married, but also a fallen, woman.[30] Her masquerade before Beatrice French is a literal enactment of this paradox because it creates in the eyes of her immediate community the fiction that she is unwed. Nancy's father once complained bitterly of women who "trollop about the streets day and night" (39–40), and his language now seems peculiarly apt to his daughter's situation. If Nancy has lost her honor, and with it her social status, she has done so in the extreme privacy, indeed seclusion, of Tarrant's hideaway at Teignmouth; but the loss of social status and the sexual taint to which that loss is here tied are complications linked to public exposure and the desire for freedom—as Mr. Lord's earlier comment pointedly revealed.

This coincidence between private and public appears again as Nancy and Lionel embark on the project of concealing their marriage—of converting a public into a private fact. Both understand that "there's a suggestion of dishonour about it" (150), but neither seems aware of how complex the concealment (or how deep the dishonor) will be. What begins as a "suggestion" of dishonor becomes, for Nancy at any rate, the entire practice of dishonor. When she receives a letter from her husband in the early days of their marriage, she tells Mary that the letter is from Luckworth Crewe: "Living in perpetual falsehood, Nancy felt no shame at a fiction such as this. Mere truth-telling had never seemed to her a weighty matter of the law. And she was now grown expert in lies"

(161). Lying quickly turns itself into "vulgar fraud" (167), and fraud is labeled what it is—criminality (173). Nancy only begins to realize the full consequences of what she has done after the encounter, described above, with Beatrice French. She is prepared to be dishonored "in the eyes of one woman" but not in the eyes of others. If Beatrice unmasks her, then, "regardless of the cost, she would proclaim her marriage, and have, in return for all she had suffered, nothing but the reproach of an attempted fraud" (248). Lionel Tarrant's response to their situation is different from Nancy's, but it too displays the complications of their situation. Tarrant still feels that, were Nancy "frankly his mistress," he would find it much easier to "play a manly part," but realizes that "the secret marriage condemned him to a course of shame, and the more he thought of it, the more he marvelled at his deliberate complicity in such a fraud" (283).

It is Nancy, however, who first suggests that fraud is linked to speculation when, in response to a letter from Tarrant announcing his return after a lengthy absence in foreign parts, she sends him money. In Tarrant's view "her imputation upon his motive in marrying her was sheer vulgar abuse, possible only on vulgar lips" (282). But the truth is that Nancy merely anticipates "the form the story has taken" in the world at large (305). Those who know about them believe that Tarrant has "made a speculation" of Nancy (307), a belief that, in others' eyes, is confirmed by Nancy taking a job at Beatrice French's dress-supply association, presumably to earn money to give to her husband (307). Later in the novel, when Tarrant learns about what he calls Samuel Barmby's "interested generosity" to Nancy—his willingness to let her draw from her father's estate even though she has violated the terms of his will—he says that "of course [Barmby] hopes to be rewarded" (311). The language of fraud, blackmail, and speculation—so much a feature of Gissing's descriptions of the public realm— is here tied, in two forms, to Nancy and Lionel Tarrant's secret marriage, which has become, as Tarrant neatly puts it, a "squalid entanglement" (311).

Finally, though Nancy lives a "veiled" life and fears exposure of her secret, her hiddenness is in turn connected to publicity of another kind. Describing her job in Beatrice French's establishment, she explains that she "advise[s] fools about the fashions" and "exhibit[s] herself] as a walking fashion-plate" (307). Her job has become self-exhibition, and in her own view and in Tarrant's, it is a kind of shame, continuous with the other degradations she has suffered— the shame of being thought unmarried, the shame of abasing herself before Jessica Morgan, Beatrice French, and Samuel Barmby. Nancy's entry into the world of new, middle-class workingwomen at the publicity-hungry dress-supply association is, oddly, an emblem of these private humiliations—and it is in response to them that Tarrant declares, "It's not too late, happily, to drag you out of this wretched slough into which you are sinking. Whatever the cost, *that* shall be done!" (308).

VI.

Tarrant declares that the solution to Nancy's problems is the revelation of their marriage: "I shall publish your marriage everywhere," he tells her. "I shall make a home for you, and have the child brought to it. . . . You are married, and a mother, and the secrecy that is degrading you shall come to an end. Acknowledge me or not, I shall acknowledge *you*" (309). Tarrant insists that secrecy is degrading and wishes, at last, for that public sanction of private experience that marriage traditionally confers. He wants to disentangle what has become entangled, to give the proper names to things (Nancy *is* married and a mother), to confer legitimacy. His willingness to acknowledge Nancy is also important because acknowledgment potentially confers both social and personal legitimacy, returning the object of acknowledgment to visibility in the social world. Given Nancy's situation, these are desirable and valuable outcomes.

Yet as the final episodes of the novel attest, Tarrant's acknowledgment is complex and unusual. Publishing his marriage means, to him, making an announcement of it "everywhere," but he has no intention of actually living with his wife. Tarrant's plan is for the couple to continue as they are—he in his lodgings, she in hers. They will come together as they wish, but they will not live together as, in the ordinary scheme of things, husband and wife would do. The objection that this arrangement prevents Nancy from experiencing the very acknowledgment of her marriage that Tarrant claims to confer is simply put aside: "The only married people . . . who can live together with impunity, are those who are rich enough, and sensible enough, to have two distinct establishments under the same roof. The ordinary eight or ten-roomed house, inhabited by decent middle-class folk, is a gruesome sight. What a huddlement of male and female! They are factories of quarrel and hate—those respectable, brass curtain-rodded sites—they are full of things that won't bear mentioning. If our income never rises above that, we shall live to the end of our days as we do now" (341). Tarrant is unnerved about what we might call the public features of private experience. His vision of the middle-class home, with its confused, indiscriminate mixing of persons of opposite sexes is a vision of the private family as a public crowd. Instead of serving as a bulwark against the disorder of public life—as Victorians liked to think it did—home here reproduces the disorder and replicates the inappropriate mixing of the sexes with which crowds are always associated. The home offers no protection against the factory; the home *is* the factory, decked out in curtains to hide things that can't be named. If Nancy's secret marriage bore an uncanny relation to the contaminated public realm, her publicly acknowledged one has the extraordinary potential to do the same.

Tarrant's reinvention of marriage means to circumvent the dangerous merger and reinterpret the problematic acknowledgment he is about to make: he will publish his marriage (acknowledge it to the world) while redesigning it in order to reduce the unacceptable public content of its private meaning. On the strange middle ground that Gissing imagines, Lionel and Nancy will affirm the public importance of marriage but will refuse the regular companionship, the ordinary society of marriage—thus affiliating themselves with marriage's authorizing power while also resisting the intimacies usually bound up with it.[31]

Or some of them, at any rate. Gissing does not mean to suggest that this is a loveless, or a sexless, marriage. Quite apart from the fact that there is no instinct in the novel to punish Nancy (at least in any final way) for the indiscretion that produced her son, Nancy's sexuality and maternity are consistently affirmed as healthy features of her life. William Greenslade has suggested that Gissing affiliated himself with Grant Allen's notion that in the 1890s there was "a 'new hedonism' through which sexual relations were to be remodelled" and that this new hedonism acknowledged the "primacy of motherhood." In "Plain Words on the Woman Question," Allen asserts solidarity with women, agreeing that "their education was inadequate; their social status was humiliating; their political power was *nil*; their practical and personal grievances were innumerable: above all, their relations to the family—to their husbands, their children, their friends, their property—was simply insupportable"—and that these features of the "woman question" indeed required redress.[32]

Allen's central notion is that "the physical impulse . . . ought to be as present in every healthy woman as in every healthy man" and that this must be so because "the race and the nation must go on reproducing themselves." He claims that he is ready to affirm "woman's just aspiration for personal independence, for intellectual and moral development, for physical culture, for political activity, and for a voice in the arrangement of her own affairs, both domestic and national"—but he feels that "the 'advanced' women will meet us on this platform"—where the "platform" invoked is not a political stage but a belief that "maternity [is] the central function of the mass of women . . . whether we have wives or not."[33]

Allen makes a biological argument (only women can replenish the population) and advances a case for free union (he argues on behalf of motherhood, not wifehood); and critics expressed, of course, serious doubts about whether such a position would free women or enslave them.[34] For all the claims it makes about "woman's just aspirations," Allen's advocacy of the primacy of motherhood would hardly have sounded liberating to the "new woman" of the 1890s— even though, as Greenslade argues, it represents a *new*, because *reinvigorated*, vision of sex and parenting, and certainly not its denial or elimination.

In his own imaginative reinvention of marriage, what Gissing hopes for is a social structure that will eliminate the unregulated, unrestrained, disorderly intimacies of everyday life—the regular fare both of the institution of marriage and of the unsorted public realm with which it is clearly homologous.[35] He wants either two separate establishments in one house or, better yet, two entirely separate houses. Ordering, sorting, separating out the members of the family/ crowd will prevent the violation of each other's individuality and integrity that crowding brings.

Thus in the place of marriage as it is typically understood (Tarrant calls it "hugger-mugger marriage," 342), Gissing envisions a marriage of separate, independent persons—neither isolated from each other nor inappropriately merged with each other. This marriage provides the social sanction and public legitimation of sexual feeling without at the same time effecting its institutionalization and, thus, its automatic affiliation with the political realm. It offers a saving vision of individual freedom and dignity that doesn't mean the loss of all intimate connection: both partners maintain their independence and privacy, but they continue to depend on each other for affection and community. Their "new" marriage means intimacy and privacy that do not monopolize and appropriate the other, freedom and mobility that are restrained and grounded by the repeated return to home. In a world in which a degraded publicity has penetrated private relations, it demonstrates how the two might be separated and yet coexist.

When Nancy arrives, with considerable difficulty, at an acceptance of her husband's position—"command[ing] her features" in an expression of what Gissing calls "rational acquiescence"—she exercises another form of that self-restraint that is a critical feature of any sane ordering of the world according to Gissing. "I am content," Nancy finally declares after a lengthy conversation in which it becomes clear that she will never live with her husband, however successful he becomes. "You are working hard, and I won't make it harder for you." His face "radiant," Tarrant replies: "Speak always like that! . . . That's the kind of thing that binds man to woman, body and soul. With the memory of that look and speech, would it be possible for me to slight you in my life apart?

It makes you my friend; and the word friend is better to my ear than wife. A man's wife is more often than not his enemy" (343). This astonishing exchange combines a number of important elements. First, though Nancy's acquiescence looks uncomfortably like conventional female submission, it also has another function. In Gissing's view, Nancy's moral growth, her "inward sincerity," must emerge as self-restraint and self-command—and particularly the kind of self-restraint and self-command that control unguarded intimacy—because the lack of these is what propelled her into, and identified her with, the degradations of the public realm. In accepting Tarrant's version of their marriage she relinquishes what he views as random access to her husband, reigns in her feelings, and thus practices *in her person* the controls and restraints that Tarrant seeks to embody in the social structure of their marriage.

Nancy's self-control also moves Tarrant to a similar expression about his command over desire. Noting that his "life apart" provides him with opportunities to "slight" her, he nonetheless insists that the memory of her "look and speech" will prevent him from doing so. (Later he comments that "each has the other's interest at heart, and each would be ashamed to doubt the other's loyalty," 344). The acknowledgment that independent lives bring with them opportunities for betrayal is here combined with an alternative vision of the way private persons might conduct themselves both in their personal and their social relations—not restrained from without by the institution of marriage or by a partner's force or supervisory capacity, but restrained from within by the love and respect each has for the other. "Salvation," as Crackanthorpe would have it, "comes from within always and everywhere." The consequence of all this—surprisingly enough—is that very union ("body and soul") that Tarrant seems in other ways so eager to regulate and restrict. Gissing both describes and celebrates real sexual intimacy here, but it has become possible only as the consequence of a unique system of personal and structural *restraints*.

It is also a consequence of the restructuring of the marital scene that Gissing has established—a restructuring at once radical and conservative. It is radical because it reinvents sexual pleasure in marriage but absolutely insists on its legitimacy. At the end of their discussion of marital infidelity, Nancy and Lionel enter the family bedroom: "Baby slept in the cot beside Nancy's bed. For fear of waking him, the wedded lovers entered their room very softly, with a shaded candle. Tarrant looked at the curly little head, the little clenched hand, and gave a silent laugh of pleasure" (344). The evidence of their earlier sexual encounter lies palpably before them. In deference to him—and very much in his presence—they enter the room "softly"; they shade the candle; he laughs in silence:

all these muffled actions anticipate the way the lovers will shield their imminent sexual encounter from their child. But they will be lovers, and they will be so very much in the context of their family situation.

Still, there is something charged about the scene: the familial setting, in particular the presence of the child as monitor and reminder, both legitimizes the sexual encounter and gives it the feel of an illicit activity. The couple must exercise caution lest they be discovered; they must be careful and quiet. But this combination, this sense of inversion, seems exactly what Gissing wants: to create the sense that there is something unusual and unexpected about the notion that married people might actually be lovers; to envision legitimate marital love and sexuality, the experience of which is charged and illicit, to ratify sexuality rather than to identify it solely with degraded public exposure.

In this new universe of marital sexuality, ordinary relations appear in a different form: friends are better than wives, ordinary wives are worse than enemies, conventional intimacy means supervision (partners watch over each other's movements, spying in order to guarantee a "nominal fidelity," 343), and only distance can create true tenderness. Nancy and Lionel's marriage confers legitimacy and restores them to social acknowledgment—and Gissing grants the (limited) importance of these.

But their marriage also resists affiliation with the public universe whose acknowledgment it simultaneously seeks: in its sorting out of households and of persons, in its various systems of restraint, Gissing seeks to distinguish their marriage from the public realm with which most marriages tend to merge; in its resistance to and inversion of publicly acknowledged forms, and finally in its rendering of marital love, Gissing constructs a social alternative poised between illicit and licit, between private and public, designed both to resist and remake the interaction of public and private realms.

For all its apparent resistance to social norms, however, Tarrant's vision is disturbingly conventional and familiar in the way it distinguishes the activities of men and women. In the conversation about marital infidelity to which I referred above, Tarrant refreshingly declares that "husband and wife should interfere with each other not a jot more than two friends of the same sex living together"; but he also asserts that "infidelity in a woman is much worse than in a man. If a man really suspects his wife, he must leave her, that's all; then let her justify herself if she can" (343; Angel Clare, in Hardy's *Tess of the D'Urbervilles*, agrees—though the debate there isn't theoretical and the consequences are tragic). The freedom from supervision that he applauds—a freedom designed to guarantee personal privacy, nonintervention, and liberty of movement—is a freedom that inevitably implies sexual liberty and hence the possibility of infidelity (as his earlier remarks about his "life apart" implied). Tarrant has already declared that he is not personally at risk here (Nancy's self-restraint will keep him faithful) and he doesn't think Nancy is either. But their conversations are nonetheless important because they identify Nancy's freedom as different from her husband's. Free at home from the supervising spouse, liberated from a confining connection, the partners in this new marriage escape one sort of bad intimacy, only to find themselves faced with the possibility of another. And yet the adultery Tarrant worries about here is strictly female adultery. Male adultery has no real meaning to him, while female adultery would be cause for termination of a marriage.

Why this insistence on the double standard? This determination, in the midst of liberated marriage, to discriminate the behavior of men from that of women, to differentiate the *talk* about equality and liberty from the irreducibly central importance of female fidelity?[36] It is all well and good, Gissing seems to suggest, to restructure marriage in order to preclude its bad mergings and unwanted violations—images, all, of the worse mergings and violations of the public realm—but only as long as the solution doesn't reproduce the problems it was designed to solve. What worries Gissing is the vision of free womanhood and the threat of female adultery and promiscuity. One of Gissing's central desires as he reimagines marriage is to invent a new form of autonomy and privacy. But while male autonomy presents the prospect of a new freedom from intervention—from surveillance, intrusion, violation—female autonomy presents the prospect of a new liberty and sexual freedom, and these in turn suggest the possible *loss* of autonomy—not the woman's loss of her own autonomy, but the man's loss of it.

Having relinquished the idea of home as the traditional space of private possession, Gissing has relocated that space in Nancy's body—and this view is consistent with the idea, as Keith Thomas has suggested, that the double standard has its origin in the "desire of men for absolute property in women, a desire which cannot be satisfied if the man has reason to believe that the woman has once been possessed by another man, no matter how momentarily and involuntarily and no matter how slight the consequences."[37] Thomas's remarks stress the need for a fundamental, and absolute, space of private possession, located outside a man's self, in a woman. Tarrant's remarks gesture toward a similar, fundamental need—consistent with the desire, everywhere expressed in Gissing's novel, to establish a space of privacy in the midst of publicity's ever-greater encroachments. In effect, Nancy's body becomes the last preserve, the final space of privacy. The reconfiguration of marriage and home means to establish freedom and mobility—freedom from oppressive surveillance, freedom from excessive intimacy and bad merging—but never at the expense of authentic privacy, that precious commodity so little in evidence in Gissing's world.

It is on this ground that Tarrant also opposes the publication of Nancy's novel: "It isn't literature, but a little bit of Nancy's mind and heart, not to be profaned by vulgar handling. To sell it for hard cash would be horrible. Leave that to the poor creatures who have no choice. You are not obliged to go into the market" (354). Nancy's novel *isn't* literature—which finds its proper place in public—but rather her "mind and heart," exposed and turned to capital. In this sense, Tarrant's view is much like Marian Yule's in *New Grub Street*: when Jasper Milvain suggests that she take up novel writing in order to make money and, in particular, that she use their love affair as material for her plot, Marian is horrified—and so are we. The exposure of intimate experience and its conversion into "hard cash" suggests that permeability of private and public realms that Gissing seeks to reform. Nancy's novel is thus "seal[ed]" and put away in "the back of a very private drawer" (356) and that, simply, is the end of her career as a writer. Her husband asserts that there is "genuine independence on both sides," yet this is not the case (he is a successful journalist; her writing career comes to an abrupt end). Nancy accepts the loss with good humor. She "subdued her natural impulse, and conformed to her husband's idea of wifehood. It made her smile to think how little she preserved of that same 'genuine independence' " (356).

That Nancy should somehow become the ultimate space of privacy, that in her self-restraint and in her fidelity she should embody privacy all the while engaging in what turns out to be only a theoretical freedom and liberty, seems a hard fate indeed. But Nancy's acceptance of the distance between Tarrant's pronouncements about their equality and his real belief in it testifies, for Gissing, to her mature acceptance of the principle of containment whose presence—or absence—is an insistent feature of all of his "woman question" novels. In *The Odd Women*, for example, Rhoda Nunn has, at the novel's start, a complex public life as the codirector of an employment agency for unmarried women, but her expansive life feels contained and even defused by her sexual narrowness. Rhoda is identified from the start with a rigid morality that inappropriately excludes sexuality and femininity, and this narrowness in her character (not, it seems, her public commitments themselves) must undergo a serious transformation—in this case as she opens herself up to sexual love. Once she does, however, Gissing must resolve the more difficult problem that emerges when a sexually mature woman contemplates life in the public realm that she clearly occupies, and it is then that the authentic principle of containment expresses itself—now, as mature relinquishment, as an acknowledgment that the sexual self-expression toward which she has been moving is the very thing she cannot have.

Nancy Lord relinquishes liberty (including sexual liberty) rather than sexuality, but in both instances the principle of containment is associated with the heroine's heightened consciousness of herself and her situation—and the contrast between the two is important. For Rhoda, whose sexual self-development is one of the novel's central themes, sexuality is relinquished just as consciousness of it is fully attained. But as Gissing describes Rhoda's mature acceptance of her limiting situation, he suggests that she too achieves what is, in effect, a *theoretical* complexity: "Passion had a new significance; her conception of life was larger, more liberal; she made no vows to crush the natural instincts. But her conscience, her sincerity, should not suffer. Wherever destiny might lead, she would still be the same proud and independent woman, responsible only to herself, fulfilling the nobler laws of her existence."[38]

Just as Rhoda affirms her proud singleness, she also makes clear that her sexual rigidity and narrowness are gone—but not because she has a lover. It is her "conception" of life that is larger, and this theoretical expansion—this fulfillment at the level of consciousness of what cannot be fulfilled in fact—acknowledges and undermines the movement toward psychological and sexual complexity with which the novel has been concerned. Rhoda retains the independence that Nancy can hold onto only theoretically—while Nancy retains access to sexuality and motherhood at the cost, it seems, of authentic sexual independence and liberty. Together, the novels suggest that Gissing was better able to imagine in theoretical than in actual terms the full range of female experience. Rhoda cannot actually live in both realms: she can only incorporate the experiences and memories of one into a life lived exclusively in the other.[39] Similarly, Nancy participates in a marriage that is theoretically complex and satisfying but whose lived experiences have about them much limitation and constraint. Unlike Brontë's Shirley, whose public restraint later makes private intimacy possible, Gissing's heroines experience restraint *on the other side* of sexual knowledge.

Gissing seems positively to seek out the limit, to look for the moment at which full human expression meets some clear sense of a defining and limiting boundary—as though it were impossible truly to believe in lives as rich as those he envisions theoretically and as though all mature persons recognized the absolute impossibility of living such lives. It is just this absence of maturity that characterizes *The Whirlpool*'s Alma Rolphe. Her debut as a musician and the dangerous public exposure she seeks have uniformly catastrophic consequences in miscarriage, illness, and eventual suicide. Here, too, Gissing identifies public exposure with illicit sexuality, secrecy, and criminality. If there is a central absence in *The Whirlpool*'s Alma Rolphe it is surely a saving principle of constraint.

In *The Odd Women* and *In the Year of Jubilee* Gissing negotiates the difficult, jeopardizing boundaries between private and public life. Perhaps he was moved to do so by the terrible sense everywhere present in his earlier novel *New Grub Street* that the gulf between private and public was absolute and irremediable, that there was no middle ground between the agonizing obscurity that seeks recognition and the consuming universe of degraded publicity that makes itself the only scene of visibility and human representation. In *In the Year of Jubilee* Gissing explores the way in which the public realm penetrates private experience, but he also seeks to reconfigure intimacy and privacy, to imagine new ways in which they might be at once protected from and enriched by their public associations. If Gissing's success is theoretical rather than actual, then the limitation has multiple and important sources—in Gissing's authentic anxiety about the dangers of public exposure in the 1880s and 1890s; in his wish to maintain some sort of privacy that is not at the same time utter obscurity; in a fear of plenitude; and in the corresponding admiration for self-restraint, an admiration easily assimilable to, but not absolutely identical with, conventional ideas about proper female behavior. Gissing's complex negotiations of public and private speak to the enormity of the task of finding authentic human space in a world increasingly and disturbingly open.[40]

V

Renovating Public Space in
The Convert

I.

AT THE TIME of George Gissing's death in 1903, Elizabeth Robins's involvement in the early militant suffrage movement was still several years in the future, but it is not difficult to imagine what Gissing's response to her political engagements might have been. Gissing valued independence and autonomy in women as long as these were acquired without exposure to the degradations and violations of the public realm. He would likely have had both a keen sense of the values of female citizenship and a powerful aversion to the spectacle of women in public that the Trafalgar Square suffrage meetings regularly offered their audiences and that the demonstrations, scuffles, and later battles with the police would also generate. So painful did Gissing find female public exposure that he was literally unable to represent it in the pages of *The Whirlpool*. When Alma Rolfe has her recital in that novel, her husband wanders about outside, looking at the placards that announce her appearance, but (like the narrator) unable to witness or report on the event itself.[1]

Though her name remains unfamiliar to many readers, Elizabeth Robins, author, actress, and activist, played a crucial role in the political life and public culture of the early twentieth-century women's movement—though she too felt uneasy about certain features of public participation. She avoided the direct confrontations that could have brought her a prison sentence, telling the suffrage leader Millicent Garrett Fawcett that she would rather die than go to jail. She was a frequent, but also anxious and hesitant, speaker for women's rights. She felt protected in her stage roles by the cover they provided, but "naked in the withdrawal of the magic cloak of invisibility" when speaking before a political audience—[2] an interesting commentary not only on her own part as public speaker but on the public speaking she would represent unambiguously in *The Convert*.

Born in the United States in 1862, Robins embarked on her acting career at the age of nineteen and was briefly (and tragically) married to a fellow actor, George Parkes, who committed suicide two years later: dressed in a suit of armor, he drowned himself in the Charles River. Robins was only twenty-four years old. She moved to London shortly thereafter and spent the better part of her life in Britain, as an actress (the first to play Hedda Gabler in English and to introduce Henrik Ibsen's Hilda in *The Master Builder*), a playwright, a novelist, and an essayist. After her conversion to "the cause," she was a friend of the Pankhursts, member of the Women's Social and Political Union (the WSPU), and president of the Women Writers' Suffrage League. Her essays, letters to the press, literary works, and speeches over several decades made a significant contribution to the cause of women's rights.

Before her conversion to the suffrage cause, in a novel entitled *George Mandeville's Husband* (1894), Robins presented her readers with a problematic vision of female public life and authorship (George Mandeville is a woman writer's pseudonym). The novel is caught between its sympathetic portrayal of a defective father (Wilbrahim) who seeks to protect his invalid daughter from what he calls "the woman horde advancing" and its unsympathetic portrayal of a defective mother (the novelist/playwright/wife of the title) who defaults on her maternal obligations. George Mandeville supervises the endless rehearsals of her latest play, and her husband meditates on the advancing horde while their daughter sickens and fades away:

> The woman horde advancing—taking by storm offices, shops, studios, and factories, each fighting with desperate success for "a place," whether in a learned profession or on the top of an omnibus, competing with men in every department of industrial life, jostling them in the streets, preaching to them, clamouring against them, crying "Anathema!" at street-corners, and "Woe! woe!" from the house-tops. . . . Rosina should never struggle and toil, she should be no more than a dignified looker-on at this new dance of death. . . . Rosina should be; the less she "did," the better.[3]

While Wilbrahim meditates, Rosina, it turns out, is dancing not the new but the old dance of death. Jane Marcus's view that Robins's "indictment of Wilbrahim for insisting on the sheltered life of his daughter is as strong as her burlesque of a presumptuous literary woman" is an accurate one,[4] but this equal distribution of fault only paralyzes, rather than rescues, the novel's plot. Both engagement and disengagement are equally poisonous and repellent, so that Rosina has little to do in the novel *but* die.

Elizabeth Robins's longtime correspondent and friend Henry James was similarly ill-disposed to the idea of female publicity. Even in 1909, two years after the staging of Robins's well-received play *Votes for Women!* and publication of her suffrage novel *The Convert* and over twenty years after the publication of *The Bostonians*, James refused to sign a women's suffrage petition, reportedly commenting that he was "not eager for the *avènement* of a multitudinous and overwhelming female electorate." Robins claims, in a preface to James's letters to her, that James responded to her play "with an ardour that astonishes even me," and biographer Angela John notes that he did write "fifty pages on the first part of the first act." But Robins felt, according to Johns, that James's intentions were to "depoliticise" the play. She resisted this, and argued for keeping "as much of the woman movement as shall put the ignorant in possession of its main facts."[5]

As soon as the play went into production, James went on a trip to France "for some eight or ten weeks," thus missing the rehearsals and the opening night, but promising his return for the end of the run. In letters written to Robins from France he begs for reports on the play but then apologizes for not responding to them in a timely fashion, describing "the newspaperisms" that she has mailed to him as "poverties and vulgarities of reportership" through which he "seem[s] to make out the impression made by the performed thing—and above all the 2nd Act—which I feel it deplorable that I have missed." This final letter on the subject (he had now been away for eight weeks) makes clear that the run is about to end and that he won't return from Paris for another month and a half. There is no correspondence about the play after this period and none about the novel (or about any other of Robins's novels). As Jane Marcus points out, James (and George Bernard Shaw as well) were Robins's "champions when she was the champion of Ibsen, but when she herself began to write, they were silent."[6]

It is not difficult to understand why James reacted as he did. Quite apart from whatever jealousy he might have felt about Robins's theatrical success (their friendship spanned the period of his own difficult association with the stage), James continued to represent public life as degrading, promiscuous association that erodes individual distinction. Even the fragmentary remarks above illustrate this: the female electorate that he imagines is a confused, disorderly crowd that engulfs men (it is "multitudinous and overwhelming"; no "man in his senses" could be eager for it), and the public press provides a set of common isms, at once unreliable, vulgar, and poor. Even Paris is described by James as "a great vessel in which one is so shaken about that one can scarcely cling to the table and chair."[7]

Robins's *Votes for Women!* and her novel *The Convert* (1907) provocatively contest this vision, offering in its place a powerful reimagination and reconfiguration of public space. Robins, it must be said, "felt some qualms" both about the play and the novel. She feared that the play was "too much in monochrome," and told her friend Lady Florence Bell that the novel "wasn't remotely a piece of Art—but just pleading, pleading, pleading." In my estimation, both the play and the novel are better than that, though Robins's limitations, especially when viewed in relation to earlier writers, are evident. Whatever their limits, however, Robins's texts show an extraordinary understanding of issues that dominated both documentary and novelistic representations of female public life in the prior century: they not only "put the ignorant in possession of [the] main facts" but reinterpret those facts in important ways.[8]

The novel and the play raise familiar issues—the misconstruction of character that women suffer when they enter the public sphere; the sexual taint that accompanies female public appearance; the danger that results from mixing private with public endeavor; the chaos and disorder that are identified with public space—and then they unmask, and refashion the issues. Robins presents women who deflect unwanted attention and create a shapely, cohesive public sphere that is the location of high moral and ethical action. She perceives the exposure and disorder to which her own earlier character, Wilbrahim, referred and from which James and Gissing recoiled, but she reinterprets the exposure and assigns the disorder and degradation to another source. *Votes for Women!* and—even more commandingly *The Convert*—conceive the possibility of female public action that is authoritative and effective. They contain and reconfigure the anxieties about publicity and sexuality that emerge and overwhelm earlier, nineteenth-century representations of female publicity. They afford us a crucial glimpse into the public realm as a sphere of activity open to women, useful to women—indeed, transformed by women. It is Robins's unique contribution to the public/private debate that she was able to imagine, in Hannah Arendt's sense of the term, a *polis*—a political realm of "words and persuasion"—that belonged not solely to men but to women as well.[9]

I will concentrate on *The Convert* because it is fuller and more interesting than *Votes for Women!*—though the latter certainly had the advantage of performance on its side. The play's second act, as James's letters confirm, must indeed have been powerful, reproducing as it did the great scenes of female public speaking that many in the audience did not have the courage to attend in Trafalgar Square. As Catherine Wiley notes in her discussion of the play, theatergoers found themselves in the position of the audience at a suffrage rally—invited actively to participate, to "comment upon the content of the play," much as the audience of a rally would comment on the speakers' performances there.[10] Surely this was one of the things that made the Trafalgar Square scenes (act 2) so compelling to audiences and reviewers alike. But whereas in *Votes for Women!* Vida Levering is converted before the play's action begins, in *The Convert* the heroine's conversion is depicted in the narrative, and thus the very action of conversion—so central to Robins's vision of a newly imagined, and newly legitimized, public sphere—is enacted before the reader's eyes.

II.

In an early scene of *The Convert*, as Vida Levering admits to her sister, Mrs. Fox-Moore, that it isn't because of its philanthropic function but rather because she "likes managing things" that she is involved in a charity concert, Robins introduces an idea that will have a profound influence on Vida as the novel unfolds. Her sister reports that their friend, Mrs. Freddy Tunbridge,

> *"was talking about you in her enthusiastic way when she was here the other day. 'Vida could administer a state,' she said. Yes, I laughed, too, but Mrs. Freddy shook her head quite seriously, and said, 'To think of a being like Vida—not even a citizen.' "*
>
> *"I'm not a citizen?" exclaimed the lady, laughing down at her sister over the banisters. "Does she think because I've lived abroad I've forfeited my rights of—"*
>
> *"No, all she means is——Oh, you know the bee she's got in her bonnet. She means, as she'll tell you, that 'you have no more voice in the affairs of England than if you were a Hottentot.' "*
>
> *"I can't say I've ever minded that. But it has an odd sound, hasn't it—to hear one isn't a citizen."* [11]

Their conversation is the first in a series of incidents that cause Vida to rethink her situation as a woman and, later, to reconsider her attitude toward the militant suffrage movement whose early activities form the background of the novel's action. In this scene Vida is struck by the assertion that she is "not a citizen," and the momentary confusion about what this means is significant. Vida believes that Mrs. Freddy uses the word *citizen* to mean something like "legal inhabitant" and that she thinks Vida has forfeited her citizenship by spending more time abroad than in England.

Mrs. Freddy uses the word *citizen* not in its geographical but in its deeper, political meaning—an inhabitant with "civic responsibilities." [12] Her sense that Vida could manage a great deal more than a charity concert (she "could administer a state") stands in stark contrast to the fact that Vida is barred not only from administering but from participating in affairs of state. Her residence or nonresidence is beside the point. The far more intractable problem is that citizenship is here denied to a citizen—in the most fundamental way and as a matter of law.

The assertion that Vida has "no more voice in the affairs of England than if [she] were a Hottentot" (an "uncultivated South African black") complicates this reading as well because it conflates Vida's first understanding of the matter— that travel in foreign parts is the problem—with the notion that Vida really *is* a foreigner, indeed, that she resembles that particularly uncultivated foreigner whose status as alien, colonized, disenfranchised Other resembles her own.[13] In one respect Mrs. Freddy uses the term *savage Hottentot* casually—it is, after all, a racial slur—to make the surprising remark that the cultivated Vida is in no better position than her "primitive," nonwhite sister. But in drawing the analogy between Englishwomen and Hottentots, she also invokes a familiar feminist discourse that compares supposedly free Englishwomen with their obviously suppressed counterparts in China and India as well as Africa.[14]

The confusion of meanings thus comes full circle. Vida may be a cultivated Englishwoman, but she is also an uncultivated foreigner; she may be, but really she may not be, a citizen. Vida initially thinks that Mrs. Freddy is making a personal judgment based on a mistaken notion of how citizenship works; but this in turn leads to a darker interpretation in which Vida must realize that neither personal judgment nor error is involved. The disability is not a matter of judgment; it is not based on anything Vida has done or might undo; and it is more far-reaching, and ontologically disturbing, than Vida's first, casual reading of Mrs. Freddy's assertion would suggest.

Interpretive errors like this one are everywhere present in Robins's novel and are central to *The Convert*. In a later scene in which the weekend guests at Ulland House debate two recent political events, Vida begins to question the accounts she hears and to reinterpret them herself. The first, a "disturbance— where was it?—in some town in the North several weeks ago" (57), refers to an event in October 1905 in which a factory girl, Annie Kenney, addressed a deputy of the newly elected Liberal Party in a meeting at the Free Trade Hall in Manchester, insisting that he explain what the new ministry planned to do about the suffrage matter; she unfurled a "Votes for Women" banner, was rushed by officials and, after a second attempt to address the deputy, was dragged from the hall. Along with Christabel Pankhurst, Kenney held a protest meeting outside, and the two were later arrested.[15] The second occurred on 25 April, 1906, when members of the WSPU were present in the Ladies' Gallery during debate of a women's suffrage resolution. The 26 April edition of the *Times*

reported the entire event, and it was recorded in even greater detail in parliamentary debate records. As *Hansard* notes, devoting a full paragraph, in brackets,
to the words of the women in the gallery: "[At this point cries were heard from
the Ladies' Gallery which completely interrupted the proceedings on the floor
of the House. Some voices were heard to shriek out 'We will not have this talk
any longer,' 'Divide, divide,' 'Divide, divide'; 'Vote, vote, vote;' 'Vote for Justice
for women,' 'We refuse to have our Bill talked out,' 'You are true liberty loving
Liberals! You do not believe in equality and justice.']" Then, according to numerous accounts—but not reported either in the *Times* or in *Hansard*—
"through the obnoxious [Ladies' Gallery] grille, a third woman thrust a little
flag and the now famous legend 'Votes for Women' made its first appearance in
the House of Commons." The Speaker, who described himself as "the only
person who [could not] see what [was] going on"—a comment that provoked
laughter—nevertheless remarked that he had given "instructions to the atten-
dants that the Ladies' Gallery should be cleared." His comment was greeted with
cheers from the floor and the police "rushed in and pulled the ladies out."
Opponents did indeed "talk out" the bill: Samuel Evans wondered "whether
there could be any argument in his favor stronger than what had just occurred.
Did hon. members desire that what had taken place in the gallery should be
repeated on the floor of the House? Did they suppose that such exhibitions were
approved of by the mass of the women in this country?" Evans ended his speech
at eleven o'clock when the rules of procedure meant that adjournment was
required. He remarked that "when they had still some hundreds of thousands
of men without a vote who took an interest in and who studied politics, surely
it was a very strong order to ask the House of Commons to agree to give a vote
to every woman at one fell swoop, and so to make the number of women electors
exceed that of the men voters of the country."[16]

The events themselves were dramatic indeed. As the guests at Ulland House
reveal, however, they also demonstrated to many members of the general public
just what Evans highlighted for his audience—the "public demonstration of the
unfitness of women for public office" (56). One of the most notable features of
the demonstration was that the women's voices were reported both in the newspapers and in *Hansard*'s account of the parliamentary debate—an unprecedented
occurrence. So, too, was the appearance inside the House of the "Votes for
Women" banner. Though these may seem small matters, their impact upon
members of the House was tremendous. The members' astonishment is even
easier to understand when it is situated in the context of the history of the
Ladies' Gallery and of women's place in the House of Commons.

The nineteenth-century Ladies' Gallery is thought to have emerged in the period before the 1832 Reform Bill, when a member placed a chair for his sister-in-law "over the ventilator . . . with the heat of the lamp in front" where "she could hear and not be seen." As early as 1822 Maria Edgeworth gave a vivid account of a visit to the Ladies' Gallery: "In the middle of the garret is what seemed like a sentry-box of deal boards and old chairs placed round it: on these we got and stood and peeped over the tops of the boards. Saw the large chandelier with lights blazing, immediately below: a grating of iron across veiled the light so that we could look down and beyond it: we saw half the table with the mace lying on it and papers, and by peeping hard two figures of clerks at the further end, but no eye could see the speaker or his chair,—only his feet; his voice and terrible 'ORDER' was soon heard." Edgeworth's colorful report emphasizes the women's exclusion and their difficulty in seeing exactly what was going on below. Standing on chairs over a hole in the attic floor of the House, and staring as they did through the blaze of the chandelier's candlelight, the eager, intent women could identify only half the table, make out some figures "by peeping hard," and detect the otherwise invisible speaker "only [by] his feet."[17]

After the destruction by fire of the House of Commons in 1834, it was moved that a more "commodious" Ladies' Gallery be built. But debate in the House addressed the concern that the establishment of such a gallery would sanction "the too great interference of ladies already in the political world," that women's presence would unduly influence the speakers since the gentlemen would be "addressing themselves to the gallery instead of to the legislative portion of the House," and that ladies would corrupt the men who had the right to choose which women should be given "preference" in seating. That women's presence in the House would redirect the interest and attention of the men points, once again, to the sexualizing force of women's presence in public spaces.[18]

Parliament did vote to establish a new Ladies' Gallery but then failed to appropriate funds for it. Now members worried about bringing ladies there "to keep bad hours, and witness proceedings that would not always be agreeable to their feelings." They argued against making "the ladies of England political partisans" and feared that granting the proposition would make it "impossible to continue society on the footing on which it now happily stood." This latter remark—typical not only of Ladies' Gallery debates but of suffrage debates as well—exposes the fear that any alteration in women's access to political knowledge or power would fundamentally change the relations between the sexes.[19]

Eventually, however, the funds were voted, and space for a Ladies' Gallery was included when the new House was completed in 1850. In 1852, when the

House of Commons was improved, however, the gallery was "concealed by a grille." Some thirty years later debates began about the necessity of removing the infamous grille. In August 1884 the First Commissioner of Work was asked whether "he would favorably consider and adopt measures for an increase of space and improved ventilation in the ladies' gallery; also for the removal of the screen." In the 30 March 1885 debate that followed, William Gladstone "doubted whether [the grille] really did exclude sound, and he thought it was quite conceivable that the grille might even improve hearing by breaking the waves of sound. Then ladies did not want light . . . to read documents and papers in the Gallery. Ladies came to see and hear what was going on in the House, and he did not think the question of light applied to the matter."[20] The motion was defeated and the grille was not removed. For more than thirty years the issue of the removal of the grille repeatedly came up—always revealing, as Gladstone's remarks did, the desire to preserve the gallery as a place from which women could watch and hear but not a place in which they could either be seen or from which they could have direct access to the floor of the House. The grille was only removed in August 1917 when women were about to gain the vote and be admitted as Members to Parliament, which happened in the following year.

Calling out from the Ladies' Gallery and thrusting the "Votes for Women" banner through the grille was perceived to be a spectacular violation of decorum because, as the above materials suggest, the grille embodied in architectural terms the desire to keep women separate, invisible, and inaccessible; to see that they not interfere in the business of politics; to guarantee that even if present in public they were essentially not present, were secluded in a marginal (unlit, unventilated, oddly situated) space. If the women in the Ladies' Gallery of Maria Edgeworth's day could neither see nor be seen, the women in the new gallery could be obscured from view while they were watching and listening. Piercing the grille and unfurling the banner represented a trespassing of boundaries, a refusal to accept containment, a threat to social arrangements as they currently stood, an insistence on being both *heard* and *seen*. No wonder the policemen were called to remove the offending women.

In Robins's novel, Vida initially takes part in the general condemnation of the women's actions—she even corrects Lady John's description of "the Woman Suffrage precipice," suggesting instead that it be called the Woman Suffrage "mud-puddle" (56). But gradually she reevaluates her position. The "scene" is described by others as "idiotic" and "revolting," the women portrayed as "sexless" and "touched," a "handful of half-insane females" (56, 57). Dick Farnborough even describes Annie Kenney, in the earlier event, as "a Red Indian" (not a Hottentot this time) whom the policemen carry out "scratching and spitting. . . . You see . . . there's something about women's clothes—*especially* their hats, you know—they—well, they ain't built for battle. . . . She's just funny, don't you know!" (58). When Lord Borrodaile remarks, "There's nothing that shakes my nerves like seeing a woman struggling and kicking in a police-man's arms," Farnborough continues to insist on the "humour" in the situation: "They say they swept up a peck of hairpins after the battle!" he remarks (59). Farnborough also offers a graphic description of the violent scene: "The cattiest one of the two, there she stood like this, her clothes half torn off, her hair down her back, her face the colour of a lobster and the crowd jeering at her" (59).

Vida now senses that the scene Farnborough describes is frightening rather than amusing: "I don't see how you could stand and look on at such a hideous scene." She thus begins to effect her separation from the group and to inaugurate a different interpretation of events. Farnborough asserts that he wasn't looking on, that the scene was told to him by a male friend who witnessed with horror the "revolting . . . scrimmage." But Vida replies: "If it was as horrible as that for Major Wilkinson to look on at—what must it have been for those girls?" (59).

Farnborough "resent[s]" Vida's pity for the suffrage women, but he par-ticularly dislikes the suggestion that there might be another point of view on their conduct. His retort is designed to challenge the legitimacy of any other perspective than his own: "It's never so bad for the lunatic . . . as for the sane people looking on" (59). This remark opens the door to a flood of denunci-ation that Vida finally interrupts with a string of questions and comments: "You know some of them? . . . But you've seen them? . . . But I suppose you've gone and listened to them haranguing the crowds . . . We're all so certain they're such abominations . . . I thought maybe some of us knew something about them" (60).

Not until the gathering breaks up do we learn the real source of Vida's angry reaction. She is disturbed by Farnborough's "talking about women like that, before women": "Of course we *all* know they aren't accustomed to treating our sex in general with overmuch respect when there are only men present," she remarks; "but—do you think it's quite decent that they should be so free with their contempt of women before us?" (61). Vida is troubled by the way that the men expose the women in what amounts to a public setting. Moreover, her sexually charged language about the absence of "decen[cy]" and about the inappropriately "free" expression of the men hints at her sense that their con-versation has the quality of a public violation—a notion that seems even more convincing because the men return so insistently to the bodily disarray of the scene—hats and hairpins falling by the peck, and women struggling in the arms of policemen.

Vida's odd acknowledgment ("of course we *all* know") that men do not speak respectfully of women in the company of other men is made even more potent by the revelation of a still uglier truth. Something has liberated these men to represent their disrespect *in mixed company.* And all of this is even more significant because the men are discussing the inappropriateness of women making themselves vulnerable in public while the men's actions replay the very exposure and "comic" disassembly of the women which they claim to abhor.

In this early scene, Vida is "jarred," and then "ruffled" (65), by the discrepancy she perceives between the men's assertions that they admire and respect women and the sign that their admiration and respect barely conceal a disrespect and even contempt that the men expose publicly in the very act of criticizing female publicity. Though Paul Wiley will later declare that he idealizes women and that this is why he cannot bear to see them "scramble off their jewelled thrones to mount the rostrum and the omnibus" (64), Vida has already begun to probe and ponder the familiar rhetoric.

II.

Vida's discomfort with the antisuffrage ideology shared by the guests at Ulland House is a prelude to the even greater incongruity she will experience at the suffrage meetings in Trafalgar Square. When she attends the first outdoor meeting with her sister, she registers the difference between the reputation of "these new Furies" and their actual appearance:

> But were these frail, rather depressed looking women—were they indeed the ones, outrageously daring, who broke up meetings and bashed in policemen's helmets? Nothing very daring in their aspect to-day—a little weary and preoccupied they looked, as they stood up there in twos and threes, talking to one another in that exposed position of theirs, while from time to time about their ears like spent bullets flew the spasmodic laughter and rude comment of the crowd   strangely unconscious, those "blatant sensation-mongers," of the thousand eyes and the sea of upturned faces!   (75)

Robins is interested both in the inconspicuousness of the women, and in their unconsciousness of what she calls their "exposed position." Quite literally, they cannot be picked out, cannot be identified in the crowd, either by their own appearances or by some consciousness they might be expected to show of their centrality to the event at hand. Vida and her sister even wonder whether "perhaps these [women] are not the ones." They stand in small, inconspicuous groups, thinking not about the crowd but about their common commitments and concerns (they are "preoccupied" and "unconscious"); their central relations are to each other and to their cause, rather than to the audience. The attention-getting behavior—spasmodic laughter and rude comment—occurs in the crowd rather than on the platform. And the "bash[ing]" is all in the other direction as well—not from the suffrage women toward the crowd, but from the crowd toward them (75).

Vida has not, she realizes here, understood the suffrage women. And when Lothian Scott (modeled on the Labour M.P. and staunch suffrage supporter Keir Hardie) speaks, she realizes that she does not understand the crowd of working-men either as they hoot a speaker thought to be their champion. Nor does she understand what Robins refers to as the "argot" of the speakers and the crowd. Significantly, she cannot judge the speaker's invocation of historical precedent for demanding the vote in public (his precedent is the Hyde Park Riot that preceded the 1867 Reform Bill) because she does not know enough history to do so. "In the midst of so much that is obscure," Vida thinks, "it is meet to reserve judgment" (86).

The early destabilizing of Vida's views begins with the surprising conversation about citizenship at the novel's start, becomes anger and confusion at Ulland House, is confirmed by the disappointment of negative expectations in the appearance of the suffrage women, and finally emerges in her recognition that she is not in a position to judge what she witnesses at the Trafalgar Square suffrage meetings. It opens up a space of consideration not present before and sets the stage for the revision and, finally, reversal of views that Vida will experience as one of the novel's central "converts."

In the first speech to which Vida listens after she suspends judgment, the task of the speaker is itself redefinition, and among other things she redefines the meaning of citizenship. In defending the right of Mrs. Pankhurst to lead a deputation to Sir Henry Campbell-Bannerman's house, Mrs. Chisholm (the meeting's leader, modeled on Mrs. Pankhurst herself) notes that

> "*she had a perfect right . . . more than a right, a duty, to perform in going with that deputation on public business to the house of a public servant, since, unlike the late Prime Minister, he had refused to women all opportunity to treat with him through the usual channels always open to citizens having a political grievance.*"
>
> "*Citizens? Suffragettes!*"

. . . . .

"It won't be the first time in history that a name given in derision has   (89)
become a badge of honour!"

In this example the audience refuses (again) to permit the women to identify themselves as citizens and insists on the derogatory term *suffragettes*. But instead of challenging the notion that the women aren't citizens, the speaker accepts the counterdesignation *suffragette*, though she insists that it is a term of honor. If the sequence began by challenging Vida's right to think herself a citizen, it begins over again here with the prospect that she might assign herself an alternative "badge of honor."

Furthermore, Chisholm will make the argument that the apparent confusion of private with public actions (going to the prime minister's *home* on *public business*) is really an acknowledgment that the private/public distinction has already been compromised by the very persons who complain that it has been unfairly violated. The man in question, a public servant, has denied women access to the usual public channels; he has failed to maintain the private/public distinction because he has disabled public action in the public arena.

A similar reworking of terms can be detected in the next exchange between the speaker and the audience:

"Yer ought to leave politics to us——"
"We can't leave politics to the men, because politics have come into the
home, and if the higher interests of the home are to be served, women must   (90)
come into politics."

This effort at revision—which appears to argue that the public sphere has already penetrated the private one, so that private life must now take up the responsibilities of the public realm—operates on a similar principle. If the first speaker claims that public business can't be carried on in public places (and *must* therefore be carried on in private ones), this speech seems to argue that public business is regularly carried on in private places by the state. Politics have "come into the home," so that there is now no choice but to serve the interests of the home by acknowledging and then reconceiving the breakdown of distinctions.

This appears straightforward enough until one realizes that what the speaker in fact means—this is the direction into which the crowd presses her—is that "politics have come into the home" in the sense that women have been forced to go out into the world to work: "You men can't always earn enough to keep the poor little home going, so the women work in the shops, they swarm at the mill gates, and the factories are full. . . . Yet, you go on foolishly echoing:

Woman's place is at home" (90). What begins as an argument that the state has intruded into the home (a common enough contention in this period) becomes an argument about an exercise of economic power (and a critique of men's inadequacy—"you men can't always") that has brought about women's emergence into the public realm.

The speaker also wants to talk about restrictive legislation in the workplace, in other words about a different way in which public policy has infiltrated the private concerns of women. But this only brings the argument around full circle: economic forces have penetrated the home, propelling women into the public realm, where again they are violated by legislation that they cannot influence. This blurring of distinctions, or breaking down of public/private boundaries, is presented as a state of affairs already in place; the idea that voting would represent an originary violation of a sacred distinction is thus actively contested.

Finally, the last section of the speech ties the failure of legislators to consult women's legislative interests with their failure to consider seriously the suffrage resolution before Parliament and with a disrespect for women that lies beneath their apparent protection. Describing the 26 April 1906 scene in the House of Commons, the speaker suggests that

> *even the woman of what are called the upper classes—even she must wince at the times when men throw off the mask and let her see how in their hearts they despise her. . . . What happened to* our *honour, that these men dare tell us is so safe in their hands? Our cause was dragged through filth. The very name "woman" was used as a signal for jests and ribald laughter, and for such an exhibition of sex rancour and mistrust that it passed imagination to think what the mothers and wives of the members must think of the public confession of the deep disrespect their menfolk feel for them.*

(91–92)

The "exhibition of sex rancour" to which she refers is a central feature of the 1906 debate, as it is of virtually all debates on women's suffrage in the period. For example, in the 1871 debate in the House of Commons on the Women's Disabilities Bill, John Henry Scourfield suggests that "every person signing a petition in favour of the extension of the franchise to women should be instructed to accompany the signature with a photographic portrait, and that Mr. Darwin or Professor Owen, who could distinguish the sex of animals from very trifling signs, should be retained to decide from an examination of the pictures as to the sex of the person represented, for he could not help suspecting that many of the signatories were not women, but men in women's clothing."[21] It is difficult to decide whose sexuality is being impugned: that of male supporters (they are not true men, but rather men in women's clothing) or the women themselves (there are no women supporters, for the women have been unsexed and are actually men dressed as women).

Charles Newdegate, in a parallel set of remarks, contested Edward Backhouse Eastwick's assertion of the equality of men and women by arguing that "there might be some differences, he could not help imagining [Eastwick] might have continued, in the physical construction of men and women, and then he could have told us that through some Darwinian process of development, these differences would eventually be obliterated."[22] Newdegate's comments suggest a similar erosion of sexual difference, the threat of which is designed to ward off any rearrangement of social positions and powers. If anything, the earlier debates are cruder and more degrading than the later ones, though the arguments do not change significantly.

In the 1906 debate to which Robins's characters refer and which one member of Parliament, William Redmond, would call "sickly—not to say disgusting," William Randall Cremer, maintaining that granting women the suffrage would mean admitting them to Parliament, points out that "there were times and periods in women's lives when they required rest not only for mind but for body, and to drag them into the political arena under those conditions would be cruel indeed. There were also periods, especially in a married woman's life, when it would be absolutely impossible for her properly to discharge her duties as a Member of this House." Cremer seems eager to protect women during what Sir Almroth Wright would later call in the *Times* their "physiological emergencies." He is surprisingly explicit here in naming both menstruation and pregnancy as reasons to exclude women from Parliament. Cremer goes on to consider how women would operate in the House of Commons: "What influences would be used by women on men and men on women in order to secure votes?" The imputation of sexual misconduct is striking, given the earlier references to women's sexual and reproductive lives, just as a later suggestion that women's interest in parliamentary affairs is essentially prurient seems to stress the dark side of female sexuality: "The way in which women rushed to hear cases in our Law Courts and listen to evidence which no woman of refinement or decency should listen to, went very far to prove that women would not introduce any higher order of morality or humanitarianism into the legislature of this country."[23]

The speaker, Mrs. Chisholm, is unwilling to accept—indeed she insists on bringing to light—the public violation of women in which the debates engaged ("our honour . . . so safe in their hands . . . was dragged through filth") and also the "public confession" of disrespect that the debates embodied. The combination of these matters is exactly what stuns Vida in the earlier episode at Ulland house. In both episodes the makers of the scene are declared to be the men themselves, the objects of their sex rancor the very women whose honor they claim to defend.

Mrs. Chisholm, however, is able to turn Vida's confusion into something clearer and more decided and to offer Vida a sense of common cause with others:

(92)

> *You blame us for making a scene in that holy place! You would have us imi-*
> *tate those other women—the well-behaved—the women who think more of*
> *manners than of morals. . . . There were* others *up there in the little pen*
> *that night!—women, too—but women with enough decency to be revolted,*
> *and with enough character to resent such treatment as the members down*
> *there on the floor of the House were giving to our measure. Though the*
> *women who ought to have felt it most sat there cowed and silent, I am proud*
> *to think there were other women who cried out,* "Shame!"

Once again Mrs. Chisholm turns meanings on their heads. It isn't the women in the gallery who are disgusting and revolting; they possess "enough decency to *be* revolted" (italics mine). Chisholm's insistence that the offended women are the women of "character" is important too, since what Vida felt at Ulland House was more like confusion and disorientation than a sense of her own integrity. Chisholm's speech offers Vida a method, a way of identifying her feelings that assigns them a different meaning.

Ironically, at the moment that Vida is recovering her identity, her sister tells her to "Pull down [her] veil," and Robins comments that "Vida's mind at the word 'veil,' so peremptorily uttered, reverted by some trick of association to the Oriental significance of that mark in dress distinctively the woman's" (92). It is no accident that Vida's mind reverts to this. Captivated—Robins actually says "dazed," by the power of Chisholm's speech and by its representation of what Chisholm has just called "a new chapter in human history" ("It began with 'Shame!' but it will end with 'Honour,' " 92)—Vida hears the instruction from her sister as a challenge to this vision of female power and of dignified publicity. "Why should I pull down my veil?" she asks, and "disobey[s] the mandate" until she sees Dick Farnborough—her nemesis at Ulland House—in the crowd (93). Though she does lower her veil to prevent him from seeing her, the association she has herself made now seems inescapable. As things currently stand, she is a woman who, like her Eastern counterpart, must hide herself in shame. She has neither social standing, nor power, nor the right to that public identity that Chisholm has described.

In the next suffrage meeting that Vida attends, a key subject is "chivalry"— the Western version of the covering and protection of women that Easterners represent in the veil. The speaker here is Ernestine Blunt (about whom I shall have more to say later); her attack on chivalry, like Mrs. Chisholm's attack on the blurring of public/private boundaries, is based on the understanding that chivalrous relations have *already* disappeared—not that the suffragettes will end them. When the audience asks "What's to become of chivalry," she replies, "What *has* become of chivalry?"

> *Don't you know that there are girls and women in this very city who are* *working early and late for rich men, and who are expected by those same* *employers to live on six shillings a week? Perhaps I'm wrong in saying the* *men expect the women to live on that. It may be that they* know *that no* *girl can—it may be the men know how that struggle ends. But do they care?* *Do* they *bother about chivalry? . . . Girls are driven—when they are not* *driven to worse—they are driven to being lodging-house slaveys or over-* *worked scullions. That's all right! . . . At Cradley Heath we make chains.* *At the pit brows we sort coal. But a vote would soil our hands!*

(118, 119)

Ernestine Blunt challenges the code of chivalry that underlies opposition to the vote, and this is important because, while Vida may shrink from the Eastern allusion above, she has yet to relinquish its Western version. Moreover, in the vision of the working "slavey," and, even worse, in the invocation of the girl forced into prostitution by low wages, Miss Blunt argues that chivalry has long been dead: it is a cover for its opposite, the exploitation of women.

The debate about chivalry—the conditions of its existence and the con-sequence of challenges to it—runs through discussion on the position of women in the nineteenth century. T. H. Lister put the problem, and the threat, suc-cinctly in an 1841 article that I have already cited (see chapter 1): "But let women be made ostensibly powerful; let a sense of competition be introduced; let man be made to feel that he must stand on the defensive—and the spirit of chivalry . . . will speedily cease; and it will be useless to expect a continuance of that feeling, to which most women can now appeal with confidence, and which lends the most essential charms to the ordinary intercourse of civilized society. Women, as a class, cannot enjoy, at the same time, the immunities of weakness and the advantages of power." Lister's final assertion indicates the peril associated with "ostensible power." Weakness (or at least the failure to exercise power) confers immunity on women, while the acquisition or display of power will result in woman's loss of man's protection.[24]

Over thirty years later, in an essay in the same journal, Louisa Shore chal-lenged the view that such chivalry can have any value at all, dependent as it is on intimidation, and constituting as it does a contract (see chapter 3: "They say, that, if they are obliged to grant women equal social and legislative rights, *i.e.,* justice, [women] will no longer receive from men that so-called 'chivalrous homage' which [men] regard apparently as sufficient compensation for every disadvantage and every humiliation attending the whole sex"). Like Robins, Shore conceives of chivalry as a "modification" of—really a cover for—"barbaric female slavery." Perhaps her keenest insight, however, is her revelation of the "bargain . . . a very one-sided bargain" that lies beneath chivalry's generosity and graciousness. Lister issues the threat, but Shore discerns that this threat conceals a devil's pact.[25]

Robins's suffrage speakers are still debating chivalry some thirty years later, though for Ernestine Blunt, the fiction has finally lost its force.[26] A powerful moment in her speech occurs when the speaker addresses the crowd on the subject of how chivalry operates:

(119)

> *"If you are intelligent you know as well as I do that women are exploited the length and breadth of the land. And yet you come talking about chivalry! Now, I'll just tell you men something for your future guidance."* She leaned far out over the crowd and won a watchful silence. "That talk about chivalry makes women sick." *In the midst of the roar, she cried, "Yes, they mayn't always show it, for women have had to learn to conceal their deepest feelings, but depend upon it that's how they feel."*

To the reinterpretation, reversal, and reassignment of meanings so central to the suffrage speakers generally, Miss Blunt here adds something new. As she leans "far out over the crowd," she unmasks the concept of chivalry and its agents in the audience and elsewhere on behalf of the very women upon whom the fiction is imposed. In her confidential assertion—"I'll just tell you men something for your future guidance"—Miss Blunt rearranges the relations between men and women, suggesting that those who believe they control the ideological content of their relations lack critical knowledge about them. The women have seen through the fiction of chivalry. They not only don't believe it; they are actually made *sick* by it. The men may not know this, she argues, because the women conceal their feelings, but this only demonstrates in another way how little the men do know about their relations with the women they thought they had under control.

Miss Blunt's dislocation of the power relations among men and women, her insinuation that the women have already seen through the manipulations of the men—and, even more, that they know what they know even though they don't reveal it—is designed to be unsettling in the extreme. Men, she says, are simply operating on a different terrain from the one on which they think they are operating. They don't know the rules of the game any more. And women's power to conceal is an instrument in the loss of power that the men experience.

Vida has an experience that epitomizes what Miss Blunt is talking about in a scene that occurs shortly after this one. Back with her friends at the Tunbridges' house, and with her particular friend, Lord Borrodaile, she finds herself engaged in a debate about the impact of the suffrage movement on contemporary manners and morals. Vida senses the risk she runs in supporting the cause, especially the risk to friendly relations with men like Borrodaile, with whom the staking out of territories and positions threatens all ordinary relations. Borrodaile's argument is that Vida belongs "to the [civilized, aristocratic] people who are responsible for handing on the world's treasure. As we've agreed, there never was a time when it was attacked from so many sides. Can't you see what's at stake? . . . Your friends want to open the gates still wider to the Huns" (146).

For a moment, in a familiar style, Vida lightens the conversation, and Lord Borrodaile remarks that he is "too fond of [Vida] to quarrel on any ground." But turning serious again, Vida comments:

> *"You don't care enough about anything to quarrel about it. . . . But it's just as well"*—she rose and began to draw on her glove—*"just as well that each of us should know where to find the other. So tell me, what if it should be a question of going forward in the suffrage direction or going back?"*
>
> *"You mean—"*
>
> *"—on from latchkeys and University degrees to Parliament, or back."*
>
> *"Oh, back," he said hastily. "Back. Yes, back to the harem."*   (147)
>
> *When the words were out, Lord Borrodaile had laughed a little uneasily—like one who has surprised even himself by some too-illuminating avowal. . . . But the revealing word he had flung out—it seemed to have struck wide some window that had been shuttered close before. The woman stood there in the glare.*

Lord Borrodaile's inadvertent acknowledgment that he prefers the subjection and sexual slavery of women—the multiple wives and concubines of the harem—to their freedom and equality (latchkeys and university degrees both represent this freedom, as does the suffrage) illuminates for Vida what is at the heart even of the most decorous, chivalrous, and "civilized" men. Standing there in the glare as Borrodaile's civility and culture are unmasked, Vida must feel, as her later remarks suggest, that the terms of the battle have been revealed to her. She has asked that they be revealed; she has told Borrodaile that "it's just as well that each of us should know where to find the other."

The conversation is important both because of the turn it takes and the context in which it is set. Borrodaile has brought to the Tunbridges' party two "squares of cardboard, tied face to face with tape" that turn out to contain carefully protected photographs of artwork unearthed during Sir Arthur Evans's (celebrated) archaeological dig at Crete. Robins describes Borrodaile's gentle handling of the reproductions as he takes them one at a time "from between [the] two bits of cardboard" and holds one up before his eyeglasses. Borrodaile tells Vida of

(147–48)

> *what was not then so widely known—details of that most thrilling moment perhaps in all the romance of archaeology—where the excavators of Knossos came upon the first authentic picture of a man belonging to that mysterious and forgotten race that had raised up a civilization in some things rivalling the Greek. . . . For here was this wonderful island folk—a people standing between and bridging East and West—these Cretan men and women who, though they show us their faces, their delicate art and their stupendous palaces, have held no parley with the sons of men, some say for three and thirty centuries. . . . At last he shared the picture . . . this proud athlete coming back to the world of men after his long sleep . . . but meeting us with a high, imperial mien, daring and beautiful.*

The photographs that Borrodaile shows are clearly from Evans's collection of works unearthed at the site of the Minoan civilization (the finds were made, and news of them disseminated, at the time Robins was writing her novel). The photographs reveal a "high degree of civilization" in a culture that had, until Evans "recovered" it, disappeared (148). Borrodaile suggests that the disappearance of the Minoan civilization is part of "a universal rhythm," but also that the work of Evans and the photographs themselves represent the preservation of culture in another way. Vida wonders whether a culture's disappearance represents something about the meaning of its history—"that an Empire maintained by brute force shall perish by brute force" (149)—an interpretation whose implications Borrodaile does not wish to pursue. Robins's intention is to show the contrast between Borrodaile's highly civilized appreciation of the beauty of ancient artifacts (he handles them with an acute sense of their delicacy and beauty) and his uncivilized views of women (he would just as soon they went back to the harem, and no one, it seems, is willing to handle them with care). Vida actively seeks out revelation in this scene; she willingly relinquishes the comfort, the decorum, the civility, the cover of chivalrous relations. And she finds, as Mrs. Chisholm might suggest, that what lies beneath these is an astonishing "sex rancour." As Ernestine Blunt would have it, the talk about chivalry makes her sick.

The impact of the suffrage speeches on Vida's own thinking also comes to a climax in this scene. First, because Vida's experience of the operations of chivalry so nearly reflects Miss Blunt's; and second, because like Ernestine, Vida begins purposefully (if tentatively) to engage in the unmasking activity that is central to the novel. Instead of accepting and participating in the cover of civil relations (as she has done in the past), she lifts the cover in this scene, and her action has as its consequence the revealing and exposing of Borrodaile. Like the other interpretive activities of *The Convert*—the rereading of key historical events, the reassignment (often the reversal) of values, the reconception of conventional boundaries—the unmasking of Borrodaile is particularly important because it is performed *by* a woman, not *on* one. Women in *The Convert* are the agents of interpretation, not, as they are in *Shirley* and *North and South*, the potential or real objects of misinterpretation and misconstruction. Moreover, instead of being problematically exposed, like Diana, for example, in *Diana of the Crossways*, or Nancy Lord in *In the Year of Jubilee*, these women expose the exposers. Though the suffrage women in the novel are revealed on the plinth— as in some sense Vida is exposed when the "window that had been shuttered close before" is opened—it is really Borrodaile who is exposed, and in ways that he can't relish.

III.

The suffrage women (and Vida is fast becoming one of them) exhibit an interpretive control of the field that has as its consequence the redirection of interpretive energy (away from themselves) and the exposure and reconstruction of *others*. Their activity reverses the usual way in which women lose protection or immunity when they enter public spaces—indeed, in Robins, those who lose immunity are not women but men.

The fact that the suffrage women are the agents of the reconstruction of others and that they seem immune to the misconstruction of character that is a concern of public women in all of the novels we have examined is particularly striking: for they *are* assaulted—verbally, psychologically, and physically—by the audiences to whom they speak. As Robins would later remark, "Woman, having ceased in some measure to be helpless, has become, in the polite phrase of Mr. Henry James, 'impeachable.' Stated bluntly, men despised her at their ease for her helplessness. From no manifestation of hers do the majority of the opposite sex recoil so sharply as from signs of her ceasing to be helpless."[27] The crowds interrupt them, taunt them, insult them, propose to them, hoot them on or off the stage, comment on their sexual attractiveness (or lack thereof), and loudly assess their fitness as speakers, electors, and women.

As Vida learns in an exchange with Miss Claxton about why the suffrage women carry dogwhips, the women are not only verbally assaulted but sexually violated at political meetings as well: "Not the police, but the stewards . . . and the men who volunteer to 'keep the women in order,' they . . as they're turning us out they punish us in ways the public don't know. . . . They punish us by underhand maltreatment—of the kind most intolerable to a decent woman" (158). Vida is shocked by this example of the actual physical defilement of women—here not a mere association between publicity and sexuality, not a suggestive imputation against the women's characters, but an actual violation of their persons that Miss Claxton is ashamed to describe.[28]

In the midst of all this, the extraordinary aspect of Robins's representation of the suffrage women remains their invulnerability to personal attack and misconstruction. Standing as they do, exposed on the plinth, the public speakers are immune to violation. Vida notes from the start that "the young girls seem to have as much self-possession as the older ones" and yet at the same time "they exhibited . . . what was perhaps even stranger—an utter absence of any flaunting of courage or the smallest show of defiance. What was this armour that looked like mere indifference? It couldn't be that those quiet-looking young girls *were* indifferent to the ordeal of standing up there before a crowd of jeering rowdies whose less objectionable utterances were: 'Where did you get that 'at?' 'The one in green is my girl!' 'Got your dog-whip, miss?' and such-like utterances" (98). Though present on the stage, the women don't make a show of their presence: they neither vaunt their courage in appearing nor make anything of the manner in which their appearance defies cultural norms. They appear without calling particular attention to the fact that they appear.

In the case of Ernestine Blunt, the most significant, and most successful, of the suffrage speakers, the "armour [of] mere indifference" turns out to be "an invincible deafness" to impertinence (115), an "inaccessibility to flattery" (178), an absence of "personal vanity" (179). Like the armor of indifference, Ernestine's deafness fails to absorb—it deflects—unwanted comments, just as her "inaccessibility to flattery" deflects praise. Robins suggests that Ernestine has no self-interest in relation to the crowd, no "personal vanity" to cultivate; she does not need or use the audience to generate a sense of self; she deflects personal interest altogether. If you wanted to "get a rise out of Ernestine," the narrator notes, "you had to talk about her 'bloomin' policy' " (115).

In a later conversation with Lord Borrodaile, Vida is on the verge of saying that Ernestine's "unselfconsciousness [is] the most surprising thing about her," but somehow this assertion goes too far. It isn't that she has no self (self-possession *is* a trait of the suffrage women) or has no self-consciousness, for "she *is* conscious, in a way, of the hold she has on the public, but it hasn't any of the deteriorating effect" that Borrodaile depreciates in public women (179). Vida means that Ernestine's consciousness of the crowd's operation is tactical: she knows how to acquire its attention, how to move it, how to sway it, how to "exercis[e] her hold over her meeting" (177). But she doesn't seem aware of, or focused on, the sense of her attractiveness to the crowd, the sense of their awareness of *her*. Being immune to flattery, and lacking even a "glimmer" of vanity, the effects of exposure on Ernestine are neutralized and, as they are, so too are the other consequences of publicity, especially the degradation and demoralization associated with seeking undifferentiated attention from a crowd. Borrodaile wants to argue otherwise in this conversation: "I don't think I ever doubted that women have a facility in speech. . . . I don't even doubt they can, as you say, sway and control crowds. But I maintain it is very bad for the women. . . . How can it fail to be! All that horrible publicity. All that concentrating of crude popular interest on themselves! Believe me, nobody who watches a public career carefully but sees the demoralizing effect the limelight has even on men's characters" (177). But Ernestine does not concentrate popular interest on herself. She deflects personal interest away from herself and thus remains immune to attacks on her person. (An earlier speaker who "encouraged personalities" lost control over the crowd and was forced to withdraw, 106.) Ernestine's fearlessness in the crowds seems significantly related to this. In an amusing scene in which Vida notices a disturbance in the streets, finds Ernestine in its midst, and tries to rescue her by getting her safely into a brougham, Ernestine insists that she is safe in the crowd. What Vida perceives as "the attack of those hooligans on a handful of defenceless women" Ernestine represents quite differently: "they weren't attacking us . . . just running after us and screaming a little" as the women run to catch a bus. "There's nothing to be frightened at," she insists (167).

The contradiction between Ernestine's apparent physical helplessness—she's so small that "unless she's on a chair, she is swallowed up" (176)—and her ability not only to survive in, but actually to manage and control, a crowd is significant as well. Even after a meeting is over, an "immense tail of boys and men (and a few women) [were] all following after—quite quiet and well-behaved—just following, because it didn't occur to them to do anything else. In a way she was still exercising her hold over her meeting" (177).

Ernestine's small size is another means of de-emphasizing her physical presence, of suggesting that her presence in the crowd is not about her body, not about herself. The odd absence of self, or deflection from self, with which her appearances are associated seems actually to be a cause of her capacity to control her audience. Instead of the crowd focusing its energies on the disassembly of her character—an activity that has as its consequence the breakdown and dispersion of the crowd itself—she offers up a blank presence that will accept neither an inflation nor a depreciation of its own value but does generate (in the absence of that other, interfering static) an alternative reading of the world that both turns the interpretive energy back on the crowd and then reconstructs the crowd in its image. Lacking a target for their misbehavior, the crowd is quiet in Ernestine's (meager) presence, listens to her, coheres around her. In a later scene the "slackly held gathering showed signs of cohesion" as soon as Ernestine appeared, and the "waiting units drew closer together" (188).

IV.

Ernestine's capacity to organize and control a crowd, to effect social cohesion, is thus contrasted with Borrodaile's view that "crude popular interest" demoralizes, disintegrates, and degrades character.[29] Vida sees none of those "evil effects among the Suffrage women." Quite the contrary: "It almost seems . . . as if there were something ennobling in working for a public cause. . . . I'm bound to admit . . . that I think the Suffrage movement in England has the advantage of being engineered by a very remarkable set of women. Not in ability alone, but in dignity of character" (178). Vida stands on its head the traditional view both of public life in general and of female publicity in particular. Unlike George Gissing's view that the public realm is chaotic and disorganized, merging as it does in *In the Year of Jubilee* "all the produce and refuse of civilization," Robins's vision is potentially cohesive, dignified, and ennobling. In Gissing's novel the only way to get around the degradations of public life and its infringement on private life (Gissing, as we have seen, describes the "ordinary middle-class home" as if it were itself a crowd) is through the elaborate maneuver of a marriage in which husband and wife do not live together, a marriage that provides intimacy without the dangers of community.[30] But in Robins's rendition, public life is dissociated from personality. Hence, it does not require Gissing's complex efforts to salvage some sort of privacy in the midst of a degrading publicity because it separates private from public life or, as we shall see again shortly, drains private life of the particular dignity and power it has in other accounts.

In Henry James's *The Bostonians*, private life holds pride of place. Publicity, like democracy, is an eroding force; it blurs distinctions of character, generalizes human pain, and diverts the self from the more critical business of identifying its "genuine vocation."[31] In Robins, public life *is* associated with the loss of a certain kind of selfhood, as James would recognize, but then it is reattached to another conception of the self—as dignified, highly conscious, historically placed. Vida is struck by this early on when she witnesses the suffrage women's power to "make history," and she sees for the first time the "possibility of historic significance" in the exhibition before her (86). In Robins's view it is public, not private, life that is the scene of noble action and of the historicizing of otherwise merely private events.

Public life is also associated with the idea of collective action, with the notion that membership in a community is an empowering, rather than a disempowering, fact. Vida betrays her growing sense of this in a conversation with Borrodaile about H. G. Wells's *In the Days of the Comet* (1906). Vida is disappointed by Wells's view that, in the utopia his novel imagines, the woman is only "a minister of pleasure, negligible in all the nobler moods, all the times of wider vision or exalted effort! Tell me . . . in the building of that City of the Future . . . shall women really have no share?" Borrodaile remarks, "I only know that I shall have no share myself"—an acknowledgment of his entirely private address to experience. But Vida replies, "Ah, we don't speak of ourselves" (208). Like Ernestine, Vida has begun to think beyond the self, and she speaks to this issue directly in her own Trafalgar Square speech. There her fear of the crowd—she first stands "like one who too much values the space between her and the mob to lessen it by half an inch" (262)—is transformed into a "camaraderie" with it, and her plea to the crowd to "join the Union" ends in an appeal to women that effects the conversion of Geoffrey Stonor's fiancée, Jean Dunbarton (266, 270).

The Convert proposes the idea that private life gains significance when it "joins on" to other things, when the idiosyncratic personal event can be illuminated and transformed by its connection to a larger cause. Robins articulates this view in her handling of the novel's romantic subplot. As a young woman, Vida took "offence at an ugly thing that was going on under my father's roof. Oh, *years* ago! I was an impulsive girl. I turned my back on my father's house" (225). She was befriended by Geoffrey Stonor, with whom she had an affair that ended in an unexpected pregnancy and then, when Geoffrey felt his inheritance threatened, an abortion. The shelter for destitute women that Vida works to create emerges from this past experience, as she openly declares—to the chagrin of her Ulland House audience.

Vida's past relationship with Geoffrey is even more potently an issue when Jean becomes aware of it. She wishes Geoffrey to make amends to Vida, though Vida feels the real debt cannot be paid: "He can't repay the one he robbed. . . . No, he can't repay the dead" (285). But, says Vida, Geoffrey can help the living: "There are the thousands with hope still in their hearts and youth in their blood. Let him help *them*. Let him be a Friend to Women" (285).

Jean thinks that Geoffrey should propose marriage to Vida, but Vida has no interest in him: in response to Lady John's assertion that "the memory of a thing like that can never die—can never even be dimmed for the woman," Vida replies: "You don't seriously believe . . . that a woman, with anything else to think about, comes to the end of ten years still absorbed in a memory of that sort? . . . Geoffrey Stonor! For me he's simply one of the far back links in a chain of evidence" (287).

Vida is willing to let Jean think, for a moment, that she will hear Geoffrey out, not because she suffers "from that old wrong" but because "I shall coin her sympathy into gold for a greater cause than mine" (288). Vida means to manipulate Jean, to trade on her innocence and affection, to convert human emotion into "gold." But the blackmail scheme is peculiar—not only because there is, in fact, no gold involved, but also because the payoff does not go to the blackmailer. As Vida notes, "The man who served one woman—God knows how many more—very ill, shall serve hundreds of thousands well. Geoffrey shall make it harder for his son, harder still for his grandson, to treat any woman as he treated me." When Lady John asks how he shall do that, Vida replies, "By putting an end to the helplessness of women" (288).[32]

When Vida and Geoffrey confront each other, she presents the situation this way: "Either her life, and all she has, given to this new Service; or a ransom if I give her up to you" (298). Vida's language is again disturbing: Jean is chattel— subject to complete possession by one owner or valuable in trade to another. Geoffrey calls Vida's threat "coercion" and "bargain-driving for a personal end" (301), but though he is right in one sense, he is wrong in another. Vida *is* driving a bargain, and Geoffrey's accurate identification of her activity recalls the earlier debates about chivalry which suggested that *it* was a bargain—power and freedom extracted from one party, protection and immunity granted by the other. But Vida's bargain is not a chivalric bargain: it is driven by a woman rather than a man and, unlike the bargain of chivalry, it operates without cover or concealment. The language of blackmail, like the language of commodification, would seem to poison Vida's activity—except that Vida neither hides what she is doing nor does what she does for personal gain. In a final interpretive reversal, Robins wants to deprive the blackmail scene both of its personality and of its taint. The bargain-driving for private ends is really bargain-driving for impersonal—or rather for collective—ends: "One woman's mishap—what is that? A thing as trivial to the great world as it's sordid in most eyes. But the time has come when a woman may look about her and say, What general significance has my secret pain? Does it 'join on' to anything? And I find it *does.* I'm no longer simply a woman who has stumbled on the way. . . . I'm one who has got up . . . and said to herself not merely—here's one luckless woman! but—here is a stone of stumbling to many. Let's see if it can't be moved out of other women's way" (303–4) This blackmail is not degrading; Vida gains Geoffrey as an important ally in the suffrage struggle and thus converts her private sorrow into collective relief.

In Gissing's *Jubilee*, blackmail is the dark underside of a world of degraded publicity. Practiced by people like Jessica Morgan, Beatrice French, and Samuel Barmby, all of whom are associated with the public realm (with university education, the fashion industry, and the newspapers, respectively), it emerges in a culture that craves, even while it perverts, privacy. But in *The Convert*, blackmail represents the de-emphasis of the personal, its "join[ing] on" to a larger set of meanings and events. As Wendy Mulford states, "Vida's personal pain is not glossed over or made to look trivial, but it is seen in perspective as one aspect of the wider forces at work which can be harnessed for change."[33]

Robins's distinctive handling of this matter is part of her more comprehensive effort to recast the meaning of private experience. Vida predicts, and then counters, the view that her private feelings are at the bottom of her joining the Women's Union: " 'The few who know about me, they'll be equally sure that, not the larger view of life I've gained, but my own poor little story, is responsible for my new departure.' She leaned over and looked into Lady John's face. 'My best friend, she will be surest of all, that it's a private sense of loss, or lower yet, a grudge, that's responsible for my attitude. I tell you the only difference between me and thousands of women with husbands and babies is that I am free to say what I think. *They aren't!*' " (289). Like Ernestine Blunt earlier, Vida leans forward to emphasize the truth she wishes to reveal. Her "own poor little story" is not responsible for her departure; there is no angry personal motive at the bottom of the thing; her political stand in fact *means more to her* than her private interests. This is the shocking truth, Vida argues, that women with husbands and babies aren't free to utter.

In a commentary on "Votes for Women!" that is equally applicable to *The Convert* Samuel Hynes says that its "tone is not that of a debate, but of a bitter, deep-felt, intimate quarrel, like a husband and wife on the brink of a divorce"; and Elaine Showalter suggests that "in representing the struggle for the vote as a sexual combat between two individuals Robins was expressing the underlying anxieties and emotions of many of her contemporaries."[34] But in my view these judgments wrongly undervalue the stance Vida takes at the end and miss the power of her final assertion. Furthermore, they wrongly affiliate Robins with other writers from whom, in their linking of publicity with sexuality, she seeks to differentiate herself. Unlike most writers about female public life who tie the publicity wars to the sex wars, Robins means to uncouple publicity and sexuality as she does earlier in her representation of the suffrage women as deflecting unwanted attention and reversing the usual pattern of female exposure and misconstruction.

Writing about *Votes for Women!* Hynes contends that women's suffering is "laid to one cause, the sexual viciousness of men. The sex war has begun, and the play is a dispatch from the front." He explains the ending in the same terms: Vida is a "woman who cannot be moved, and to whom no amends can be made, and because she is implacable, she wins her battle. But the price, for her, is total separation from men and their world: at the end . . . the alienation of the sexes is complete." Although it is true that sex rancor is an important theme both in the play and novel, it is not the only theme. In any case, as Robins herself noted elsewhere, "of all the sacrifices women lay on the altar of the new faith, none perhaps costs so much as the alienation from friends. Only the unintelligent will continue long to mistake the sacrifice for sex-antagonism."[35]

Recent critics, like Sheila Stowell and Wendy Mulford, seem better able to distinguish *The Convert* from novels characterized by what Stowell calls "conservative plotting." Stowell compares *The Convert* with other novels that have at their center "the woman with a past": "Robins reinvests [Vida] with a future, not the traditional future of the long suffering heroine [presumably marriage] . . . but a future of public service to the cause of female emancipation." Mulford, too, sees the force of the novel's impersonal (or apersonal) ending and the foregrounding, rather than the mere contextualizing, of its political meanings: "It is rare enough to find a bourgeois novel that deals directly with social movements rather than using them to contextualize the drama of interpersonal relations. But Robins's novel not only counterpoints the development of the 'heroine' with her growing awareness of the developing forces of the movement, but it also affirms, structurally, the triumph of the cause in despite, or in disregard, of personal happiness."[36]

Robins pries apart the familiar identification of sexuality and publicity in Vida's assertion that intimate, sexual material has lost its sting; it is useful, now, only as an instrument of change. Moreover, Vida twice remarks that the real debt simply *cannot* be paid: "You can never," she tells Stonor, "give me back my child" (303). The pain Vida refers to is not sexual pain; it is the pain of a woman disappointed in her hopes not of romance but of motherhood.[37]

The dissociation between sexuality and publicity contrasts with the related treatment of it in *Diana of the Crossways*. Meredith too uncouples publicity and sexuality even as his heroine engages not in blackmail but in the actual exchange of secrets for money. But Meredith's heroine restrains herself with difficulty from sexual engagement; hers is a struggle that Meredith wages as a means of generating his heroine's salvation. Gissing also treats the issue in *Jubilee*, where pub-

licity and sexuality are entwined and Nancy's sexuality is connected with motherhood: she gets pregnant in one premarital encounter with Lionel, and in the
scene near the end the wedded lovers enter quietly the bedroom in which their
child is also sleeping and consummate their marriage (again) in a familial setting.
Gissing seeks to legitimize, and simultaneously delegitimize, marital love—
wanting its benefits without its suffocating containment; wanting what is at once
socially normative and sexually illicit.

Robins, on the other hand, means to sever the connection between sexuality and motherhood. As Vida tells Stonor, the baby "showed me no barrier
is so impassable as the one a little child can raise. . . . Day and night there it was
between my thought of you and me" (297). Perhaps we are witnessing here
Robins's opposition to the notion, popularized by Havelock Ellis and others,
that the "new woman" might be, as Jill Davis puts it, "fecund, and thus sexual,
rather than a bodiless angel."[38] H. G. Wells found this appealing, but as Robins's
comments on Wells suggest, she did not. *The Convert*, however, does not simply
reject sexuality; it evokes and validates a vision of motherhood that is actually
divorced from sexuality.

Still, whatever Robins's sharp dissent from Wells, it is wrong to insist, as
Samuel Hynes has, that the significance of Robins's work lies in its "passionate,
irrational, vengefulness." Comparing Robins and Wells, and mindful of Wells's
own opposition to the suffrage movement in *Ann Veronica* (1909), Hynes declares
that it "seems understandable enough": "Wells' own liberating movement was
toward the liberation of sexual love from economic and legal restrictions (as Ann
Veronica says). He saw heterosexual union as a great human fulfillment, and
obviously a sex war was not the way to go about it. . . . Wells clearly identified
the suffrage movement with women's failure *as women*; Ann Veronica does not
belong in it because she is successful—she likes men, and they like her." As the
beginning of *The Convert* attests, Vida Levering is successful too: she likes men,
and they like her. Stowell points out that Robins is at pains to describe Vida's
womanliness, her style, her attractiveness, in a "deliberate attempt to counter
prevailing stereotypes of suffrage supporters as 'unnatural' masculinized women.
. . . Much of this portrait rested upon traditional caricatures of the frustrated
spinster, which depicted repressed sexuality manifesting itself in hysterically
fostered manly guises." Hynes is right to distinguish Robins's story from *Ann
Veronica* and to identify the real energy in the latter as an impressively liberated
female sexual energy. But he is mistaken in proposing that this is the only liberation available to "successful" women and suggesting that the only "great
human fulfillment" is a private, sexual one.[39]

Like the rewriting of the blackmail plot, Robins's rewriting of the seduction story is also important: it reverses the privatizing movement of novels like *The Bostonians* and offers something in their place. Instead of the containment both of Verena's public identity and of her sexuality in James's novel, Robins chronicles Vida's movement from private to collective action. And she recasts the public realm itself. Instead of the identification of publicity and commodification typical of *Jubilee* or the association between publicity and a dismantling exposure characteristic of *The Bostonians*, Robins has already suggested that the female public realm is cohesive, shapely, meaningful. Vida even asserts at the end, much as Ernestine has done earlier, that she is "quite safe in the crowd" and that "a man can't keep a rowdy meeting in order as well as a woman" (291). If James's and Gissing's visions of female publicity are complicated by a general sense that life in the public realm is inevitably degrading, Robins's vision makes possible the emergence of a heroine who can enter a public realm because she has reclaimed and redefined it.[40]

Robins's vision is closer, then, to Hannah Arendt's representation of a public realm that acknowledges the limitations, rather than always extolling the virtues, of privacy:

> *To live an entirely private life means above all to be deprived of things essential to a truly human life: to be deprived of the reality that comes from being seen and heard by others, to be deprived of an "objective" relationship with them that comes from being related to and separated from them through the intermediary common world of things, to be deprived of the possibility of achieving something more permanent than life itself. The privation of privacy lies in the absence of others; as far as they are concerned, private man does not appear, and therefore it is as though he did not exist. Whatever he does remains without significance and consequence to others, and what matters to him is without interest to other people.*[41]

Robins recognizes the possibility for women of authentic human action in the public realm, of public appearance as ennobling, significant, and consequential.

That Robins's public figure relinquishes the rewards of privacy in exchange for a life lived exclusively in public—rather than moving back and forth between the two as Arendt's public man would surely do—speaks to the penalties and costs still associated with public action for women. Vida affirms the greater importance, and greater significance, of the "larger view of life" she now possesses, de-emphasizing, as other suffrage women insistently do, her "own little story." But though the novel ends forcefully, with Vida securing Geoffrey Stonor's support and affirming the meaning of her own struggle, it also seems conscious—as, in their different ways, all of the novels I have treated do—of the limitations of its own position. Vida ends with a "sombre flare of enthusiasm" (304)—acknowledging, in the midst of her avowal, the human cost that such affirmations, however fervent, entail.[42]

Perhaps the most telling prediction of the constrained energy of the novel's end, on the sense of pain at the moment of victory, is Robins's own set of remarks made at the "The Prisoners' Banquet" at the Savoy Hotel, on 11 December 1906. "It is an argument for haste," she notes, "that should the Suffrage be granted tomorrow, the world may still have to wait for the generation that is to grow up in the exercise of public duty, before women can take the personal satisfaction in it that so many men do":

> *I am reminded of that happy tribe in the inclement North called the Acheto-Tinneh, which being interpreted out of the Esquimau tongue is:* The People Who Live Out of the Wind.
>
> *Enviable folk these, for in the Arctic it is not still cold, but the wind that kills. The vast majority of women would belong to the Acheto-Tinneh if they could with honour—though some of you may tell me that preference has its origin in the defects of our training. But, as I say, the women of the future, brought up in the exercise of public duty, may find it not duty alone, but pleasure as well.*
>
> *For this generation, the fighting and the sacrifice.*[43]

Robins's speech is a moving commentary on the difficulties associated with public action for this generation of women. The pain of exposure, the longing for privacy, the sense of relief in shelter—all these are evoked in the midst of her call to arms. Robins's sense that there might one day be "satisfaction" and "pleasure" in publicity gestures toward a future in which public life might be less impersonal than she imagines it in *The Convert.* But the present is characterized by sacrifice—even in this, the most positive of public novels.

Conclusion:
The Fate of Public Women

THE TEXTS I have examined in this study are situated between two key events: the 1840 Antislavery Convention, when women delegates were fenced off behind a bar to screen them from public view; and the removal in 1917 of the Ladies' Gallery grille, whose purpose was, similarly, to prevent women's interference in political affairs and whose removal immediately preceded the granting of female suffrage in 1918 and the anticipated election of women members to the House of Parliament. These two events, emblematic as they are both of historical continuity and of historical change, provide the context for a subgenre of literary texts that I have called the feminine political novel. In all such novels the struggle to provide a means for female public appearance is central—however guarded or enigmatic, however complicated or unusual the manifestation of female political life may appear. Scenes of female publicity are indeed often vexed ones—troubled by the anxiety about female exposure, by the fear that female publicity might fundamentally alter the foundations of society, and by the concern that women's engagement in public life could obliterate sexual difference altogether. Of course such scenes are also complicated by changing attitudes toward women's public lives—by perspectives that make it possible, even in the midst of resistance, to create space for female political activity, to describe its complex operations, and even in some cases to refashion the very terms by which it must be understood.

I have described Charlotte Brontë's representation of the self-screening of her heroine as a transitional stance in the history I am presenting. In *Shirley* Brontë takes the notion of coverture—a legal term that speaks to the restraint upon a woman's intercourse with the world by defining her incorporation and disappearance into her husband—and transforms coverage into a term of (limited) power. Self-screening is a voluntary act by a heroine who understands the cultural constraints with which she lives and sees the advantages both of protection and of the measured liberty that protection affords. Shirley's various screens allow her to "see without being seen," to gain access to knowledge that she would normally receive only in mediated forms, and to baffle male interpreters who would otherwise use their knowledge to gain advantage over her. Navigating the territory between constraint and cover, finding space for the exercise of her faculties in the context of known limitations, Shirley's complex roles—from male mimic, to disguised philanthropist, to secretive witness—challenge conventional understandings of the distribution between male and female action. Even Brontë's conversion of public themes into private spectacle suggests that she manipulates the terms of the public/private debate: the spectacle of intimacy with which *Shirley* concludes is both an acknowledgment of Brontë's sense of limits (no public spectacle would be safe) and an expression of her desire to manifest the self where self-manifestation is truly possible.

In the next decade Elizabeth Gaskell depicts a heroine for whom active engagement in politics is the most central feature of her experience. *North and South*'s Margaret Hale at first unwillingly relinquishes her domestic Eden and enters the universe of Milton-Northern—a world of political discussion and industrial debate. The novel describes her gradual insertion of herself into the streets, conversation, and political life of Milton, and finally her emergence as a political actress on the stage of an industrial strike. She leaves behind the womanly protections of privacy, enters the crowd, speaks on behalf of the millowner, and even covers *him* so that he can be protected from his workers. Shirley's restraint and self-screening become Margaret Hale's freedom and exposure—but the misreading of motives that Shirley fears is the unavoidable consequence of Margaret's problematic self-exhibition. Gaskell's heroine is vulnerable to multiple misconstructions of her character and to a sexual misreading of her actions that seem to deprive of her of the very power conferred upon her as she entered the world of Milton and moved freely within it.

But Gaskell also insists—quite stunningly I believe—that the loss of moral purity that Margaret experiences is positive and educative. She emerges from her ordeal with a more complex conception of woman's mission, now understood not as the moral influence exercised at home by (pure) women upon (faulty) public men but, rather, as the public labor that women must perform in the world if they are to have what Margaret later calls "freedom in working." Margaret's revision of this notion is connected to her own sense that she is not herself a pure woman at home, that she has indeed lost that moral status. But Gaskell accepts and values Margaret's defective human nature, converting our sense of her sexual shame into a vision of her sexual maturity. Gaskell thus intimates that exposure, indiscretion, and sexual taint are emphatically *not* stigmatizing, and also that the engagement of women in public affairs is at once possible, risky, and transforming.

If Margaret Hale must relinquish her sense of home as Eden, then George Meredith's Diana, though houseless and thus vulnerable at the beginning of *Diana of the Crossways*, quickly discovers that the domestic cover she had sought

brings the extreme regulation of intimacy, the imposition of restraint, the en-
forcement of subjection. Meredith thus begins by representing domestic privacy
as a violation, rather than a preserve, of personal liberty, and he moves to release
his heroine from its grip. But the loss of cover brings with it categorical confusion—Diana is neither married nor unmarried, neither imprisoned nor free—
and the ambiguity of her condition highlights Meredith's sense of woman's ambiguous place. Meredith is also quick to associate his heroine with the sort of
taint that Margaret Hale experiences (though Diana's is the taint of scandal) and
then to reveal that he has no interest in false purity. Meredith de-etherealizes
morality (as in a different manner Gaskell does as well), intimating that he values
a heroine with intellectual power who will gain strength through education,
work, and the exposure to public life.

Like Brontë and Gaskell before him, Meredith also reveals the difficulty of
distinguishing private from public action as his heroine, Diana, and her "lover"
Dacier, mix romance and politics, love and larceny. Diana is a parliamentarian
by proxy, a writer, and a source of political advice; Dacier is a member of
Parliament, a character in Diana's fiction, and a producer of political information. Their slide from sex to politics and back again is repeated frequently as
Diana buys love with money; Dacier buys love with political knowledge; she
betrays her lover for money; and he buys off scandal with marriage to another
woman. Like Shirley, Diana has political knowledge that others don't know she
possesses, but unlike Shirley, Diana uses her knowledge not just to enjoy the
tilting of power in her direction but to participate in the exchanges that constitute her world. Meredith's mergers are both perilous and promising: they are
dangerous occasions of confused action, but they are also opportunities to experience love in the world of deeds.

The fluidity of Meredith's public and private worlds is astonishing, but
Meredith preserves his ability to make them so by insisting upon the chastity of
his heroine. Diana may defy boundaries and represent an extraordinary level of
hybridity in her own person, but Meredith severs the connection between publicity and sexuality that threatens Shirley and perturbs Margaret. In doing so, he
suggests that female access to public life and the perilous, if promising, exchanges
between worlds that he describes are possible precisely because he excludes sexuality from the equation.

Freedom from restraint is the note on which Gissing begins *In the Year of
Jubilee* as well—as Nancy Lord shakes off her chaperons and wanders alone
through the streets of London during Victoria's Jubilee Day celebrations. Unlike
her predecessor, Shirley, who restrains both herself and her friend Caroline during the riot at the mill, Nancy restrains no one: she moves from city streets, to

public monuments, to commodified self display in a sequence of events that Gissing finds problematic indeed. Nancy's experience of life in the public arena is an experience of bad publicity—of dangerous exposure in a world where everyone wants his (or her) name in the newspaper. When Nancy's private life mimics her dissolute public one, when public marriage mimics illicit sexuality, and when homes are described as "factories of quarrel and hate," then Gissing suggests that some means must be found to recreate privacy in a world whose boundaries seem to have disintegrated.

His resolution represents an odd inversion of Meredith's notion of female freedom: if Diana's categorical suspension is liberating, Nancy's condition as a married woman who loves but does not live with her husband is intriguingly not. Gissing's "new marriage" represents the need both to generate community (through the public acknowledgement that marriage confers) and to guarantee personal liberty (husband and wife are free agents), but Nancy finds the freedoms of her new marriage rather less satisfying than she might wish. Gissing's novel is also interesting for the way it reintroduces sexual intimacy into its plot. Unlike Meredith's heroine whose very chastity seems to make possible the fluid relations between privacy and publicity, Gissing's heroine is sexually alive, perhaps dangerously so. Gissing seems eager both to represent her sexuality and also to cordon it off, assigning to Nancy a life that is theoretically interesting and complex but that in its lived reality seems, finally, both constrained and limiting.

Elizabeth Robins's *The Convert* represents a deliberate effort to rewrite the terms of this debate. She begins by suggesting, as in other ways Gaskell and Meredith do, that the private sphere is not a realm of privileged intimacy but a world penetrated and even constituted by politics. Men who expose women to public ridicule in private, like politicians whose legislative acts penetrate family life, reveal that the blurring of the public/private boundary is not an invention of suffragists but rather a state of affairs already in place. Because Robins's novel is both art and propaganda, it makes its point about the breakdown of distinctions more aggressively and argumentatively than other novels do, but the point is one that we have seen before. Robins will use it, however, to disarm opposition to women's bold entry into political life, suggesting that they need not veil or restrain themselves because they have already been uncovered, that they must not fear violation because, at least in a certain sense, they have already been violated, and that they should not fear exposure because their knowledge of the public realm puts them in a position to unmask the unmaskers.

Indeed, one of the most powerful features of Robins's novel is its representation of women as agents, rather than objects, of interpretation, as figures who control the interpretive field rather than serving as occasions of others'

misinterpretation and exposure. The suffrage speakers are exposed on the platform, but they exercise their power to expose persons in the crowd as they turn
taunts back on their makers; expose ideas as they redefine them; and remake
social history as they reread key events. The novel *assumes* the supple intercon-
nection of public and private realms, but it practices quite openly a different
kind of fluidity—the conversion of persons, history, and ideas.

What makes this possible is Robins's representation of the suffrage women
as invulnerable to attack because they lack what she calls personal vanity. They
are knowing but selfless; they are indifferent to what is said about them. The
dissociation of public life from personality is critical in the novel because it
reintroduces in yet another form the notion that publicity and sexuality must be
uncoupled if women are successfully to occupy public space. Robins complicates
this notion by making her heroine at once sexually attractive (she is a woman
with a past) and someone who relinquishes that past on behalf of a cause that
she values more highly than self. She also complicates it by suggesting that what
her heroine really wants is not sexuality but motherhood—that she is a woman
who knows the cost of what she relinquishes but wishes, as she bids it farewell,
to remake even that familiar notion.

The story that these novels tell extends itself interestingly, but uneasily, into
the modern period. To be sure, some of the hard-won advances of nineteenth-
century novels become commonplaces in twentieth-century fiction: E. M. Forster's heroines in *Howards End* (1910) are avowed feminists who live alone, chap-
eroned only by an ineffective, effeminate brother (unthinkable in the prior century). The conflict between the Schlegels, invested in a world of "personal
relations," and the Wilcoxes, who have their "hands on the ropes," replays Margaret Hale's conflict between private values and public engagements—except
that Forster is more suspicious than Gaskell about the value of the Wilcox's
world of "grit" (as Margaret Schlegel calls it), of "telegrams and anger" (as Helen
names it).[1]

The marriage of Margaret to Henry (of Schlegel to Wilcox) and the effort
to "connect" that it represents has catastrophic consequences (195). Pursued past
marriage (as Margaret Hale's marriage to Thornton is not) the narrative traces
Henry's failure—not to connect private to public, but to connect parts of himself
to each other. The defensive posture of Forster's characters at the end, recovering
from the breakup of their lives and returning to the country to "pick up the
pieces" as London encroaches (354, 355), argues both for the power of personal
relations and also for the renewed sense of danger associated with public industry
and its urban complications.

D. H. Lawrence's *Women in Love* (written in 1916 but not published until

1920) begins with a similar vision of free women whose opening dialogue in the novel punctures the conventions of love and marriage. Ursula, a school-teacher, and Gudrun, an art student returning from London (like Mary Ward's Marcella in an 1894 novel of the same name)—are new women who do what they wish in their work and in their love lives and who openly voice their unconventional views about men and sex: Gudrun and Ursula are only tempted "*not* to" marry. Ursula "loathes" her own house, despises the "sordid familiar place!" But when the sisters take a walk through the colliery town that evokes similar walks in nineteenth-century novels—Margaret Hale's and Nancy Lord's—both are repelled as well by "the whole sordid gamut of pettiness, the long amorphous, gritty street." Like the underground train station in *In the Year of Jubilee*, the mining town is, to Gudrun, "like a country in an underworld"; Gudrun's brightly colored stockings are an object of comment to the colliers' wives, much as Margaret Hale's clothing brought verbal attention in the streets of Milton. But Gudrun wishes to annihilate the colliery women's world; she has no interest in moving outward into it, as both Shirley Keeldar and Margaret Hale wish to do. This is a function of her already occupying a different public world (in Chelsea and Sussex, the more sophisticated precincts of London), but it is also related to Lawrence's sense that the public realm to which Victorian feminists wished to gain access was now, early in the twentieth century, defaced, unworthy, beyond redemption.[2]

The sexual freedom that nineteenth-century novelists contemplated as their female heroines entered the public sphere is a central feature of the lives of twentieth-century heroines, but it isn't necessarily tied to public commitments. Freedom from constraint lets Gudrun Brangwen be "drawn out at evening into the main street of the town" with its "shops . . . blazing and packed with women," its streets with "men, mostly men," and money "spent with almost lavish freedom" (175). Like Nancy Lord in the Jubilee Day scenes of Gissing's novel, Gudrun here finds her "boy," though he isn't as "common" as Luckworth Crewe. An electrician, "a scientist with a passion for sociology" (176), he and Gudrun have an undescribed affair. Freedom from constraint, not social engagement, generates sexual experimentation (as it also does in Gissing's novels, and with similar difficulties).

But there is no *polis*, no sphere of moral engagement that generates, for good or ill, the connection between public life and sexuality that the novels I have examined either embrace or reject. It is difficult to know why this particular feature of the movement outward into the public realm has so few proponents in novelists of the modern period. The specter of the Great War, the war itself, and then its aftermath; the movement toward aesthetic experimentation; perhaps even the disappointment that followed the granting of limited female suffrage in 1918 (as some feminists predicted, it did not radically transform women's lives or, in Gladstone's worried phrase, "uproot all the landmarks of society")—all of these contributed to the domination on the literary scene of novels that explored interiority and consciousness rather than politics and publicity. Dorothy Richardson, Katherine Mansfield, and Virginia Woolf, for example, de-emphasize plot and action and, thus, accounts of a complex, highly public social world. In Virginia Woolf's *To the Lighthouse* (1927), the unmarried, liberated artist Lily Briscoe finds freedom in her work (she paints), but Lily doesn't even care about having her paintings displayed. The interest in and anxiety about exposure in nineteenth-century novels becomes in early twentieth-century nov-els an interest in interior revelation: "I have had my vision," Lily declares at the end of the novel, when she paints her final brushstroke.[3] No exhibition follows.

Jean Rhys's heroines, in novels of the 1930s, offer the most interesting examples of female characters who have been liberated from their families, re-leased into the world, set adrift—and find themselves with nothing to do. The heroine of *After Leaving Mr. Mackenzie* (1931) moves from one hotel room, and one city, to another: she is Gissing's "rootless lodger" gone wild. Her only resource is her body, and she uses it to make her way in a world that provides (again) no real work for women to do. The public sphere that they are free to inhabit is empty of meaning, resourceless; when the body wears out, so do the funds. Rhys's frank treatment of the trade in women suggests that access to the public sphere, once acquired, creates a new set of problems to be solved. In what meaningful ways can public space be occupied? Is there a shared culture toward which women turn when access to it is opened? What work in the public realm are women free to do? Does sexual freedom bring liberation, or is sexuality (as it seems to be in Rhys) just another opportunity for failed connection? Is female privacy a new resource, or merely an old prison?

The questions that Rhys articulates are new questions, but they build on the legacy of exploration and inquiry that writers before her undertook. The nineteenth-century controversy about separate realms, and about the conse-quences of moving, gradually, from privacy toward publicity, was a complex debate, incorporating at virtually every stage protections, contradictions, and concerns that reflected the values and possible dangers of public experience. If nineteenth-century feminists and those who learned from them sought and gained access to the public realm, they were also aware of the risks that public exposure might bring, and they illuminated those risks even while they took them.

The early twentieth-century writers to whom I have briefly referred lived in a public world that their precursors had opened. Sometimes they take that world as a given, moving about in it, as Forster's and Lawrence's women do, with a freedom that some nineteenth-century writers would have found astonishing. Often, modernist writers find the public realm bleaker than their predecessors would have guessed, and they withdraw their attention to a private realm associated not with "abstract principles of right and wrong" but, like Woolf's heroines, with imagination and aesthetic exploration. At other times early modern writers find the world bleak but without alternative: Rhys's heroines are wanderers who have no interior illumination but also nowhere else to go. Their stark exposure raises new questions about women's lives in the unprotected public sphere—questions that our nineteenth-century predecessors launched, and carried forward, with a poignant sense of their difficulty, complexity, and power.

Notes

Bibliography

Index

Notes

Introduction: In Promiscuous Company

1. *Times*, 13 June 1840.
2. Phillips, quoted in Stanton, *History of Woman Suffrage*, 60, 61; Garrison and Garrison, *Garrison*, 2:382.
3. There is no evidence that Brontë read the reports on the convention, but her family were avid consumers of newspapers in general and of political news in particular. She may well have seen the newspaper accounts of this event.
4. The phrase is from Emily Davies, *The Higher Education of Women*, 18.
5. Sarah Lewis, *Woman's Mission*, 53.
6. Blackstone, *Laws of England*, 1:430; Norton, *English Laws*, 166 (see also Kaye, " 'Non-Existence,' " 558); Cobbe, "Criminals, Idiots, Women and Minors," 789.
7. Coleridge, quoted in da Costa, "Criminal Law," 178; Linton, "Judicial Shock to Marriage," 691 (also quoted in Shanley, *Marriage and Law*, 182).
8. *Hansard*, 3d ser., 192 (1868): 1360 (also quoted in Holcombe, *Wives and Property*, 153); *Hansard*, 3d ser., 200 (1870): 611.
9. Stephen, *Girton College*, 99; Clough, *Anne Jemima Clough*, 232, 295–96, 257, 240.
10. Aytoun, "Rights of Woman," 194, 197.
11. *Hansard*, 3d ser., 187 (1867): 831, 841.
12. *Hansard*, 3d ser., 206 (1871): 80, 201 (1870): 620, 206 (1871): 81.
13. Gladstone, *Female Suffrage*; also quoted in Hollis, 320.
14. Ibid.
15. For the association between female publicity and prostitution, see Walkowitz, *Prostitution and Victorian Society*; Nead, *Myths of Sexuality*; Anderson, *Tainted Souls and Painted Faces*; Michie, *Outside the Pale*. I have not discussed here novels about actresses, though a comprehensive study of this subject is surely needed. Novels in this category might include, Geraldine Jewsbury's *The Half Sisters*, Wilkie Collins's *No Name*, Henry James's *The Tragic Muse*, and George Gissing's *The Nether World*. See also Auerbach, *Ellen Terry*; Davis, *Actresses as Working Women*; Rosen, "At Home upon a Stage."
16. See also Holcombe, *Victorian Ladies at Work*; Walkowitz, *Prostitution and Victorian Society*; Vicinus, *A Widening Sphere* and *Independent Women*; Lewis, *Women in England*. With the exception of Holcombe's book (1973), all were published during the 1980s. The phrase "a widening sphere" is, as noted above, the title of Vicinus's well-known collection of essays and a response to the term *proper sphere,* commonly used to describe woman's rightful (domestic) place in Victorian society.

17. Gallagher, *Industrial Reformation*, 115. In *The Politics of Story*, published three years after Gallagher's groundbreaking book, Rosemarie Bodenheimer returned to the subject of industrial fiction and to women's roles in it. Bodenheimer seems less inclined than Gallagher to see women's public engagements, their movements "into the social frey" either as inevitably reinforcing the public private split or as examples of the way that public forays throw into stark relief their cultural opposites (*Politics of Story*, 8). Indeed, because she focuses both on social history and on "story," she is more inclined to credit fictional resolutions and find them authentic—though as I shall note in chapter 1, she discounts female public experience when it fails to meet the criterion of social *effectiveness*. Still, because Bodenheimer views novelistic work as "a mixture of social knowledge, social wish, documentary material, and literary convention, invoked or overturned" (6–7), her readings seem both more powerful and less imprisoned by the cultural materials through which she reads them.

18. Poovey, *Uneven Developments*, 2, 4, 78, 144. Poovey examines, among other things, Caroline Norton's contribution to the Matrimonial Causes Act of 1857, the relationship between Brontë's *Jane Eyre* and the social construction of the governess, and the life and writings of Florence Nightingale.

19. Armstrong, *Domestic Fiction*, 26, 27.

20. Ryan, *Banners to Ballots*, 4, 17.

21. Walkowitz, *City of Dreadful Delight*, 7, 18, 22.

22. Nord, *Walking Victorian Streets*, 12, 3, 13, 14.

Chapter 1: Public Restraint and Private Spectacle in *Shirley*

1. Wise and Symington, *Brontës: Lives, Friendships, Correspondence*, 30 October 1852, 3:331. Brontë scholars eagerly await Margaret Smith's forthcoming edition of the Brontë letters. In the meantime I have used the often disputed, but still widely cited and familiar, Shakespeare Head edition of the letters edited by Wise and Symington (hereinafter referred to as *LFC*). I will also cite on occasion excerpts from letters that do not appear in Wise and Symington but do appear in Juliet Barker's magisterial *The Brontës*—a book that questions the authenticity of Wise and Symington's letters and also the sanitation of them (they correct the Brontës' spelling, especially in the juvenile writings, and in the letters they also eliminate dashes in favor of traditional punctuation). I will (briefly) quote Barker where she quotes from manuscripts not otherwise available in print.

2. *LFC*, 12 January 1853, 4:34–35.

3. On the Brontë-Taylor correspondence, see Barker, *The Brontës*, 353; the letters to Mary do not survive. In a letter to Williams, Brontë notes that "both men and women should have the power and the will to work for themselves. . . . both sons and daughters should early be enured to habits of independence and industry" (*LFC*, 15 June 1848, 2:220; see also 3 July 1849, 3:4–5). She encouraged him to support his daughters in their educational endeavors, noting she was "glad that Louisa has a chance of presentation at Queens' College. I hope she will succeed. Do not—my Dear Sir—be indifferent—be earnest about it" (*LFC*, 3 July 1849, 3:4). She also noted with approval a work on female education by the first principal of Owens

College, John Alexander Scott, which suggested to her that it was at last becoming possible to be "thoughtful and well read without being universally stigmatised" (*LFC*, 19 March 1850, 3:88).

4.   Brontë, *Jane Eyre*, 39; further citations will appear in the text.

5.   *LFC*, 15 January 1850, 3:67; *Compact Edition, Oxford English Dictionary*, s.v. "mêlée."

6.   Brontë's remark about her visibility appears in *LFC*, 1 November 1849, 3:29; the comment about the Literary Fund Society Dinner is in Barker, *Brontës*, 638; on Brontë's trip to London, see Peters, *Unquiet Soul*, 288; both Peters and Barker quote Brontë's response to her visit to the Ladies' Gallery: see *Unquiet Soul*, 288, and *Brontës*, 640–41.

7.   Brontë's letter to Williams appears in *LFC*, 12 May 1848, 1:215; the response to Gaskell is in *LFC*, 27 September 1850, 2:149; the review article to which Brontë refers is "Woman's Mission." Bauer and Ritt attribute the essay to T. H. Rearden, but the *Wellesley Index to Victorian Periodicals* cites "——Adams." The essay's authorship is apparently unclear.

8.   See Lister, "Rights and Conditions," 189, 190. If Brontë did not know Lister's essay, she would surely have known others like it and would have been familiar at some point with the texts it reviews. In addition to Lewis's *Woman's Mission*, Lister considers *Woman's Rights and Duties* (an 1843 review of which, by J. G. Phillimore, the Brontë family would certainly have seen in *Blackwood's Magazine*), Ellis's *Women of England*, and Lady Morgan's *Woman and Her Master*. Ellis later wrote a review critical of the unwomanliness of the author of *Jane Eyre*, and in 1851, in one of his many packages of books, Smith Williams included Lady Morgan's tract among a group of books on "feminine issues"; Brontë indicated that she felt he had chosen well (Barker, *Brontës*, 634).

9.   Lister, "Rights and Conditions," 204.

10.   "Woman's Mission," 352, 353.

11.   Ibid., 354, 366.

12.   Lewis, *Woman's Mission*, 53, 50, 54, 67–68, 68.

13.   Ibid., 68.

14.   "Woman's Mission," 358, 359.

15.   Ibid., 361, 370, 371.

16.   Brontë, *Jane Eyre*, 141; *LFC*, 27 September 1850, 2:150; "Woman's Mission," 359, 361, 362.

17.   Taylor, "Enfranchisement of Women," 291, 293, 295; *LFC*, 20 September 1851, 3:278

18.   Taylor, "Enfranchisement of Women," 300, 301; *LFC*, 20 September 1851, 3:278.

19.   Brontë, *Shirley*, 19; further citations will appear in the text.

20.   Greg, "Why Are Women Redundant?" quoted in Hollis, *Women in Public*, 33.

21.   I focus most of my attention in this chapter on the character of Shirley. Other critics speak interestingly and well about Caroline's plight (Gilbert and Gubar) and about Caroline and Shirley's relationship (Cosslett).

22.   Moglen, *Self Conceived*, 176; Gilbert and Gubar, *Madwoman in the Attic*, 381, 382; Bodenheimer, *Politics of Story*, 49. I treat Gilbert and Gubar's reading of *Shirley* at length in my own "Playing at Being a Man."

23.   Garber, *Vested Interests*, 16. Much of Shirley's (male) behavior is prototypical of the

"new woman" of a much later decade—the 1890s. See Cunningham, *New Woman*, 42: "She separates fighting dogs as efficiently as she deals with squabbling curates, wields a pistol with confidence, and when bitten by a supposedly rabid mongrel, calmly cauterizes the wound herself." Cunningham finds Shirley's eventual romantic interest completely incompatible with such extraordinary behavior, a position with which I shall later take issue.

24. Chase, *Eros and Psyche*, 59.

25. Briggs, "Social Themes," 213.

26. Brontë herself disliked, and was extremely anxious about, "scenes." She visited the Smith family following the completion of *Shirley* and wrote to her father after a dinner party given in her honor by her hosts (Thackeray was also present): "I get on quietly. Most people know me, I think, but they are far too well bred to show that they know me, so that there is none of that bustle or that sense of publicity I dislike" (*LFC*, 4 December 1849, 3:54; also quoted in Gerin, *Evolution of Genius*, 405). Gerin describes the special preparations the Smiths made on Brontë's behalf, knowing her "dislike of fuss" (*Evolution of Genius*, 406). Though the issue is broader and more complex than this, it seems important to note that the cultural anxiety about publicity obviously has in Brontë a psychological source as well.

27. The uneasiness about exposure in *Jane Eyre* is related to, but clearly different from, the apprehension about exposure in *Shirley*. Shirley desires to "see without being seen" at the mill; Jane uses the same words to describe her first response upon seeing Rochester's guests arrive at Thornfield (195) and about her presence amidst Rochester's company where she also hopes to "gaze without being observed" (203). The difference between the two novels is instructive: Shirley's dangerous public setting contrasts with Jane's social and domestic one; Shirley's invisibility contrasts with Jane's partial obscurity (she is veiled or obscured behind a curtain in the first scene and sits in the shade, half hidden behind a window curtain in the second). No one knows of Caroline's and Shirley's presence at the mill; Rochester knows that Jane is there and will soon veil himself (in gypsy's garb), to meet her mediated gaze with his own.

28. Bodenheimer, *Politics of Story*, 48–49; Eagleton, *Myths of Power*, 46, 47, 50.

29. Gilbert and Gubar, *Madwoman in the Attic*, 384, 375; Keefe, *World of Death*, 140, 141.

30. Gilbert and Gubar, *Madwoman in the Attic*, 376–80, 388–92.

31. See Tayler, *Holy Ghosts*, 199. Tayler does not perceive this section as the "weak spot in *Shirley*" that other critics claim it to be. But she also does not discern its relation to the Louis/Shirley story: "To render its themes in novel form was the work of Charlotte's final masterpiece, *Villette*." But there are similarities between Louis and Paul Emmanuel which suggest that the themes of this devoir are at work in both: the two men are violators of the privacy of the women they love: M. Paul goes through Lucy's desk in the same way that Louis goes through Shirley's—poking his cigar into all of her most private spaces. The sparring, aggressive, master/pupil relation is a significant version of the male/female love relation in Charlotte Brontë's imagination.

32. The movement from public to private concerns is often cited as an example of the novel's lack of coherence or unity. The debate, however, is as old as the remark that

"in 'Shirley' . . . all unity is wanting" (G. H. Lewes, "Currer Bell's 'Shirley,'"
159). As Bodenheimer correctly points out, the unity problem "was the central
issue in *Shirley* criticism for some time" (*Politics of Story*, 39), and in a certain sense
it remains so. Bodenheimer cites early essays by Briggs, Korg, and Shapiro, and
many more could be added to the list. The issue variously entails the displacement
of public themes by private ones (nearly all critics agree that this occurs), the
relation of the Luddite problem to the "woman question" (Bodenheimer, Eagleton, Webb), the concern that claims to realism are overwhelmed by the romantic
conclusion (Donald Stone), and the belief that the promise of radical feminism is
contained or even defeated by disappointingly conservative marriages (Gilbert and
Gubar, Cunningham, Boumehla). These divisions and oppositions are sometimes
read—as they were first by Lewes—as signs of defective art and internal inco-
herence; but they are also read as evidence of Brontë's instinct to compromise
(Eagleton) or, conversely, as her active refusal to do so (Bodenheimer). I acknowledge the conflicts and oppositions that these readings represent but will propose
a more "unified" reading of Brontë than most critics feel inclined to press, a
reading that, among other things, will argue that there are social and political
origins for the move from public to private.

33. John Kucich usefully describes relationships like the one between Louis and Shirley
as examples of "eroticized combativeness." He suggests that they can be "an effective
instrument of mastery over others, as well as a sign of social authority, and not
simply submission" (*Repression in Victorian Fiction*, 77, 39). Other critics have noted
the erotic features of Shirley and Louis's relationship, though not always in ways
that suggest its subversive power. Eagleton identifies the "pronounced dialectic of
power and submissiveness . . . in the strongly sadomasochistic relationship between
Shirley and Louis Moore," but he sees it as an attempt to occupy "a middle ground
between the most objectionable extremes of reverence and rebellion" (*Myths of
Power*, 57–58). Igor Webb argues that the contradictory demands of such a relationship are not resolved in the novel: "The need for a full life for women as for
men leads to the demand for equality—but this demand is not compatible with the
need for a master" (*Custom to Capital*, 154).

34. Moglen, *Self Conceived*, 186. Like Moglen, Stone regards as "the greatest disappointment" of the novel "Brontë's inability to think of any fate for her independent-
minded co-heroine, with her masculine name and magisterial ways, other than to
be consigned to the arms of the least interesting of all Brontë's heroes" (*Romantic
Impulse*, 124). Gilbert and Gubar similarly deplore the fact that "by the end of the
novel . . . Shirley is a 'bondswoman' in the hands of 'a hero and a patriarch'"
(*Madwoman in the Attic*, 395). Shirley Fister echoes this view when she declares that
"both Caroline and Shirley are finally 'mastered' and tightly bound in matrimonial
chains, a fate which strikes us as incommensurate with their earlier vigorously-
voiced protest against restrictive sexual ideologies" (*Victorian Women's Fiction*, 98).
Nancy Armstrong even suggests that Shirley's marriage requires her to "relinquish
her masculine qualities and grow to resemble the unextraordinary" and in her view
"unattractive" Caroline Helstone (*Desire and Domestic Fiction*, 214). On the other
side of the argument, Kucich reminds us that "our sense of fatal compromise and
of emotional constraint in Brontë's fiction is emphatically a modern one." Contem-

porary audiences, as Kucich notes, found the novels "shamelessly passionate" (*Repression in Victorian Fiction*, 38).

35.   Ewbank, *Proper Sphere*, 41.

Chapter 2: Woman's Work in *North and South*

1.   Chapple and Pollard, *Letters of Mrs Gaskell*, 7 April 1853, 228 (hereinafter referred to as *Gaskell Letters*).
2.   Ibid., 7 April 1853, 227.
3.   Ibid., ? early February 1853, 223.
4.   See Herstein, *Smith Bodichon*, 80. See also Cornwallis, "Property of Married Women," 336–38, in which the petition was reprinted in its entirety along with a selection of signatories.
5.   Smith, "Most Important Laws," 6, 8, 14; petition, quoted in Cornwallis, "Property of Married Women," 338.
6.   *Gaskell Letters*, 26 April 1850, 113; ?April 1850, 109; 21 March 1848, 54. The letters to Chapman include 2 April 1848, 55; 13 April 1848, 55–56; 5 December 1848, 64; 7 December 1848, 65. The final quotation is from Smith's petition, quoted in Cornwallis, "Property of Married Women," 336.
7.   See Strachey, *Cause*, 63. F. D. Maurice is described as having "rendered an immense service to the Women's Movement." Queen's College, though nonresidential and limited in its range of intellectual offerings (it identified itself as teaching "all brands of female knowledge"), was still very important as a first step toward higher education for women. Entrance examinations for university education were not open to women until 1866, and Emily Davies opened her college at Hitchin in 1869.
8.   For Gaskell's complaint about difficult schoolmistresses, see *Gaskell Letters*, 12 December 1850, 138; comments about Meta's career are from Uglow, *Habit of Stories*, 317; the final quotation is, again, from Barbara Smith's petition, quoted in Cornwallis, "Property of Married Women," 337.
9.   Herstein, *Smith Bodichon*, 80; Uglow, *Habit of Stories*, 311; *Gaskell Letters*, 5 April 1860, 607, 606, 607.
10.   *Gaskell Letters* 14 May 1850, 115–18; February 1850, 106.
11.   *Gaskell Letters*, 27 October 1854, 316, 320; see Strachey, *Cause*, 24.
12.   Gaskell, *North and South*, 508; further citations will appear in the text.
13.   See Cazamian, *Social Novel in England*; Tillotson, *Novels of the 1840s*; Williams, *Culture and Society*, 104; Pollard, *Novelist and Biographer*, 10, 138.
14.   Wright, *Basis for Reassessment*, 10, 14, 132; Dodsworth, Introduction, 20; Hardy, "Gaskell and Eliot," 170.
15.   Bodenheimer, *Politics of Story*, 66; David, *Fictions of Resolution*, 41.
16.   Gallagher, *Industrial Reformation*, 149, 172, 179, 168, 113; Nord, *Walking the Victorian Streets*, 173, 174. See also Yeazell's notion that political novels with female heroines often shift from "dangerous aggression to . . . modest evasion and restraint" as a "maneuver of [political] containment" ("Why Political Novels Have Heroines," 143). In a more recent book on Gaskell, Schor censures critics who have been "quick to read the heroine's progress as only into subjectivity and sexuality," but see my statement of this position in "In Promiscuous Company," which predates Schor's

book. Schor correctly identifies the movement of *North and South* "into the density of Industrial England and its economic and sexual politics" but believes that the novel raises "its own criticism of the condition-of-England novel," of Margaret's role as "mediatrix," and of Gaskell's relation to her own novelistic authority (*Scheherezade in the Marketplace*, 120). In her account of urban women, Nord acknowledges my position on female publicity in the novel but disagrees with my analysis of the ending. Nord argues—like David, Yeazell, Gallagher, and others—that Gaskell is unable to "resist the interpretation of public gestures as private ones" (*Walking the Victorian Streets*, 174 n. 58).

17. *Gaskell Letters*, 6 December 1853, 255–56.
18. See Milton, *Paradise Lost*, 4.335–36, 4.132–42.
19. Gallagher, *Industrial Reformation*, 178.
20. Parkes, "Educated Women," 290, 295–96, 290.
21. Bodenheimer identifies the tradition that places *North and South* in the context of Jane Austen's *Pride and Prejudice* (53 n. 27) but doesn't mention the example of the postponed marriage plots. It is interesting to note in the context of those common plots that Margaret does not marry the man who proposes to her "in spite of" himself, while Elizabeth Bennett eventually does. Henry Lennox belongs to the wrong world—indeed, to Margaret's old Harley Street world—and would not make for Margaret an appropriate match in a novel that concerns her relation to the world of industrial work.
22. As I suggested in my Introduction, it was commonplace both in novels and in nonfictional sources to identify publicity with sexuality. Parkes focuses on the problems associated with loss of caste, but she notes too that "no sane person will tolerate the notion of flinging girls into those very temptations and dangers which we lament and regret for boys." She points out that if mothers are "less stringent than fathers" about the circumstances of working life for their daughters, that is only because they "know less what external life is than because they would shrink less from exposing their daughters to evil example." Parkes's solution is to protect "every woman in the exercise of her profession" ("Educated Women," 296). Gaskell imagines no such protections for Margaret.
23. Parkes, "Condition of Working Women," 3.
24. Felicia Bonaparte describes Margaret in this scene "as a man" and claims that Margaret and Thornton's business partnership at the novel's end must remain intact "if Margaret is to maintain her identity as an independent, male, woman" (*Gypsy Bachelor of Manchester*, 192, 193). To assign male status to Margaret is to diminish rather than to highlight the transgressive quality of her activity. After all, if this is what men do, and Margaret is a male, then she will not experience the exposure or misconstruction of character that is such a central experience in the novel and to which the novel's language insistently points.
25. Pikoulis, "Varieties of Love and Power," 189 n. 1.
26. *Gaskell Letters*, 14 May 1850, 115; Gaskell and Brontë had not yet met.
27. David, *Fictions of Resolution*, 43.
28. Bodenheimer, *Politics of Story*, 66.
29. Brontë, *Shirley*, 336, 337.
30. Lister, "Rights and Conditions," 204.

31. Gaskell, *Mary Barton*, 351–52; further citations will appear in the text.

32. Lewis, *Woman's Mission*, 53; *North and South*, 247.

33. Keith Thomas has argued that, historically, "female chastity has been seen as a matter of property . . . the property of men in women." Thus, a wife's adultery "immeasurably diminishe[s]" its value. He also observes that "the language in which virginity is often described" is the language of "the commercial market," where "girls who have lost their 'honor' have also lost their saleability" ("The Double Standard," 210). Thomas's argument sheds light on Margaret's self-condemnation: speaking of herself as damaged property is a way of registering her sexual taint.

34. Secrecy cannot, of course, be identified absolutely with privacy, as Sissela Bok has pointed out, but the two are still significantly connected. Bok argues that the "practice of secrecy" is frequently tied to "concepts of sacredness, intimacy, [and] privacy," as well as to "silence, prohibition, furtiveness and deception" (*Secrets*, 6). In *North and South* secrecy is a kind of deep privacy that intentionally conceals what privacy conceals anyway, namely intimacy.

35. Coral Lansbury affirms that Margaret is not a traditional Victorian heroine but a woman who "demands the right to be an active member of society, unconfined to any particular region or class." But Lansbury refuses to see the ways in which publicity and sexuality coincide. Instead, she upholds Margaret's defensive and, in my view, mistaken belief that the sexual reading of her experience during the strike is an unfair one—a confusion of "social responsibility with personal infatuation" (*Novel of Social Crisis*, 118).

36. For Molly's sense of guilt about Osmond Hamley's secret marriage, see Gaskell, *Wives and Daughters*, 246; for Cynthia's indiscretions with Mr. Preston, see 528; further citations will appear in the text.

37. Elliott, "Female Visitor," 33.

38. Summers, "Women's Philanthropic Work," 58, 45.

39. See Barrett, *Ellice Hopkins*. Barrett's biography of a "lady visitor" explains that "having the old ideas as to woman's work, Mrs Hopkins [Ellice Hopkins's mother] shrank from publicity for women, and was herself very gentle, quiet and domestic. Hence it must often have been a severe trial to her that her daughter should take up work which led her along such thorny roads, and into such a glare of publicity, and even of opprobrium" (Barrett, 23; also quoted in Summers, "Women's Philanthropic Work," 60). Margaret, it is clear, plans to operate on just such "thorny roads"— though even Edith suggests that she is more at risk of soiling her clothes than her character. See also F. K. Prochaska's chapter 4, "In the Homes of the Poor," 97–137. Prochaska offers a more positive interpretation of the impact on the poor of lady visitors. Prochaska claims that though visitors were often single, they were not always so: Margaret might well maintain her interest in visiting even as a married woman.

40. Nord suggests that "Margaret tries to reproduce in London the kind of independent urban rambling in the neighborhoods of the poor to which she had become accustomed in Milton. It is striking, however, that the narrative only hints obliquely at this activity and never describes Margaret's experience of it" (*Walking the Victorian Streets*, 172). I agree with Nord that Gaskell's portrait is oblique, but I also believe that Gaskell is suggesting work that amounts to more than "independent rambling."

41. For additional proponents of this view, see, for example, Basch, *Relative Creatures*, 250; Newton, *Women, Power and Subversion*, 164, 168; and Stoneman, *Elizabeth Gaskell*, 120.

Chapter 3: Rectitude and Larceny in *Diana of the Crossways*

1. Stevenson, *Ordeal of George Meredith*, 261; C. L. Cline, *The Letters of George Meredith*, 1 March 1876, 3:1704 (hereinafter cited as *Meredith Letters*).
2. *Dictionary of National Biography*, "Louisa Shore," 151–52. In 1877, the year following the exchange of letters to which I refer, the article was reprinted as a pamphlet entitled *The Citizenship of Women Socially Considered* and was signed with the initials "L. S." Arabella Shore identifies the article as her sister's in her own "Memoir" attached to *Poems by A. and L.* (1896). The *Wellesley Index to Victorian Periodicals* confirms the attribution (3:650).
3. Shore, "Emancipation of Women," 137, 138; Cobbe, " 'Criminals, Idiots, Women, and Minors,' " 778.
4. Morley, *Recollections*, 1:47, quoted in J. S. Stone, *Meredith's Politics*, 48; Mill, *Subjection of Women*, 6–7; Shore, "Emancipation of Women," 137, 138, 139; Mill, *Subjection of Women*, 13; Shore, "Emancipation of Women," 140.
5. Shore, "Emancipation of Women," 142; Mill, *Subjection of Women*, 16.
6. Meredith, *The Egoist*, 87; further citations will appear in the text.
7. Mill, *Subjection of Women*, 12.
8. Shore, "Emancipation of Women," 144; *Hansard*, 3d ser., 206 (1871): 86; Shore, "Emancipation of Women," 144; *Hansard*, 85; Shore, "Emancipation of Women," 148. Shore regularly refers in her essay to the 3 May 1871 debate on the Women's Disabilities Bill.
9. Shore, "Emancipation of Women," 146, 147.
10. It would be difficult to identify every source in which this point is made. Two instructive examples from the 1870s and 1880s are Anne Isabella Robertson, "Women's Need for Representation" (1872; reprinted in Jane Lewis, *Before the Vote Was Won*), and Elizabeth Wolstenholme Elmy, "The Parliamentary Franchise for Women" (1884; also reprinted in Lewis). Robertson points out that "politics so frequently affect the minutest particulars of household life and economy—all that is acknowledged even now to be within the range of what is called 'women's sphere'—[that] it cannot be denied that women should take an interest in such affairs" ("Women's Need for Representation," 145). Elmy argues in favor of the vote as a means of opposing invasive legislation such as the Contagious Diseases Acts. She insists that "our exclusively male Legislature is perfectly capable, under the guise and pretence of 'protection,' of exposing to the same insecurity and possible outrage every girl and woman in these kingdoms" ("Parliamentary Franchise for Women," 406).
11. *Hansard*, 3d ser., 206 (1871): 100; Shore, "Emancipation of Women," 150–51, 152–53.
12. Shore, "Emancipation of Women," 171.
13. First, Meredith defends his "Ballad," arguing that he isn't describing the "present situation" of women "but one in which it is to be understood that the beautiful *i.e.*

the most thoughtless of the sex hitherto, turn the chief weapon of the sex to the benefit of their sisters . . . and thus partly by beauty, partly by earnest argument, win one champion, and make their antagonist melancholy" (*Meredith Letters*, 1:568). The ballad is peculiar, invoking familiar clichés about women that Meredith himself surely did not believe and yet suggesting that the convert to the cause is a "fool-flushed old noddy" (l. 267). It is also odd because it is hard to see the ballad apart from "the present situation" (*Meredith Letters*, 1:520–21).

14. Meredith, *Beauchamp's Career*, 262; further citations will appear in the text. It is generally agreed that Seymour Austin was modeled on Russell Gurney, member for Southampton from 1865 to 1878. But Gurney was an open advocate both of the Married Women's Property Bill and of women's suffrage—more activist, in other words, than Meredith's Seymour Austin. This contradiction in Meredith's representation of his women's rights activist is reflected in disagreements among critics about the nature of Meredith's feminism. To take just two examples: J. S. Stone identifies Austin with Meredith, noting that the former is "much more radical than either Shrapnel or Beauchamp [in *Beauchamp's Career*]—as radical, in fact, as George Meredith himself was becoming in this matter" (*George Meredith's Politics*, 71). But Austin's point of view—that the professions should be opened and that the growing strength of increasingly worldly women would permit them to alter their own situation—was certainly not the perspective of the parliamentary advocate of legal reform. Penny Boumehla disagrees with Stone in her essay on the novel: "Diana's venture into the 'men's phrases' of the public world proves to be the very thing that brings about collapse into the generic fate of narrated woman"—that fate being silence ("Rattling of her Discourse," 207).

15. Meredith, "Uses of the Comic Spirit," 3, 15, 15, 31–32.

16. Williams, "Unbroken Patternes," 47; Meredith, "Uses of the Comic Spirit," 41, 46; Meredith, *Diana of the Crossways*, 17; further citations will appear in the text.

17. *Meredith Letters*, 13 June 1889, 2:964; January 1905, 3:1513; 19 May 1904, 3:1497; 13 June 1889, 2:964; 28 April 1885, 2:769. For additional insight into Meredith's opinions on women's suffrage, and especially on the militant movement, see also *Meredith Letters*, 13 June 1889, 2:1206 in which he (humorously) berates Mrs. Leslie Stephen for signing the infamous Petition against Woman Suffrage that appeared in the *Nineteenth Century* in 1889; 28 October 1906, 3:2331, in which he defends, in a letter to the *Times*, the spirited demonstration of 23 October that led to the imprisonment of Christabel Pankhurst and others. His letter of 13 April 1907, 3:2359, is less forgiving of the intemperateness of the militant suffrage women. Meredith also explains in a 1908 letter why he would not sign the petition circulated by Violet Hunt, insisting that he was "not in harmony with the present militant movement, and for the reason that I am, as I have for long been, in favour of the suffrage for women. I like them for the high spirit they show, but think them erratic in policy" (26 February 1908, 3:2442).

18. See Huddleston, Introduction, xii.

19. Caroline Norton, *English Laws for Women*, 166; Huddleston, Introduction, i, ii.

20. Fowler, "Prophecy for Feminism," 32; Boumehla, "Rattling of her Discourse," 202. Boumehla's point is that "as a *witty* woman," as "foreigner and criminal, outcast and outlaw, Diana stands outside the narrative of the 'women of waxwork' and 'women of happy marriage.' " Like the figure in Meredith's "Idea of Comedy," she is dan-

gerous to the social order for all these reasons. In the end, however, she must be "recuperated into the marriage plot"—returned to "the generic fate of narrated woman" (which is to stop talking). Boumehla sees this as Meredith's means of "explor[ing] the limits and enact[ing] the problems of writing that 'sketch of the women of the future,'" (204–7). Fowler, "Prophecy for Feminism," 32. Fowler generally takes a more moderate position: Diana is "one of the first moderns . . . the woman repressed, yet . . . the woman who revolts and prophetically achieves a measure of self-determination" (35–36). I will offer a different reading of the novel's conclusion.

21. See *Macbeth* 5.1.38.

22. See also Shore, "Emancipation of Women," 139.

23. Egeria was the nymph known in legend for her wise counsel to the second king of Rome.

24. Sir Lukin's praise of Diana's manliness recalls Mill's comment in parliamentary debate that "unless there are manly women, there will not much longer be manly men" (*Hansard*, 3d ser., 187 [1867]: 823). Mill puts the matter positively, though it is more common to see it put negatively. Shore refers to the familiar complaint that women who favor the suffrage are "strong-minded women" and that these are thought to be "women of masculine character and idiosyncracies"—a "formidable" objection ("Emancipation of Women," 149). Shore comments that a "freer culture" will "ennoble" woman, "not transform her into man—why was such a senseless misrepresentation ever dragged in to degrade a serious discussion into burlesque?" ("Emancipation of Women," 172–73). It is noteworthy that Meredith imagines Diana's sexual hybridity in such positive terms—and especially that he does so in the words of Sir Lukin.

25. Shore focuses on what she calls "the old fetish worship of husbands . . . that curious religion which made it a wife's highest virtue to pay the obedience of a slave to a master, however cruel, capricious, or irrational he was, however noble and wise she, might be—in short, the greater his mental and moral inferiority to her, the greater the merit of her absolute submission. . . . This fetishism continues in a modified shape to be represented by the law of the land" ("Emancipation of Women," 167). Meredith is more interested in the fetishizing of the sexual purity of the wife, but the two are obviously related.

26. Norton was romantically linked with George Herbert, a young statesman; when news of the Corn Law Repeal was leaked to the *Times*, Norton was thought to have been the responsible party. Meredith's disclaimer, now always printed at the front of the novel, emerged from complaints by Norton's friends that he was reviving the old scandal. See for example Fowler, "Prophecy for Feminism," 31.

27. McGlamery, "In His Beginnings," 483–84; Marcus, "Clio in Calliope," 189; Beer, *Change of Masks*, 160.

28. Wilt, *Readable People*, 55.

29. Deis, "Marriage as Crossways," 22; Marcus, "Clio and Calliope," 189, 190.

30. Jenny Calder discusses this scene at length but oddly does not point out the monetary metaphors that dominate it ("Cash and the Sex Nexus," 40–45).

31. Jan B. Gordon argues that the "blurred barrier" between public and private in the novel is associated with an "increasing volume of gossip" and that "long the object of gossip . . . [Diana] must eventually become its instigator" ("Internal History,"

258, 259). Dacier's response is to associate Diana with *prior* gossip about her *after the fact*. Moreover, although he recognizes himself as the "leaky vessel," as (an unwitting) player in the general circulation of gossip, he does not see his participation in the translation of love into larceny.

32. It is a commonplace of debates on women's suffrage that women in the West are connected to women in the East, though Englishmen did not like to think so. In the 3 May 1871 parliamentary debate this likeness appears as a remark made by Edward Backhouse Eastwick, that England serves as an example to India where women are "degraded to a state little better than slavery. How could we expect that Indian women would be emancipated from the imprisonment of the zenanah [the harem] . . . as long as we proclaim the inferiority of women in this country" (*Hansard*, 3d ser., 206 [1871]: 78).

33. Wilt describes Constance Asper as "spun-sugar" (*Readable People*, 51), but Meredith's point about Constance is that she represents a negative, fetishized version of chastity from which he wishes to distinguish Diana. For a view closer to my own, see Baker, "Sanctuary and Dungeon," 75.

34. Elam, "Conjugating Romance," 181.

35. Baker, "Sanctuary and Dungeon," 75.

36. Conrow, "Ideal of Purity," 205.

37. Baker, "Sanctuary and Dungeon," 80.

38. Wilt, *Readable People*, 59.

39. Ibid., 74; Beer, *Change of Masks*, 165; Lindsay, *Life and Work*, 268; Stone, *Meredith's Politics*, 151; Elam, "Conjugating Romance," 194, 196.

40. When Meredith wanted to portray relationships as submission and relinquishment of self, he did so in the words of Sir Willoughby Patterne: "Give all and claim all; cancel and create; extinguish and illuminate" (333). Clara describes what feels like the "death of the imagination"—a much stronger term—as Willoughby "dragged her through the labyrinths of his penetralia, in his hungry desire to be loved more" (417).

41. Shore, "Emancipation of Women," 176.

42. Forster, *Aspects of the Novel*, 91. For an excellent summary of the history of critical opinion on Meredith, and particularly on his reputation for "novelty and unorthodoxy" (3), see chapter 1 of Joseph Moses's *The Novelist as Comedian* (3–15).

43. Stevenson, *Ordeal of George Meredith*, 231.

44. Another parallel should be noted—between *Beauchamp's Career* and *Shirley*. In *Shirley* the women are reluctant to break into the men's room at the mill for fear that their characters will be misconstrued. They must be content with witnessing rather than preventing the battle that ensues, though Shirley declares that "seeing without being seen" is surely better either than being absent or being misunderstood. Cecilia Halkett does (in the mid 1870s) what Shirley cannot do (in the late 1840s): she enters the men's smoking room with her friend Mrs. Lespel to uncover the men's plot against Nevil. She tears down and burns some "animated verses" about Renée, "the French Marquees [sic]" that are pinned to the wall along with Nevil's electoral address (180–81). She also breaks her word to her father and alerts Nevil to the plan, saving him from the "scandal of the public entry into Bevisham on the Tory wash-box" secretly designed by his friends to "burlesque [him] in the sight of the

town" (he is a Radical, not a Tory, 197). Meredith thereby dramatizes Cecilia's growing independence of her father, her willingness to cross the line into the men's preserve, and her independent, effective political action.

45. Howard, " 'Delicate' and 'Epical' Fiction," 168.

46. Shore, "Emancipation of Women," 171.

Chapter 4: Crowds and Marriage in *In the Year of Jubilee*

1. Gissing, *In the Year of Jubilee*, 22; further citations will appear in the text.

2. Mathiessen et al., *Collected Letters of George Gissing*, 2 June 1893, 5:113. Hereinafter referred to as *CL*.

3. *CL*, 5:114; some proponents of women's education, including Emily Davies, acknowledged but feared the connection between the agitation for the suffrage and the struggle for women's education (Strachey, *Cause*, 141); *Times*, 5 January 1869.

4. *Daily News*, quoted in *Englishwoman's Review* no. 17, (1874): 43–45.

5. Strachey, *Cause*, 258; Rubinstein, *Before the Suffragettes*, 18.

6. See Showalter, *Sexual Anarchy*, 3.

7. *CL*, 2 September 1885, 2:345.

8. *CL*, 21 June 1887, 3:125.

9. See Korg, *Critical Biography*, 185; *CL*, 2 June 1893, 5:113; Fernando, "Aspects of Anti-Feminism," 109.

10. See Coustillas, "Gissing's Feminine Portraiture," 101; Goode, *Ideology and Fiction*, 170; Cunningham, *New Woman*, 151.

11. James, *Notebooks*, 82. James would later take up the subject of this entry in a novella about newspapers entitled *The Reverberator* (1888); *CL*, 21 June 1887, 3:125, 126.

12. Grand, "New Aspect," 271; Ouida, "The New Woman," 610. Ellen Jordan, David Rubinstein, and Ann Ardis have all explored what Ardis calls the "genealogy" of the term *new woman* and have suggested how the debate about her evolved (see Ardis, *New Women, New Novels*, 179 n. 1.). Jordan dates the first use of the term to Grand's May 1894 essay ("Christening of the New Woman," 19). Rubinstein traces it to a group of essays that appeared two months earlier in the March 1894 issue of *Nineteenth Century* magazine (*Before the Suffragettes*, 16–23); these essays include "The Revolt of the Daughters I. A Last Word on 'the Revolt,' " by B. A. Crackanthorpe; "The Revolt of the Daughters II. Daughters and Mothers," by M. E. Haweis; and a pair of responses to these, including "A Reply from the Daughters I," by Kathleen Cuffe, and "A Reply from the Daughters II," by Alys. W. Pearsall. Crackanthorpe's first piece, "The Revolt of the Daughters," to which the above are sequels, appeared in the January number of *Nineteenth Century* and is also a key part of the genealogy.

13. Linton, "Wild Women," 79, 83, 80.

14. Linton, "Social Insurgents," 597, 600.

15. Rubinstein, *Before the Suffragettes*, 12; Crackanthorpe, "Revolt of the Daughters," 25.

16. Crackanthorpe, "Revolt of the Daughters," 26, 29.

17. Ibid., 30.

18. Ibid., 26.

19. See Cunningham, *New Woman*, 145: Nancy "chafes against her father's old fashioned

ideas of ladylike behavior, and signals her dissatisfaction with his insistence on chaperonage by sallying forth alone into the midst of the jubilee-night crowds." As I will shortly suggest, Nancy has other reasons, as well, for "sallying forth."

20. Thomas Richards points out—contra Gissing—how well organized and orderly the celebration was. "Well before the long procession wound its way around the streets of London, preparations had been underway in the office of Works to insure that the Jubilee would come off like clockwork." Richards also notes that "many of the Jubilee's leading events were designed primarily to show how smoothly Victorian institutions functioned" ("Image of Victoria," 10, 11). Richards does affirm the instinct toward "maximum possible exposure" and the spectacular "commodification of Victoria's image" that lay at the heart of the event (12, 13), but the connections that Gissing draws among self-exposure, social confusion, and sexual abandonment are very much the novelist's own.

21. Baedeker, *London and Its Environs*, 154.

22. For a different reading of this important scene, see Goode, *Ideology and Fiction*, 173–75. See also William Wordsworth's poem "Composed Upon Westminster Bridge, September 3, 1802," which this scene calls to mind. Wordsworth's speaker *is* at the mid point of his universe, but the awakening city he describes, though it includes "ships, towers, domes, theaters and temples" (l. 6), is at the same time "asleep" and "still" (l. 13, l. 14); it does not present the viewer with the problems that Gissing's urban vista does, in part because Wordsworth has imagined away the city's occupants.

23. Welsh, *George Eliot and Blackmail*, 61; Warren and Brandeis, quoted in Welsh, 62; the jurists also note that "the intensity and complexity of life, attendant upon advancing civilization, have rendered necessary some retreat from the world, and man, under the refining influence of culture, has become more sensitive to publicity, so that solitude and privacy have become more essential to the individual." Their assertion could easily function as an epigraph to the last Gissing novel published in his lifetime, *The Private Papers of Henry Ryecroft* (1903).

24. Rachel Bowlby identifies the difficulties associated with attaining "success in a cultural sphere already defined as degraded" and points to the identification of "femininity and commercialization" that results when women do appear in public ("Review," 28).

25. Mabel Collins Donnelly notes the connection when she states that the Jubilee night scene "serves as a foreshadowing of [Nancy's] yielding to primitive impulse when a crisis comes" (*Grave Comedian*, 171). John Sloan also makes the connection, and argues, further, that the latter scene's "very explicitness would seem to betray a hidden fascination with the liberating possibility of woman's active sexuality" ("Worthy Seducer," 358).

26. Gillian Tindall observes that railroad stations are "a source of incidental emancipation for Gissing's women, who are thus enabled to go about town on their own much more fully than their mothers would have" (*Born Exile*, 259). In this instance Jessica Morgan experiences her freedom in a destructive way: it stimulates her to lose control of her judgment and to engage in battle with her friends.

27. Welsh explains the relationship between publicity, privacy, and blackmail in the

Notes to Pages 134 to 143   203

market economy of nineteenth-century England this way: "So much exposure of personal qualities among agents unacquainted or unaccustomed to one another has in turn enhanced the value of privacy and created the need for intimacy. A very natural resistance to publicity has encouraged the sharing of secrets as a deliberate means to intimacy. Secrecy in turn becomes a temptation to betrayal, or to the threat of betrayal that is blackmail" (*George Eliot and Blackmail*, 72–73). Welsh's description is pertinent here, though it doesn't fully convey the sense in which degraded financial dealings that are tied to intimate relations reproduce the marketplace conditions they seek to escape.

28. Fernando argues that "the real mark of Gissing's resistance to emancipation rests in the way he implied in his novels that emancipationist ideas gave direct rise to the social vulgarity he detested" ("Aspects of Anti-Feminism," 112). This oversimplifies matters. As the train station scene suggests, the real problem in Gissing's novels is the impossibility of identifying the source of the vulgarity.

29. As Korg notes, "Marriage, which was supposed to sanctify the relations between the sexes, often proved to be its ultimate corruption" (*Critical Biography*, 186).

30. Tindall points out in her Introduction to the Harvester edition of *Jubilee* that Nancy's situation "is exactly like that of an unmarried mother" (xvi). Adrian Poole rightly says that "the novel deliberately goes *beyond* the supposedly crucial cataclysm of the heroine's sexual 'fall' " (*Gissing in Context*, 197). In my view it does so in a surprising fashion—both marrying and, in a sense, unmarrying the heroine so that she escapes official shame but fully experiences her own fallenness.

31. Cunningham highlights Gissing's "proud" suggestion that "here is one type of relation . . . which will never be sullied by jealousy and will not drive a long-suffering husband mad" (*New Woman*, 148). Tindall concurs, describing this as "the fantasy of the faithful wife with whom one doesn't actually have to live" (*Born Exile*, 187). In a certain sense both are right. But I am trying to suggest that Gissing's vision is both evasive and constructive.

32. Greenslade, "Disease of Civilization," 518, 519 (the phrase "new hedonism" is Allen's); Allen, "Plain Words," 455.

33. Allen, "Plain Words," 457, 458.

34. See Showalter, *Sexual Anarchy*, 49–54.

35. Tony Tanner's thesis is relevant here: "Rules of marriage, economic rules, and linguistic rules" are "systematically interdependent" so that "the breakdown of one implies the breakdown of all three. The failure of marriage as a binding form may either presage or be isomorphically related to the imperilment of the particular economic system in which it is embedded and to a possible crisis in the status and ownership of the accepted discourses" (*Adultery in the Novel*, 85).

36. Deirdre David suggests that Gissing is "both resistent to and immersed in, patriarchal systems of belief and practice"; the result of this is that the "novel of patriarchal generation is firmly rejected. But the novel of female independence is not fully embraced" ("Ideologies," 119). John Sloan puts the case somewhat differently, but his formulation is useful: "The voice of protest and freedom for oppressed womanhood is never completely silenced, but it can only be heard athwart the novel's own declarations, with their shoring up of the traditional claims of authority, pa-

triarchy, and class" ("Worthy Seducer," 58). Instead of paralysis and enervation, these critics find the embodiment of a complex social process whose successes were at once significant and compromised, real and partial.

37. Thomas, "The Double Standard," 216.

38. Gissing, *The Odd Women*, 291. Further citations will appear in the text.

39. According to Rubinstein, many middle-class women who pursued careers in the labor market of the 1890s did so at great cost: "arduous years of training, the sacrifice of marriage and, in some cases, of a normal private life" (*Before the Suffragettes*, 80). Gissing presents these costs as ideological commitments at the beginning of *The Odd Women* and as felt losses at the novel's end.

40. I explore a different version of this problem in "Joy behind the Screen: The Problem of 'Presentability' in George Gissing's *The Nether World.*"

Chapter 5: Renovating Public Space in *The Convert*

1. Gissing, *The Whirlpool*, 308, 312.

2. John, *Staging a Life*, 150.

3. Robins, *George Mandeville's Husband*, 158–59.

4. Marcus, "Art and Anger," 125–26.

5. James, quoted in Hunt, *I Have This to Say*, 52; Robins, *Theatre and Friendship*, 19; John, *Staging a Life*, 147.

6. *Theatre and Friendship*, 5 March 1907, 261; 1 May 1907, 263; Marcus, "Art and Anger," 73.

7. *Theatre and Friendship*, 1 May 1907, 263.

8. John, *Staging a Life*, 147; Gates, *Actress, Novelist, Feminist*, 166.

9. Arendt, *Human Condition*, 26.

10. Wiley, "Matter with Manners," 112.

11. Robins, *The Convert*, 42; further citations are in the text.

12. *Compact Edition, Oxford English Dictionary*, s.v. "Citizen."

13. Ibid., s.v. "Hottentot."

14. As I have already noted, the relationship between suppressed Englishwomen and their counterparts in the East is a frequent subject of discussion in materials about women's suffrage (see chapter 3, note 32) and it will arise repeatedly in *The Convert*. In a lecture delivered at New Hall, Tavistock, 11 March 1871, Millicent Garrett Fawcett considers the argument "that the exercise of political power by women is repugnant to the feelings and quite at variance with a due sense of propriety." But she notes that "in Turkey, a woman who walked out with her face uncovered, would be considered to have lost all sense of propriety—her conduct would be highly repugnant to the feelings of the community. In China, a woman who refused to pinch her feet to about a quarter of their normal size, would be looked upon as entirely destitute of female refinement. We censure these customs as ignorant, and the feelings on which they are based as quite devoid of the sanction of reason" (quoted in Lewis, *Before the Vote Was Won*, 114).

15. Strachey, *Cause*, 293–95.

16. For the entire debate, see *Hansard*, 4th ser., 155 (1906): 1570–88; for the bracketed comments from the Ladies' Gallery see 1584–85; the account of the banner's ap-

pearance in the gallery is from Robins, *Way Stations*, 24; see Strachey's description of the Speaker of the House and of the removal of the protestors (*Cause*, 299); Evans's comments were reported both in the *Times*, 26 April 1906, and in *Hansard* 1586, 1587. According to Sylvia Pankhurst, it was Irene Miller who called out, "Divide! Divide!" and Teresa Billington (later Greig) who "thrust [the] little white flag . . . through the grille" (Pankhurst, *Suffragette Movement*, 210). Billington-Greig, it should be noted, is the model for Ernestine Blunt.

17. *Englishwoman's Review* no. 77 (1879): 397, 398; Edgeworth, *Memoirs*, 182.
18. *Englishwoman's Review* no. 77 (1879): 398; *Hansard*, 3d ser., 29 (1835): 632, 638; 33 (1836): 530.
19. *Hansard*, 3d ser., 35 (1836): 1076, 1077.
20. On the renovations of the House that led to the installation of the grille, see Port, *Houses of Parliament*, 148; on the commissioner of work's recommendation that the screen be removed and for Gladstone's comments, see *Hansard*, 3d ser., 192 (1884): 107–8, and 296 (1885): 1004.
21. *Hansard*, 3d ser., 206 (1871): 88.
22. Ibid., 120.
23. *Hansard*, 4th ser., 155 (1906): 1578, 1574; *Times*, 28 March 1912; *Hansard*, 4th ser., 155 (1906): 1574, 1575.
24. Lister, "Rights and Conditions," 204 (see chapter 2 for a fuller discussion of Lister).
25. Shore, "Emancipation of Women," 150, 151 (see chapter 3 for a fuller discussion of Shore).
26. Robins explored the issue again in 1924: "Women who sit in the sun of private benevolence have been soothed to a mean complicity in the misery of the mass. In the eyes of many a woman to whom men have been "very nice" there seems an ungraciousness too raw in pointing out that man's private attempt to right the public balance by compensatory kindness to individuals, by conferring special immunities and privileges, by all that he has thought of as chivalry, is to offer a dole of bright farthings in lieu of the gold of equal inheritance" (*Ancilla's Share*, xliv–xlv).
27. Ibid., 85–86.
28. Detailed accounts of bodily violence became commonplace during the period of the militant suffrage movement, though forcible feeding—an infamous example of bodily violation—would not emerge as an issue for several years. The women who were imprisoned in the aftermath of a violent suffrage demonstration outside Bingley Hall, Birmingham, on September 17, 1909, went on a hunger strike, and the first reports of forcible feeding appeared in the press one week later, on September 24, 1909 (Mackenzie, *Shoulder to Shoulder*, 124–25).
29. Lisa Tickner notes that, in the aftermath of the great Mud March of 1907 (so named because of the wet weather), women involved in the planning of the 1908 procession "responded to the accusation that they were 'making a spectacle of themselves' by doing precisely that. . . . They were part of the spectacle, but they also produced and controlled it; as active agents they need not passively endure the gaze of onlookers. . . . They could invite it, respond to it, work with it and move on. Their bodies were organized collectively and invested politically and therefore resistant to any simply voyeuristic appropriation" (*Spectacle of Women*, 81).
30. Gissing, *Jubilee*, 280, 374.

31. James, *Bostonians*, 374.
32. Joanne Gates observes that, unlike Olive Chancellor in *The Bostonians*, Vida does not actually want to take Jean away from Stonor, and she has no personal designs on the young woman. She uses Jean as she crafts her bargain with Stonor; she wants what Jean can win her in the larger scene of action. (*Actress, Novelist, Feminist*, 165).
33. Mulford, "Women's Suffrage Literature," 183.
34. Hynes, *Edwardian Turn of Mind*, 202; Showalter, *Literature of Their Own*, 221.
35. Hynes, *Edwardian Turn of Mind*, 202, 204; Robins, *Way Stations*, 187.
36. Stowell, *Stage of Their Own*, 18; Mulford, "Women's Suffrage Literature," 183.
37. The end of the novel explains Vida's interest in the Tunbridge children at the novel's beginning. As Ilmberger notes, these are "the children she can never have" (*Love and Friendship*, 51).
38. Davis, "New Woman and New Life," 20.
39. Hynes, *Edwardian Turn of Mind*, 203, 206; Stowell, *Stage of Their Own*, 21.
40. The manufacturers in Gaskell's *North and South* are described in terms similar to those that describe Robins's suffragettes: "There was much to admire in their forgetfulness of themselves and the present, in their anticipated triumphs . . . at some future time which none of them should live to see" (217). In Gaskell's universe, however, private and public are always collapsing into each other, in ways that are finally exhilarating and transforming. This is not true of Robins's more pained and painful vision.
41. Arendt, *Human Condition*, 58.
42. Vida Levering and *The Odd Women*'s Rhoda Nunn find themselves in similar circumstances at the novels' conclusions. Both commit themselves to lives of noble duty, and both relinquish the pleasures of private experience. Gissing's narrator even says about Rhoda, after she has relinquished her lover and returned to her work, that her "conception of life was larger" (291). But what Gissing means is that Rhoda returns to her life of public commitment with a real understanding of the sacrifices that such a life entails. The novel explores Rhoda's sexual self-development, so her "larger" conception of life is one that includes the significance of a passion she now knows, but must live without. Vida, on the other hand, begins with sexual knowledge. Her larger conception of life is based on a changed assessment not of the significance of passion but of the significance of public commitment.
43. Robins, *Way Stations*, 35. Robins spoke following the release from Holloway Gaol of the women arrested in the lobby of the House of Commons on 3 October 1906. The women had gone, as Robins records, to send a message to the prime minister "asking whether the Government proposed to do anything" about the suffrage question. When the answer came back "no," there were protests and ultimately arrests in the lobby. The Prisoners' Banquet followed the women's release from prison (*Way Stations*, 29).

Conclusion: The Fate of Public Women

1. Forster, *Howards End*, 28; further citations are in the text.
2. Lawrence, *Women in Love*, 54, 57, 58; further citations are in the text.
3. Woolf, *To the Lighthouse*, 209.

Bibliography

Acland, Alice. *Caroline Norton.* London: Constable, 1948.

Allen, Grant. "Plain Words on the Woman Question." *Fortnightly Review* 52 (1889): 448–58.

Anderson, Amanda. *Tainted Souls and Painted Faces: The Rhetoric of Fallenness in Victorian Culture.* Ithaca, N.Y.: Cornell Univ. Press, 1993.

Ardis, Ann. *New Women, New Novels: Feminism and Early Modernism.* New Brunswick, N.J.: Rutgers Univ. Press, 1990.

Arendt, Hannah. *The Human Condition.* Chicago: Univ. of Chicago Press, 1958.

Armstrong, Nancy. *Desire and Domestic Fiction.* New York: Oxford Univ. Press, 1987.

Auerbach, Nina. *Ellen Terry: Player in Her Time.* New York and London: W. W. Norton, 1987.

[Aytoun, William E.]. "The Rights of Woman." *Blackwood's Magazine* 92 (1862): 183–201.

Baedeker, Karl. *London and Its Environs: Handbook for Travellers.* 14th rev. ed. London: Dulau and Co., 1905.

Baker, Robert S. "Sanctuary and Dungeon: The Imagery of Sentimentalism in Meredith's *Diana of the Crossways.*" *Texas Studies in Literature and Language* 18 (1976): 63–81.

Barker, Juliet. *The Brontës.* New York: St. Martin's, 1994.

Barrett, R. M. *Ellice Hopkins.* London: Wells & Gardner, 1907.

Basch, Françoise. *Relative Creatures: Victorian Women in Society and the Novel.* New York: Schocken, 1974.

Bauer, Carol, and Lawrence Ritt. *Free and Ennobled: Source Readings in the Development of Victorian Feminism.* New York: Pergamon, 1979.

Beer, Gillian. *Meredith: A Change of Masks.* London: Oxford Univ. Press, 1970.

Blackstone, William. *Commentaries on the Laws of England.* 4 vols. 1765–69. Reprint, Chicago: Univ. of Chicago Press, 1979.

Bodenheimer, Rosemarie. *The Politics of Story in Victorian Social Fiction.* Ithaca, N.Y.: Cornell Univ. Press, 1988.

Bok, Sissela. *Secrets: On the Ethics of Concealment and Revelation.* New York: Vintage, 1984.

Bonaparte, Felicia. *The Gypsy-Bachelor of Manchester: The Life of Mrs. Gaskell's Demon.* Charlottesville: Univ. Press of Virginia, 1992.

Boumehla, Penny. *Charlotte Brontë.* Bloomington: Indiana Univ. Press, 1990.

———. " 'The Rattling of Her Discourse and the Flapping of Her Dress': Meredith Writing the 'Women of the Future.' " *Feminist Criticism: Theory and Practice.* Ed. Susan Sellers. Toronto: Univ. of Toronto Press, 1991.

Bowlby, Rachel. "Review of *The Whirlpool.*" *Gissing Newsletter* 21 (1985): 22–29.

Briggs, Asa. "Private and Social Themes in *Shirley*." *Brontë Society Transactions* 13 (1958): 203–14.

Brontë, Charlotte. *Jane Eyre*. 1847. Reprint, Harmondsworth: Penguin, 1966.

———. *Shirley*. 1849. Reprint, Harmondsworth: Penguin, 1974.

———. *Villette*. 1853. Reprint, Harmondsworth: Penguin, 1979.

———. *The Professor*. 1857. Reprint, Harmondsworth: Penguin, 1989.

Calder, Jenny. "Cash and the Sex Nexus." *Tennessee Studies in Literature* 27 (1984): 40–53.

Cazamian, Louis. *The Social Novel in England, 1830–1850*. Trans. Martin Fido. 1903. Reprint, London: Routledge and Kegan Paul, 1973.

Chapple, J. A. V., and Arthur Pollard, eds. *The Letters of Mrs. Gaskell*. Cambridge: Harvard Univ. Press, 1967.

Chase, Karen. *Eros and Psyche: The Representation of Personality in Charlotte Brontë, Charles Dickens, and George Eliot*. New York: Methuen, 1984.

Cline, C. L. *The Letters of George Meredith*. 3 vols. Oxford: Clarendon Press, 1970.

Clough, Blanche Athena. *A Memoir of Anne Jemima Clough*. London: Edward Arnold, 1897.

Cobbe, Frances Power. "Criminals, Idiots, Women, and Minors." *Fraser's Magazine* 68 (1868): 777–94.

Collins, Wilkie. *No Name*. 1862. Reprint, Oxford: Oxford Univ. Press, 1992.

Conrow, Margaret. "Meredith's Ideal of Purity." *Essays in Literature* 10 (1983): 199–207.

Cornwallis, Caroline Frances. "The Property of Married Women." *Westminster Review* 66 (1856): 331–60.

Cosslett, Tess. *Woman to Woman: Female Friendships in Victorian Fiction*. Atlantic Highlands, N.J.: Humanities Press International, 1988.

Coustillas, Pierre. "Gissing's Feminine Portraiture." *George Gissing: Critical Essays*, Ed. Jean Pierre Michaux. Totowa, N.J.: Barnes and Noble, 1981.

Crackanthorpe, B[lanche] A[lethea]. "The Revolt of the Daughters." *Nineteenth Century* 35(Jan. 1894): 23–31.

Cunningham, Gail. *The New Woman and the Victorian Novel*. New York: Barnes and Noble, 1978.

da Costa, Mendes. "Criminal Law." In *A Century of Family Law 1857–1957*. Ed. R. H. Graveson and F. R. Crane. London: Sweet and Maxwell, 1957.

David, Deirdre. *Fictions of Resolution in Three Victorian Novels: North and South; Our Mutual Friend; Daniel Deronda*. New York: Columbia Univ. Press, 1981.

———. "Ideologies of Patriarchy, Feminism, and Fiction in *The Odd Women*." *Feminist Studies* 10 (1984): 117–39.

Davies, Emily. *The Higher Education of Women*. London: Alexander Strahan, 1866.

Davis, Jill. "The New Woman and the New Life." In *The New Woman and Her Sisters: Feminism and Theatre, 1850–1914*. Ed. Vivien Gardner and Susan Rutherford. Ann Arbor: Univ. of Michigan Press, 1990.

Davis, Tracy C. *Actresses as Working Women: Their Social Identity in Victorian Culture*. London: Routledge, 1991.

Deis, Elizabeth J. "Marriage as Crossways: George Meredith's Victorian-Modern Compromise." In *Portraits of Marriage in Literature*. Ed. Anna Hargrove. Essays in Literature. Macomb, Illinois: Western Illinois Univ., 1984.

Dodsworth, Martin. Introduction. *North and South*. New York: Penguin, 1970.

Donnelly, Mabel Collins. *George Gissing, Grave Comedian*. Cambridge: Harvard Univ. Press, 1954.

Eagleton, Terry. *Myths of Power: A Marxist Study of the Brontës*. London: Macmillan, 1975.

Edgeworth, Maria. *A Memoir of Maria Edgeworth with a Selection from Her Letters by the Late Mrs. Edgeworth*. 3 vols. London: Joseph Masters and Son, 1867.

Elam, Diana. " 'We Pray to Be Defended from Her Cleverness': Conjugating Romance in George Meredith's *Diana of the Crossways*." *Genre* 21 (1988): 179–201.

Eliot, George. *The Mill on the Floss*. 1860. Reprint, Harmondsworth: Penguin, 1982.

———. *Middlemarch*. 1871–72. Reprint, Harmondsworth: Penguin, 1982.

Elliott, Dorice Williams. "The Female Visitor and the Marriage of Classes in Gaskell's *North and South*." *Nineteenth-Century Literature* 49 (1994): 21–49.

Ellis, Sarah Stickney. *The Women of England, Their Social Duties and Domestic Habits*. London: Fisher, 1839.

The Englishwoman's Review of Social and Industrial Questions. 40 vols. 1866–1910. Reprint, New York and London: Garland, 1980–85.

Ewbank, Inga-Stina. *Their Proper Sphere: A Study of the Brontë Sisters as Early Victorian Female Novelists*. Cambridge: Harvard Univ. Press, 1966.

Fernando, Lloyd. "Gissing's Studies in Vulgarism: Aspects of His Anti-Feminism." In *George Gissing: Critical Essays*, Ed. Jean Pierre Michaux. Totowa, N.J.: Barnes and Noble, 1981.

Fister, Shirley. *Victorian Women's Fiction: Marriage, Freedom, and the Individual*. Totowa, N.J.: Barnes and Noble, 1985.

Forster, E. M. *Howards End*. 1910. Reprint, New York: Vintage, 1989.

———. *Aspects of the Novel*. 1927. Reprint, New York: Harcourt Brace, 1954.

Fowler, Lois Josephs. "*Diana of the Crossways*: A Prophecy for Feminism." *Carnegie Series in English* 12 (1972): 30–62.

Gallagher, Catherine. *The Industrial Reformation of English Fiction: Social Discourse and Narrative Form, 1832–1867*. Chicago: Univ. of Chicago Press, 1985.

Garber, Marjorie. *Vested Interests: Cross-Dressing and Cultural Anxiety*. London: Routledge, 1992.

Garrison, Wendell Phillips, and Francis Jackson Garrison. *William Lloyd Garrison*. 4 vols. 1805–79. Reprint, New York: Arno Press and the New York Times, 1969.

Gaskell, Elizabeth. *Mary Barton*. 1848. Reprint, Harmondsworth: Penguin, 1985.

———. *North and South*. 1854–55. Reprint, Harmondsworth: Penguin, 1970.

———. *Ruth*. 1853. Reprint, London: Dent, 1982.

———. *The Life of Charlotte Brontë*. 1857. Reprint, Harmondsworth: Penguin, 1981.

———. *Wives and Daughters*. 1866. Reprint, Harmondsworth: Penguin, 1980.

Gates, Joanne E. *Elizabeth Robins, 1862–1952: Actress, Novelist, Feminist*. Tuscaloosa: Univ. of Alabama Press, 1994.

Gerin, Winifred. *Charlotte Brontë: The Evolution of Genius*. Oxford: Oxford Univ. Press, 1967.

Gilbert, Sandra M., and Susan Gubar. *The Madwoman in the Attic: The Woman Writer and Nineteenth-Century Literary Imagination*. New Haven: Yale Univ. Press, 1979.

Gissing, George. *The Nether World*. 1889. Reprint, Brighton: Harvester, 1982.

———. *The Emancipated.* 1890. Reprint, Rutherford, N.J.: Fairleigh Dickinson Univ. Press, 1977.

———. *New Grub Street.* 1891. Reprint, Harmondsworth: Penguin, 1985.

———. *The Odd Women.* 1893. Reprint, New York: W. W. Norton, 1977.

———. *In the Year of Jubilee.* 1894. Reprint, London: Dent, 1994.

———. *The Whirlpool.* 1897. Reprint, Rutherford, N.J.: Fairleigh Dickinson Univ. Press, 1977.

———. *The Private Papers of Henry Ryecroft.* 1903. Reprint, Brighton: Harvester, 1982.

Gladstone, William. *Female Suffrage: A Letter from the Right Honorable W. E. Gladstone to Samuel Smith, M.P. April 11, 1892.* London: John Murray, 1892.

Goode, John. *George Gissing: Ideology and Fiction.* New York: Barnes and Noble, 1978.

Gordon, Jan B. "*Diana of the Crossways*: Internal History and the Brainstuff of Fiction." In *Meredith Now,* Ed. Ian Fletcher. London: Routledge and Kegan Paul, 1971.

Grand, Sarah. "The New Aspect of the Woman Question." *North American Review* 158 (1894): 270–76.

Great Britain. *Hansard Parliamentary Debates,* 3d and 4th series.

Greenslade, William. "Women and the Disease of Civilization: George Gissing's *The Whirlpool.*" *Victorian Studies* 32 (1989): 507–23.

Hardy, Barbara. "Mrs. Gaskell and George Eliot." In *The Victorians.* Ed. Arthur Pollard. Vol. 6 of *A History of Literature in the English Language.* 10 vols. London: Barrie and Jenkins, 1970.

Hardy, Thomas. *Tess of the D'Urbervilles.* 1891. Reprint, Harmondsworth: Penguin, 1978.

Harman, Barbara Leah. "In Promiscuous Company: Female Public Appearance in Elizabeth Gaskell's *North and South.*" *Victorian Studies* 31 (1988): 181–94.

———. "Joy behind the Screen: The Problem of 'Presentability' in George Gissing's *The Nether World* (1889)." In *The New Nineteenth Century: Feminist Readings of Underread Victorian Fiction.* Ed. Harman and Susan Meyer. New York: Garland, 1996.

———. "Playing at Being a Man: The Genesis of Publicity according to *Shirley.*" In *Making Feminist History: The Literary Scholarship of Sandra M. Gilbert and Susan Gubar.* Ed. William E. Cain. New York: Garland, 1994.

Herstein, Sheila R. *A Mid-Victorian Feminist, Barbara Leigh Smith Bodichon.* New Haven: Yale Univ. Press, 1985.

Holcombe, Lee. *Victorian Ladies at Work: Middle-Class Working Women in England and Wales 1850–1914.* Hamden, Conn.: Archon Books, 1973.

———. *Wives and Property: Reform of the Married Women's Property Law in Nineteenth-Century England.* Toronto: Univ. of Toronto Press, 1983.

Hollis, Patricia. *Women in Public, 1850–1900: Documents of the Victorian Women's Movement.* London: Allen and Unwin, 1979.

Howard, David. "George Meredith: 'Delicate' and 'Epical' Fiction." In *Literature and Politics in the Nineteenth Century.* Ed. John Lucas. London: Methuen, 1971.

Huddleston, Joan, ed. *English Laws for Women in the Nineteenth Century,* by Caroline Norton. Chicago: Academy Chicago, 1982.

Hunt, Violet. *I Have This to Say: The Story of My Flurried Years.* New York: Boni & Liveright, 1926.

Hynes, Samuel. *The Edwardian Turn of Mind.* Princeton, N.J.: Princeton Univ. Press, 1968.

Ilmberger, Frances M. *Love and Friendship in the Life and World of Elizabeth Robins*. M. A. Thesis, California State University at Hayward, 1988.

James, Henry. *The Bostonians*. 1886. Reprint, Harmondsworth: Penguin, 1984.

———. *The Reverberator*. 1888. Reprinted in *A London Life and The Reverberator*. New York and Oxford: Oxford Univ. Press, 1988.

———. *The Tragic Muse*. 1890. Reprint, Harmondsworth: Penguin, 1984.

———. *The Notebooks of Henry James*. Ed. F. O. Matthiesen and Kenneth B. Murdock. New York: Oxford, 1961.

Jewsbury, Geraldine. *The Half Sisters*. 1848. Reprint, Oxford: Oxford Univ. Press, 1994.

John, Angela V. *Elizabeth Robins: Staging a Life, 1862–1952*. London: Routledge, 1995.

Jordan, Ellen. "The Christening of the New Woman: May 1984." *Victorian Newsletter* 63 (1983): 19–21.

[Kaye, J. W.]. "The 'Non-Existence' of Women." *North British Review* 23 (1855): 536–59.

Keefe, Robert. *Charlotte Brontë's World of Death*. Austin: Univ. of Texas Press, 1979.

Kelvin, Norman. *A Troubled Eden: Nature and Society in the Works of George Meredith*. Stanford, Calif.: Stanford Univ. Press, 1961.

Kestner, Joseph. *Protest and Reform: The British Social Narrative by Women, 1827–1867*. Madison: Univ. of Wisconsin Press, 1985.

Korg, Jacob. "The Problem of Unity in *Shirley*." *Nineteenth-Century Fiction* 12 (1957): 125–36.

———. *George Gissing: A Critical Biography*. 1963. Brighton: Harvester Press, 1980.

Kucich, John. *Repression in Victorian Fiction: Charlotte Brontë, George Eliot, and Charles Dickens*. Berkeley and Los Angeles: Univ. of California Press, 1987.

Lansbury, Coral. *Elizabeth Gaskell: The Novel of Social Crisis*. New York: Barnes and Noble, 1975.

Lawrence, D. H. *Women in Love*. 1920. Reprint, Harmondsworth: Penguin, 1982.

[Lewes, George Henry]. "Currer Bell's 'Shirley.' " *Edinburgh Review* 91 (1850): 153–73.

Lewis, Jane. *Women in England, 1870–1950: Sexual Divisions and Social Change*. Brighton: Wheatsheaf, 1984.

———. *Before the Vote Was Won: Arguments for and against Women's Suffrage 1864–1896*. London: Routledge & Kegan Paul, 1987.

[Lewis, Sarah]. *Woman's Mission*. 1839. Reprint, Philadelphia: Willis P. Hazard, 1854.

Lindsay, Jack. *George Meredith: His Life and Work*. London: Bodley Head, 1956.

Linton, Eliza Lynn. "The Judicial Shock to Marriage." *Nineteenth Century* 29 (1891): 691–700.

———. "The Wild Women as Politicians." *Nineteenth Century* 30 (1891): 79–88.

———. "The Wild Women as Social Insurgents." *Nineteenth Century* 30 (1891): 596–605.

[Lister, T. H.]. "Rights and Conditions of Women." *Edinburgh Review* 73 (1841): 189–209.

Mathiessen, Paul F, Arthur C. Young, and Pierre Coustillas, eds. *The Collected Letters of George Gissing*. 5 vols. Athens: Ohio Univ. Press, 1990–94.

Mackenzie, Midge, ed. *Shoulder to Shoulder*. New York: Random House, 1975.

Marcus, Jane. " 'Clio in Calliope': History and Myth in Meredith's *Diana of the Crossways*." *Bulletin of the New York Public Library* 79 (1976): 167–92.

———. "Art and Anger." *Feminist Studies* 4 (1978): 69–98.

McGlamery, Gayla. "In His Beginnings, His Ends: The 'Preface' to Meredith's *Diana of the Crossways.*" *Studies in the Novel* 23 (1991): 470–89.

Meredith, George. *The Egoist.* 1875. Reprint, Oxford: Oxford Univ. Press, 1992.

———. "A Ballad of Fair Ladies in Revolt." *Fortnightly Review* 20 (1876): 232–41.

———. *Beauchamp's Career.* 1879. Reprint, Oxford: Oxford Univ. Press, 1988.

———. *Diana of the Crossways.* 1885. Reprint, New York: Norton, 1973.

———. "Essay: On the Idea of Comedy and the Uses of the Comic Spirit." *Miscellaneous Prose.* Vol. 23 of *The Works of George Meredith.* New York: Scribner's, 1910.

Michaux, Pierre, ed. *George Gissing: Critical Essays.* Totowa, N.J.: Barnes and Noble, 1981.

Michie, Elsie B. *Outside the Pale: Cultural Exclusion, Gender Difference, and the Victorian Woman Writer.* N.Y.: Ithaca: Cornell Univ. Press, 1993.

Mill, John Stuart. *The Subjection of Women.* 1869. Reprint, Cambridge: M.I.T. Press, 1982.

Moglen, Helene. *Charlotte Brontë: The Self Conceived.* New York: Norton, 1976.

Moses, Joseph. *The Novelist as Comedian: George Meredith and the Ironic Sensibility.* New York: Schocken, 1983.

Mulford, Wendy. "Socialist-Feminist Criticism: A Case Study, Women's Suffrage Literature, 1906–14." In *Re-Reading English.* Ed. Peter Widdowson. New York: Methuen, 1982.

Nead, Lynda. *Myths of Sexuality: Representations of Women in Victorian Britain.* New York and Oxford: Blackwell, 1988.

Newton, Judith Lowder. *Women, Power, and Subversion: Social Strategies in British Fiction, 1777–1860.* Athens: Univ. of Georgia Press, 1981.

Nord, Deborah Epstein. *Walking the Victorian Streets: Women, Representation, and the City.* Ithaca, N.Y.: Cornell Univ. Press, 1995.

Norton, Caroline. *The Separation of Mother and Child by the Law of Custody of Infants Considered.* London: Roake and Varty, 1838.

———. *A Plain Letter to the Lord Chancellor on the Infant Custody Bill.* London: James Ridgway, 1839.

———. *English Laws for Women in the Nineteenth Century.* 1854. Reprint, Ed. Joan Huddleston. Chicago: Academy Chicago, 1982.

———. *A Letter to the Queen on Lord Chancellor Cranworth's Marriage and Divorce Bill.* London: Longman, Brown, Green and Longmans, 1855.

Ouida. "The New Woman." *North American Review* 158 (1894): 610–19.

Pankhurst, Sylvia. *The Suffragette Movement.* 1931. Reprint, London: Virago, 1984.

Parkes, Bessie Rayner. "What Can Educated Women Do?" *English Women's Journal* 4 (1860): 289–98.

———. "The Condition of Working Women in England and France." *English Women's Journal* 8 (1861): 1–9.

Peters, Margot. *Unquiet Soul: A Biography of Charlotte Brontë.* New York: Doubleday, 1975.

Pikoulis, John. "*North and South*: Varieties of Love and Power." *Yearbook of English Studies* 6 (1976): 176–93.

Pollard, Arthur. *Mrs. Gaskell: Novelist and Biographer.* Cambridge: Harvard Univ. Press, 1966.

Poole, Adrian. *Gissing in Context.* Totowa, N.J.: Rowman and Littlefield, 1975.

Poovey, Mary. *Uneven Developments: The Ideological Work of Gender in Mid-Victorian England*. Chicago: Univ. of Chicago Press, 1988.

Port, M. H. *The Houses of Parliament*. New Haven and London: Yale Univ. Press, 1976.

Prochaska, F. K. *Women and Philanthropy in Nineteenth-Century England*. Oxford: Clarendon Press, 1980.

Rhys, Jean. *After Leaving Mr. Mackenzie*. 1931. Reprint, New York: Norton, 1997.

Richards, Thomas. "The Image of Victoria in the Year of the Jubilee." *Victorian Studies* 31 (1987): 7–32.

Robins, Elizabeth. *George Mandeville's Husband*. New York: D. Appleton, 1894.

———. *Votes for Women*. 1907. Reprinted in *How the Vote Was Won and Other Suffragette Plays*. Ed. Dale Spender and Carol Hayman. London: Methuen, 1985.

———. *The Convert*. 1907. Reprint, New York: The Feminist Press, 1980.

———. *Way Stations*. New York: Dodd, Mead, 1913.

———. *Ancilla's Share: An Indictment of Sex Antagonism*. 1924. Reprint, Westport, Conn.: Hyperion Press, 1976.

———. *Theatre and Friendship: Some Henry James Letters*. New York: G. P. Putnam's Sons, 1932.

Rosen, Judith. "At Home upon a Stage: Domesticity and Genius in Geraldine Jewsbury's *The Half Sisters*." In *The New Nineteenth Century: Feminist Readings of Underread Victorian Fiction*. Ed. Barbara Leah Harman and Susan Meyer. New York: Garland, 1996.

Rubinstein, David. *Before the Suffragettes: Women's Emancipation in the 1890s*. New York: St. Martin's, 1986.

Ryan, Mary P. *Women in Public: Between Banners and Ballots, 1825–1880*. Baltimore: Johns Hopkins Univ. Press, 1990.

Schor, Hilary M. *Scheherezade in the Marketplace: Elizabeth Gaskell and the Victorian Novel*. New York: Oxford Univ. Press, 1992.

Shanley, Mary Lyndon. *Feminism, Marriage, and the Law in Victorian England*. Princeton, N.J.: Princeton Univ. Press, 1989.

Shapiro, Arnold. "Public Themes and Private Lives: Social Criticism in *Shirley*." *Papers on Language and Literature* 4 (1968): 74–84.

Shore, Arabella. *Poems by A. and L.* London: G. Richards, 1897.

[Shore, Louisa]. "The Emancipation of Women." *Westminster Review* (1874): 137–74.

Showalter, Elaine. *A Literature of Their Own: British Women Novelists from Brontë to Lessing*. Princeton, N.J.: Princeton Univ. Press, 1977.

———. *Sexual Anarchy: Gender and Culture at the Fin de Siècle*. Harmondsworth: Penguin, 1990.

Sloan, John. "The Worthy Seducer: A Motif under Stress in George Gissing's *In the Year of Jubilee*." *English Literature in Transition* 28 (1985): 354–65.

Smith, Barbara Leigh. *A Brief Summary in Plain Language of the Most Important Laws concerning Women*. London: John Chapman, 1854.

Stanton, Elizabeth Cady, Susan B. Anthony, and Mathilda Joslyn Gage. *History of Woman Suffrage*. Rochester, N.Y.: Charles Mann, 1886.

Stephen, Barbara. *Emily Davies and Girton College*. London: Constable, 1927.

Stevenson, Lionel. *The Ordeal of George Meredith: A Biography*. New York: Scribners, 1953.

Stone, Donald David. *Novelists in a Changing World: Meredith, James, and the Transformation of English Fiction in the 1880's.* Cambridge: Harvard Univ. Press, 1972.

———. *The Romantic Impulse in Victorian Fiction.* Cambridge: Harvard Univ. Press, 1980.

Stone, J. S. *George Meredith's Politics: As Seen in His Life, Friendships, and Work.* Ontario: P. D. Meany, 1986.

Stoneman, Patsy. *Elizabeth Gaskell.* Bloomington: Indiana Univ. Press, 1987.

Stowell, Sheila. *A Stage of Their Own: Feminist Playwrights of the Suffrage Era.* Ann Arbor: Univ. of Michigan Press, 1992.

Strachey, Ray. *The Cause: A Short History of the Women's Movement in Great Britain.* 1928. Reprint, London: Virago, 1978.

Summers, Anne. "A Home from Home: Women's Philanthropic Work in the Nineteenth Century." In *Fit Work for Women.* Ed. Sandra Burman. New York: St. Martin's Press, 1979.

Tanner, Tony. *Adultery in the Novel: Contract and Transgression.* Baltimore: Johns Hopkins Univ. Press, 1979.

Tayler, Irene. *Holy Ghosts: The Male Muses of Emily and Charlotte Brontë.* New York: Columbia Univ. Press, 1990.

[Taylor, Harriet]. "The Enfranchisement of Women." *Westminster Review* 55 (1851): 289–311.

Thomas, Keith. "The Double Standard." *Journal of the History of Ideas* 20 (1959): 195–216.

Tickner, Lisa. *The Spectacle of Women: Imagery of the Suffrage Campaign, 1907–14.* Chicago: Univ. of Chicago Press, 1988.

Tillotson, Kathleen. *Novels of the Eighteen Forties.* Oxford: Oxford Univ. Press, 1954.

Tindall, Gillian. *The Born Exile: George Gissing.* London: Temple Smith, 1974.

———. Introduction. *In the Year of Jubilee.* Hassocks: Harvester Press, 1976.

Uglow, Jenny. *Elizabeth Gaskell: A Habit of Stories.* New York: Farrar, Strauss, Giroux, 1993.

Vicinus, Martha. *A Widening Sphere: Changing Roles of Victorian Women.* Bloomington and London: Indiana Univ. Press, 1980.

———. *Independent Women: Work and Community for Single Women, 1850–1920.* London: Virago, 1985.

Walkowitz, Judith. *Prostitution and Victorian Society: Women, Class, and the State.* Chicago: Univ. of Chicago Press, 1980.

———. *City of Dreadful Delight: Narratives of Sexual Danger in Late-Victorian London.* Chicago: Univ. of Chicago Press, 1992.

Webb, Igor. *From Custom to Capital: The English Novel and the Industrial Revolution.* Ithaca, N.Y.: Cornell University Press, 1981.

Wells, H. G. *In the Days of the Comet.* 1906. Reprint, London: Hogarth Press, 1985.

———. *Ann Veronica.* 1909. Reprint, London: Dent, 1993.

Welsh, Alexander. *George Eliot and Blackmail.* Cambridge: Harvard Univ. Press, 1985.

Wiley, Catherine. "The Matter with Manners: The New Woman and the Problem Play." In *Themes in Drama: Women in Theatre.* Ed. James Redmond. New York: Cambridge Univ. Press, 1989.

Williams, Carolyn. "Unbroken Patternes: Gender, Culture, and the Voice in *The Egoist.*" *Browning Institute Studies* 13 (1985): 45–70.

Williams, Raymond. *Culture and Society: 1780–1950.* 1958. Reprint, New York: Penguin, 1976.

Wilt, Judith. *The Readable People of George Meredith.* Princeton, N.J.: Princeton Univ. Press, 1975.

Wise, T. J., and J. A. Symington. *The Brontës: Their Lives, Friendships and Correspondence.* 4 vols. Oxford: Shakespeare Head Press, 1934.

Woolf, Virginia. *To the Lighthouse.* 1927. Reprint, New York: Harcourt Brace, 1981.

Wordsworth, William. "Composed Upon Westminster Bridge." *William Wordsworth. Selected Poetry.* Ed. Mark Van Doren. New York: Random House, 1950.

Wright Edgar. *Mrs. Gaskell: The Basis for Reassessment.* Oxford: Oxford Univ. Press, 1965.

Yeazell, Ruth Bernard. "Why Political Novels Have Heroines: *Sybil, Mary Barton,* and *Felix Holt."* *Novel* 18 (1985): 126–44.

Index

Victorian Literature and Culture Series

Karen Chase, Jerome J. McGann, *and* Herbert Tucker, *General Editors*

Daniel Albright
    Tennyson: The Muses' Tug-of-War

David G. Riede
    Matthew Arnold and the Betrayal of Language

Anthony Winner
    Culture and Irony: Studies in Joseph Conrad's Major Novels

James Richardson
    Vanishing Lives: Style and Self in Tennyson, D. G. Rossetti, Swinburne, and Yeats

Jerome J. McGann, Editor
    Victorian Connections

Antony H. Harrison
    Victorian Poets and Romantic Poems: Intertextuality and Ideology

E. Warwick Slinn
    The Discourse of Self in Victorian Poetry

Linda K. Hughes and Michael Lund
    The Victorian Serial

Anna Leonowens
    The Romance of the Harem
    Edited by Susan Morgan

Alan Fischler
    Modified Rapture: Comedy in W. S. Gilbert's Savoy Operas

Emily Shore
    Journal of Emily Shore
    Edited by Barbara Timm Gates

Richard Maxwell
    The Mysteries of Paris and London

Felicia Bonaparte
    The Gypsy-Bachelor of Manchester: The Life of Mrs. Gaskell's Demon

Peter L. Shillingsburg
    Pegasus in Harness: Victorian Publishing and W. M. Thackeray